Writing Islam from a South Asian Muslim Perspective

Writing Islam from a South Asian Muslim Perspective

Rushdie, Hamid, Aslam, Shamsie

Madeline Clements
Research Lecturer in English Studies, Teesside University

First published 2016 by
PALGRAVE MACMILLAN

Palgrave Macmillan in the UK is an imprint of Macmillan Publishers Limited, registered in England, company number 785998, of Houndmills, Basingstoke, Hampshire RG21 6XS.

Palgrave Macmillan in the US is a division of St Martin's Press LLC, 175 Fifth Avenue, New York, NY 10010.

Palgrave Macmillan is the global academic imprint of the above companies and has companies and representatives throughout the world.

Palgrave® and Macmillan® are registered trademarks in the United States, the United Kingdom, Europe and other countries.

ISBN 978–1–137–55437–6

This book is printed on paper suitable for recycling and made from fully managed and sustained forest sources. Logging, pulping and manufacturing processes are expected to conform to the environmental regulations of the country of origin.

A catalogue record for this book is available from the British Library.

A catalog record for this book is available from the Library of Congress.

To the people who have most believed in me, often more than I have myself: Mum, Dad, Peter – and Saud

Contents

Illustrations

Acknowledgements

I would like to thank all who have advised, encouraged and supported me in various ways during the years over which this book has evolved: Aamer Hussein, for inspiring my interest in Pakistani literature in English, introducing me to the novels of Kamila Shamsie and encouraging me to write for publication; Peter Morey for early conversations which informed the initial hypothesis, and for his rigorous and clear-sighted advice throughout the writing process; Suroosh Irfani for supporting my application for the Junior Residency I undertook at Lahore's National College of Arts in spring 2012, where I first made the acquaintance of many of the artists whose beautiful and challenging works form the chapter illustrations in this study; Khadim Ali, Komail Aijazuddin, Jamil Baloch, Saud Baloch, Ali Kazim, Sajid Khan, Imran Qureshi and Salman Toor for granting permission to use those artworks, and Corvi Mora, Toni Hafkenscheid, Sameera Raja of Canvas Gallery, VASL Artists' Collective and Sohail Zuberi for supplying photographic images; Rehana Ahmed, Peter Morey, Ruvani Ranasinha and Amina Yaqin for providing me with drafts of their conference papers and book chapters prior to their publication; Ben Doyle at Palgrave for taking the book on after its slightly eventful history, and Tomas René for his patience and stalwart assistance putting the final touches to the manuscript; Taylor & Francis for granting permission to reuse my material, originally published as 'Enchanted Realms, Sceptical Perspectives: Salman Rushdie's Recent Fiction' in Chambers, C. and Herbert, C. (eds) (2014) *Imagining Muslims in South Asia and the Diaspora: Secularism, Religion, Representations*, London: Routledge, 127–41; Claire Chambers for inviting me to contribute an essay to that volume; Christopher Butler for his energetic responses to an early draft of the Aslam chapter; John Taylor for his sympathetic reflections on the task of writing; Lindsay Duguid for giving me the opportunity to review international fiction for the *Times Literary Supplement*, and her excellent guidance during that period; Coral Ann Howells for her continuing warmth and wise reflections on the world of academia; and David Johnson, whose perceptive comments about my craft of writing, confidence in my abilities and unstinting support with the final stages of editing have meant a very great deal to me.

1
Writing Islam from a Contemporary South Asian Muslim Perspective

1.1 Sajid Khan

In the introduction to the revised edition of *Covering Islam: How the Media and the Experts Determine How We See the Rest of the World*, Edward Said (1997: xii) expressed increased concern that 'malicious generalisations about Islam have become the last acceptable form of denigration of foreign culture in the West'. He went on to describe his disturbance on being asked, presumably because of Middle Eastern – and mistaken Muslim – identity, to provide the media with an insider's insight into the bomb attack in Oklahoma City in April 1995:

> I must have received twenty-five phonecalls...The entirely face-tious connection between Arabs, Muslims, and terrorism was never more forcefully made evident to me; the sense of guilty involvement which, despite myself, I was made to feel struck me. (xiv)[1]

These observations point to a reductive trend in Anglo-American discussions of Islam, and highlight its potentially unsettling impact on those actual and assumed Muslim writers who might be called upon to comment in the Western public sphere.[2] They provide a means of entry into this study, which asks how four South Asian Muslim authors have responded to the challenge of writing about Islamic faith ties in the aftermath of the attacks on New York of 11 September 2001, which replaced the Oklahoma City bombings as the most destructive on US soil to date.

Writing Islam explores the hypothesis that the international novels of Salman Rushdie, Mohsin Hamid, Nadeem Aslam and Kamila Shamsie can be read as part of a post-9/11 attempt to revise modern "knowledge" of the Islamic world, using globally disseminated literature to reframe Muslims' potential to connect with others. It considers how the "world literature" they create and shape maps spheres of Islamic affiliation and affinity, questioning where their subjects turn in seeking a sense of connection or identification, and why. It provides a detailed examination of the inter-cultural and intra-cultural affiliations and affinities the characters pursue in these texts, asking what aesthetic, historical, political and spiritual identifications or commitments could influence such connective attempts. It also analyses popular discourses and critical discussions surrounding these texts, offering a critical examination of the explanations offered by the authors in their non-fiction writing and commentary for privileging, problematising or prohibiting one (Islamic) affiliation or affinity instead of another, and scrutinising how the writers are appropriated as authentic and hence authoritative spokespeople by dominant political and cultural forces. Finally, it explores how, as authors of Indian and Pakistani origin, Rushdie, Hamid, Aslam and Shamsie negotiate their identities and the tensions of being seen to act as Muslim spokespeople in (conscious) relation to the complex international and geopolitical contexts in which they write.

For the purposes of this study, I use 'affiliation' to describe the more active and selective of the modes of Islamic connection which may be traced in the novels. According to the *OED Online* (2013a, 'affiliate, v.'), the would-be 'affiliate', an adoptive son, seeks to attach himself to an institution, organisation, political group or society, expressing in his choice a desire to belong. In Edward Said's (1983: 18–19) conception, this may constitute what he describes as a 'turn' from a lost or outmoded natural familial 'filiation' to a critically created and 'compensatory' cultural and societal system of 'affiliation'. Further, it may demonstrate an individual's desire to become an 'agent' or 'bearer' of a particular notion of 'civilisation' or 'culture' (Gilroy 2004: 65).

The term 'affinity', in contrast, variously defined in the *OED Online* (2013b, 'affinity, n.') 'by position' as a 'relationship of kinship generally between individuals or races', and 'by inclination' as a 'voluntary social... companionship [or] alliance' and 'psychical or spiritual attraction', may point to a more natural, unplanned or even involuntary sense of being drawn to a particular community grouping, geographical area or imaginative realm. Nederveen Pieterse (2007: 186–8) uses the term to describe the 'multiple circuits of [cultural] identification and integration' within which migrant communities participate in a global multicultural context. However, the term need not be confined solely to this usage. 'Affinitive' may also refer, for example, to the kind of feelings ignited between Muslims of radically different social, educational and doctrinal backgrounds when engaging in Islamic rituals or contemplating a common heritage or culture in their South and Central Asian homelands.

In drawing attention to different ways in which contemporary Muslim connections are established and experienced, the literature by authors of South Asian origin which I examine begins to take leave of the colourful, hybrid and darkly comic multicultural visions offered in the popular postcolonial writing of the 1980s and 1990s. This period, bookended in the UK by Salman Rushdie's *Midnight's Children* (1981) and Zadie Smith's *White Teeth* (2000), and punctuated by Hanif Kureishi's *The Black Album* (1995), perhaps did more to juxtapose the religious and secular than to explore their interrelationship. Yet the twenty-first-century fictions I consider remain in dialogue with these novels, with works of world literature like Michael Ondaatje's *The English Patient* (1992) and with contemporary fiction by other Pakistani writers in English, such as Aamer Hussein's story collection *Turquoise* (2002) and novella *Another Gulmohar Tree* (2009). They are also indebted to the precedents set by earlier postcolonial South Asian Muslim authors in English, for example Attia Hosain in *Sunlight on a Broken Column* (1961), and to writers from the Urdu literary tradition including the poets Habib Jalib and Faiz Ahmad Faiz, and the prose writers Intizar Husain and Saadat Hasan Manto, whose often controversial works have contributed to a wider history of writing and contesting Islam in subcontinental contexts. The novels by Rushdie, Hamid, Aslam and Shamsie I consider are also composed in conscious relation to such (anti-)colonial antecedents as E. M. Forster's *A Passage to India* (1924), Ahmed Ali's *Twilight in Delhi* (1940), Graham Greene's *The Quiet American* (1955) and Albert Camus' *The Fall* (1957), which resurface in places as intertexts. However, without negating the importance of such earlier literary trends and traditions as shaping influences, in particular subcontinental Muslim ones, it is my purpose in *Writing Muslims* to present a contextualised study of novels produced in the post-9/11 decade by four "Muslim" writers whose names are now prominent in Western academia and publishing, and to explore their contents and creation in relation to the demands of this particular period.

After 9/11: Muslims in the frame

The "terror" attacks of 9/11 and, later, 7/7, brought a militant "jihadist" Islam sharply into world view. Racing to decode the 'message' of 11 September 2001, commentators and critics in the British press such as Martin Amis (2008: 3) interpreted the launching in Afghanistan of this 'Intercontinental Ballistic Missile' as an alien culture's wake-up call to the unassuming West.[3] As Amis put it, 'America, it is time you learned how implacably you are hated' (3). Social anthropologist Pnina Werbner (2002: 1) would later observe that it seemed to parties on both sides of the proposed ideological divide 'that the clash of civilizations predicted by Huntington...between Islam and the West had finally materialised'.

The language used to narrate the violent historical events of 9/11 and defend the invasion of Muslim nation states in the weeks and months following the collapse of New York's twin towers both reflects and sustains this assumption. The 'rhetoric of "evil" ' deployed by George W. Bush in his State of the Union Address in January 2002 (Kellner 2002: 344) and the 'moral' pronouncements of British Prime Minister Tony Blair in anticipation of the renewed war with Afghanistan (Gilroy 2004: 67–8) are typical. For, as Werbner (2002: 2) went on to note, in the immediate aftermath of 9/11, it seemed the civilisational ' "clash" – or its denial – had become the jargon of politicians and the media': an evolving 'newspeak' (Hobsbawm 2007: 163) of 'ideological shortcuts' (Nederveen Pieterse 2007: 179) that could potentially be manipulated in the interests of revised geopolitical agendas, and ultimately therefore in support of the ensuing "war on terror". Since that time, this discourse has continued to penetrate discussions of globalisation and culture in the US and in Europe (179), tending to separate individuals of different faiths into opposing categories of "us" and "them"; to position Muslims and Arabs as premodern or, as Salaita (2008) puts it, 'uncultured' in relation to the West; and perhaps even, as Bayoumi (2008: 4–5) proposes, to 'degrade the language' to such an extent that it 'structure[s] the thinking [of American citizens] about the Muslims living among [them]'.

The articles, interviews, commentaries and notices published by writers such as Martin Amis, Christopher Hitchens and Salman Rushdie in the international English-language press since 2001 have attempted in various ways to furnish Western readers with a deeper understanding of Islam and Islamism and to justify the compromising of (Muslims') civil liberties in a language that perpetuates the notion of a clash of values.[4] In making their arguments, such intellectuals have typically pitched the reason, modernity and secularity for which they claim to stand against the evils of an irrational, encroaching religious extremism, and promoted freedom of expression over what they consider to be a suspect cultural relativism. This was the case, for example, with the 'manifesto' against a 'new global [Islamic] totalitarianism threat' signed by 12 public figures including Rushdie, which appeared in the French political weekly *Charlie Hebdo* in March 2006 (H. Ali et al., cited in *BBC News* 2006). Prompted by Muslim dissent over the handling of sensitive issues such as the Danish cartoons controversy, its authors tried to use a liberal, secular and democratic rhetoric to distance themselves from accusations of 'Islamophobia' while fostering a fearless and 'critical' discourse on 'Islam' (*BBC News* 2006). But the resulting anti-fundamentalist press statement sounded more like anti-Islamic 'moral posturing' (Nederveen Pieterse 2007: 190–1) than a precursor to reasoned discussion on equal terms.

The slew of fictional narratives produced by either Western or Westernised writers, both in North America (DeLillo 2007; Safran Foer 2005; Updike 2006) and in the UK (Amis 2008; Faulks 2009; McEwan 2005; Rushdie 2005c) in the wake of 9/11 have juxtaposed such similar values and principles when describing imaginary terrorist threats or suspect Muslim subjects. Their attempts to grapple with what the critic Robert Eaglestone (2010: 361) has termed 'the melange of anxiety and anger that make up the West's fuzzy understanding of the current multiple and interlinked crises' have therefore tended to reinforce binary oppositions between Islam and the West, rather than seeking to understand why they occur. In Ian McEwan's *Saturday* (2005), for example, the novel's rational, secular neurosurgeon protagonist, Henry Perowne, perturbed by a burning plane bound for Heathrow, seen as symbolic of a looming 'attack' not just on London but on 'our whole way of life' (35), muses about what might happen to his 'innocuous' musician son under a radical regime characterised by 'hatred' and 'the purity of nihilism' (33). His grim conclusion, that 'in the ideal Islamic state, under strict Shari'a law, there'll be room for surgeons. [But] Blues guitarists will be found other employment' (33), re-articulates the underlying notion of a clash of values, pitching in fiction the innocent and expressive individual against an intolerant, absolute, unknown Other.

Critical commentators across disciplines and cultures have begun to expose how such a totalising rhetoric can demonise and demean the Muslim subjects it attempts – and fails – to represent. Analysing in *The Uncultured Wars* instances of anti-Arab racism amongst American intellectuals, Steven Salaita shows how, in these very public and political representations of an unerringly 'strange and violent Islam' (2008: 152), Islamic peoples have come to 'exist…as characters, never narrators': always spoken for, but rarely permitted the space or the power to speak for themselves (165–6). So, through the essays of Rushdie (2002: 395), we may learn that the Islam of 'a vast number of "believing" Muslim men' stands for 'a loathing of modern society... riddled as it is with music, godlessness and sex'. Meanwhile, in fictionalised accounts, we may enter the stream-of-consciousness of the radicalised Muslim youth as he surveys with distaste the alluring bodies of bare-bellied teenage girls, 'weak Christians and non-observant Jews' (Updike 2006: 3); or "understand" the misanthropic motivations and beliefs of the 9/11 attackers, absent from the scene, through the collective litanies of their numbed New York victims:

'It's sheer panic. They attack out of panic.'

'This much, yes, it may be true. Because they think the world is a disease. This world, this society, ours. A disease that's spreading', he said.

'There are no goals they can hope to achieve... Kill the innocent, only that.'

(DeLillo 2007: 46)

This tendency of (mostly) white, Western "men of letters" to act as pundits, passing judgements on Muslims and Islam even as they attempt to speak for them, has become a cause for concern in a period of increasingly authoritarian anti-terror legislation, heightened security and rising Islamophobia in the West. It has also been a catalyst for calls to respond. The comments of Amis and others, if not exactly tolerated, were at least perhaps ignored, trivialised and un(der)-addressed in the immediate aftermath of 9/11. Since then such authors' pronouncements have drawn direct responses from their literary peers, including Terry Eagleton (2007a), Ronan Bennett (2007) and Kamila Shamsie (2007b).[5] Each of these critics has attempted to reveal racisms and hypocrisies, or to point to the defective logic of 'leading luminar[ies]' (Eagleton 2007a: x) like Amis. But they have also emphasised that the critic's greater task is to challenge the authority of such 'self-styled expert[s]' (Bennett 2007: n.p.) to propose their often limited and uninformed opinions on complex and emotive subjects without censure.

Ronan Bennett explained in 2007 that to do so – i.e. to challenge Amis et al. – is not to launch an attack on freedom of speech, far from it. 'As a novelist', he suggested in his comment piece for *The Guardian*, 'Amis is free to do whatever he wants with his characters', even if his 'flamboyant [anti-Islamic] clichés' prove 'poor substitutes for understanding, reason and real knowledge' of contemporary Muslim experiences (Bennett 2007: n.p.). However, what is not acceptable, he suggests, is for the 'odious' public endorsements of anti-Muslim prejudice and expressions of racist sentiment published by leading literary and cultural figures to be allowed to continue to pass without comment. Years after 9/11, Bennett urges, critics and authors English and Indian alike must 'start writing' to express their inability to remain silent in the face of such an 'outrage'. The novelist Kamila Shamsie (2007b: n.p.), replying to his comment, summarised the factors that convinced her, Pakistani and a Muslim, to take up the challenge to break her strategic silence and 'write a heated response':

> The failure to express outrage cannot easily be distinguished from a lack of outrage . . . Those who didn't stand up to condemn Martin Amis bear responsibility . . . because . . . he is still recognised as one of Britain's most significant writers, and has the moral authority which comes with that recognition . . . I don't advocate any form of censorship . . . But in worlds without censorship, the way to respond to odious views which are given space in the press is to, well, respond! (2007b)

The post-9/11 period has certainly seen a growth of Muslim interventions in contemporary debates about Islamic peoples, not only via the media channels of news articles and comment, but also via the more enduring literary modes of memoir and fiction (also part, perhaps, of a new wave of Pakistani English writing within South Asian fiction); and a concomitant rise in the analysis of strategies for representing Muslims by academics and practitioners.

In her annual survey of Pakistani English Literature produced in 2005, Muneeza Shamsie (2006: 161) noted, perhaps unsurprisingly, that 'in the wake of 9/11, 7/7, and the Afghan and Iraq wars a number of Pakistani writers chose to explore the relationship between Muslims and the West, whether they examined the experience of the Pakistani diaspora' – as Aslam's (2004a) novel *Maps for Lost Lovers* had done – 'or excavated episodes from Muslim and European history', as her daughter, Kamila Shamsie, would go on to do.[6] Muneeza Shamsie's (2008: 21) anthology *And the World Changed* proceeded to draw attention to works by anglophone Pakistani writers which, in 'touch[ing] on ideas of religion, identity and otherness', offered timely responses to geopolitical events. These themes of course surface in her earlier short story collections (1997, 2001) and in regional, diasporic and vernacular works, not just global English ones. Yet Shamsie's introduction to the 2008 selection firmly situates the short fictions she anthologises in the context of:

> The last decade, [in which] Pakistan has been strongly affected by political events in neighbouring Muslim lands, including the rise of the Taliban and al-Qaeda, the politicisation of religion, exacerbated by Western rhetoric of Crusades, and the clash of civilizations. (21)

Significantly, she claims these diverse stories, anthologised under a 'Pakistani' national umbrella, are 'part of a new world literature in English that gives voice to experiences beyond the traditional canons of Anglo-American literature' (24–5).[7]

Global orientations in Rushdie, Hamid, Aslam and Shamsie

I argue that Rushdie, Hamid, Aslam and Shamsie orient themselves towards the "global" in their internationally disseminated novels, both in terms of their geopolitical subject matter and selection of settings which are of symbolic and strategic significance to world powers; and in terms of the intra- and inter-cultural Muslim affinities and affiliations that they map within these zones of conflict and contact. They do this at a time when ordinary experiences of multicultural contact have been rendered suspect, and there is a desire (at least in Western spheres) for writers and academics to attempt to expose where in the world Muslim loyalties lie. This is also a moment when alternative, perhaps more positive, ways of understanding both international faith connections (such as Islamic cosmopolitanism) and responsibility to others as planet-sharing humans could usefully be revived and revised.

In *After Empire*, Paul Gilroy (2004: viii, 65) highlights how, in the 'states of permanent emergency' created out of the "war on terror", 'ordinary experiences of contact, co-operation, and conflict' between people of different races and ethnicities have come to be viewed with scepticism. For Gilroy, these experiences are symptomatic of multiculture's 'conviviality' – of its capacity to facilitate 'processes of cohabitation and interaction' in social life, in both national (British) and global (cosmopolitan) contexts (xi–xii). 'The cosmopolitan desire to presume the equal worth of alien cultures and … proliferat[e] encounters with otherness', which he goes on to defend, can also be identified in the fictions I examine in my book (65). Gilroy proceeds to observe that, in the current climate of suspicion towards non-Western others, the idea of initiating close contact, communicating or acting in concert with different ethnic (and religious) groups may be censured as inappropriate (65–70). At the same time, the potentially unifying discourses of 'cosmopolitanism' and 'human rights', which might be rallied in support of such exchanges, have become 'tainted'; they are used by dominant powers to 'justify intervention' into the sovereignty of people judged less 'civilized' (65–6, 70). He seeks to bracket the ordinary (non-elite, decentred, anti-racist and humanist) cosmopolitanism he advocates from the 'armored' cosmopolitanism he considers tantamount to 'ethical imperialism', and to explore how it might be 'sustained and even elevated' (66–9, 74–5, 79–80).

In spirit with Gilroy, I contend that the selected novels attempt to explore a range of Muslim experiences of ordinary cosmopolitan contact, co-operation and conflict, both within South and Central Asian Islamic contexts and beyond them. Doing so, Hamid, Aslam, Shamsie and (to an extent) Rushdie hint at an 'ability to live with alterity without becoming anxious, fearful or violent' (Gilroy 2004: xi), even as they investigate tensions and intolerances. It is my argument that, in dramatising aspects of subcontinental Muslim connectivity, the chosen novelists eschew a simplistic revival of the colourful, celebratory visions offered by a "saris, samosas, and steel bands" brand of commercial multicultural fiction produced by postcolonial writers in English. They also avoid reproducing cosmopolitan perspectives which may be easily aligned with totalising worldviews.

When discussing fictional depictions of incidences of both interfaith harmony and cross-cultural tension, I remain alert to the commercial and political contexts in which they are produced and how these may shape and contain them. In particular, I retain an awareness of how "exotic" literary products have been prized in late-twentieth-century Western multicultural contexts for their convenient 'levelling out of different histories, and [their] aestheticised celebration of diversity that disguises the lack of sociohistorical change' (Huggan 2001: 117). I am also conscious of the writers' potential to exploit what Timothy Brennan (1997: 36–7) has termed their 'transcultural' ('nonexilic, world-travelling') statuses in order to present an 'appropriate cosmopolitan view' (appropriate, that is, to Western audiences), which seems to betray the ideas about the assumption of equal worth which Gilroy would uphold. Brennan describes this 'new' cosmopolitanism as forming a 'geopolitical aesthetic' which foregrounds the 'roving' and 'fundamentally estranged' "third-world" individual's experiences of transcultural 'hybridity', and 'mute[s] antagonistic political objectives' (36–8). Its literary purveyors are attentive instead to 'the requisites of metropolitan assumptions' about 'disparate cultural identities'; they may, Brennan concedes, be 'critical of the West', but their 'sympathies' coalesce with prevailing Euro-American perspectives and attitudes (36–9).

Hence, my transnational authors could engage in the 'politico-exotic' (Huggan 2001:11–12) suppression of expressions of disharmony with contemporary Western, neoliberal ways of thinking about certain Muslim Others, thus ensuring their tastes are aligned with those of Anglo-American markets. So too they might mute Muslim voices of dissent, and demonise or trivialise Islamic acts of resistance to neo-imperial (Western) hegemonies, in order to secure their entry into the "global" public sphere. Furthermore, those who seek to question Western cultural values and assumptions by staging 'repoliticised' (Huggan 2001: ix) visions of Muslim South Asia to curious Western eyes may end up reinforcing exoticist myths of identity. Depictions intended to 'unsettle metropolitan expectations of cultural otherness and to effect a grounded critique of differential relations of power' (ix–x) may, ironically, gain a kind of cachet for their capacity to thrill or disturb the reader, the result being that their more critical dimensions are misread or overlooked.

Yet the twenty-first-century novels by diasporic and transnational South Asian writers which I analyse in this book collectively offer no such comfortable or compatible "cosmopolitan" visions of global multiculture to the Western reader/consumer. In different ways, each confronts and exposes the historical, religious and cultural differences, actual and perceived, which threaten to divide Muslim and non-Muslim peoples in complex geopolitical contexts – not only in rural Afghanistan and suburban Karachi, for example, but also in New York and other Western metropolises. Such fictions demonstrate the diversity of South Asian Muslim affiliations and affinities and the richness of Islamic culture's intellectual and aesthetic inheritances, which may be used to forge links between disparate communities. They may not only satisfy neo-Orientalist demands for Muslim "exotica" to some extent, but also function strategically to subvert the stereotypes that would feed Occidental assumptions and appetites. For the authors of these novels remain conscious of how the connections and perspectives they map can be manipulated and limited by political and cultural authorities – global and local, Western and Islamic – and this awareness, to varying extents, shapes the form and content of their fictions.

The fictions I examine feature a wide variety of Muslim protagonists, from indigenous peoples to migrants and refugees, diasporic settlers, moneyed expatriates and privileged world travellers. These characters find and follow feelings which may resemble Gilroy's (2004: 80) 'cosmopolitan solidarity' across actual and virtual borders; they offer a 'translocal commitment' (in his terms) to Muslims and non-Muslims 'slightly different' from themselves with whom they share a common humanity (88–9). I suggest that my authors' characters are drawn to connect with bodies and groups on grounds which not only resemble but also differ slightly from those envisaged by Gilroy. His focus when developing his ideas about 'cosmopolitan solidarity' is on largely white, Western intellectuals and travellers with what he terms 'rights-bearing bodies' (89). These individuals are empowered to extend gestures of 'translocal commitment' to those 'rights-less' people in parts of the world which are subject to neo-imperial 'brutality and arbitrary power', whom they might 'shield' or 'protect' (89). The fictions I consider do include characters – for example elite Pakistani expatriates, well-connected Japanese holocaust survivors and European Muslim converts – who might indeed (like their authors) qualify as significantly more 'rights-bearing' than either their illegal Afghan immigrant or ghettoised diasporic compatriots. Shamsie's *Burnt Shadows* (2009b), Aslam's *The Wasted Vigil*

(2008) and Hamid's *The Reluctant Fundamentalist* (2007b), among others, also feature protagonists of nominal Islamic affiliation who can be seen to go to considerable measures to avoid 'being forcibly attached by patriotism and nationalism to cultural and political formations that' in their opinion, and Gilroy's (2004: 75) terms, 'are wrong, unjust, evil, or misguided and therefore unrepresentative'. Yet, crucially, these novels also attempt to dramatise the experiences of "rights-less" (or considerably less privileged) Asian Muslim subaltern characters, whose lived experiences of quotidian cosmopolitanism are at times less edifying, and differently nuanced.

In *Ethnicities and Global Multiculture*, Nederveen Pieterse (2007: 155) looks beyond Western cosmopolitan legacies to other, 'non-Western cosmopolitanisms', such as a multivalent 'Islamic cosmopolitanism', which may shape the Muslim world's 'self-perception' and present a means of 'bridging' societies, globally. He defines cosmopolitanism 'broadly, as perspectives and sensibilities that stress human bonds and interconnectedness across cultural and political boundaries', and identifies these ideas as common to various religions: 'Buddhism, Hinduism, Confucianism, and so forth' (155). Given cosmopolitanism's accrual of 'elite and urban overtones' (156), Nederveen Pieterse suggests that the term 'global solidarity' may be preferable. This seems to echo Gilroy's (2004) 'cosmopolitan solidarity' both lexically, and in its recognition of human beings' 'essential similarity' and (global) communicability (89, 4). But whereas Gilroy's ideas are inspired by a 'postmodern planetary consciousness' derived from an 'unabashed humanism that...is...licensed by a critique of racial hierarchy and the infrahuman life forms it creates' in global, multicultural contexts (83, xii), Nederveen Pieterse (2007: 160) seeks, quoting Osman Bakar, to make a case for the idea of Islam as a 'bridging' civilisation whose 'consciousness is deeply rooted in such Quranic ideas as common human ancestry, common humanity...[and] the wisdom of ethnic and cultural pluralism' being 'a major part of Islamic self-awareness'.

Certainly, 'cosmopolitan' readings of Islamic scripture, and aspects of its heterodox spiritual traditions and aesthetic heritage which endorse and express ideas of tolerance and openness to others, inform and facilitate the fictive affinitive connections I consider here. But Islamic cosmopolitanism can manifest itself in different ways, categorised by Nederveen Pieterse as 'geopolitical, geo-economic, and cultural' (157). In its current militant, political and expansionist manifestations, it could also be seen as an aggressive contemporary 'cosmopolitanism' which operates in parallel to 'neo-liberalism and belligerent American hegemony', and yet is invariably set 'beyond the pale of [Western] modernity and globalization' (156). For, as Nederveen Pieterse proceeds to observe, 'contemporary Islam is both co-dependent with Western modernity and deeply wired to the career of global capitalism and neoliberalism *and* an alternative cosmopolitanism that is interspersed with other cultures' (166) – in other words, Islamic cosmopolitan has diverse, and divergent profiles.[8]

Likewise, the 'global' affiliations and affinities that Rushdie, Hamid, Aslam and Shamsie map are not only convivial or humanely cosmopolitan. They are also awkward and conflicting, and make for uncomfortable reading at times, while their origins and significance are sometimes hard to pinpoint or define. Literature produced by South Asian Muslim authors today reflects both the complicated nature of contemporary global Muslim experiences of connection, and the concerns held about them by the (largely Western) world for which they write.

The inter-cultural and intra-cultural connections charted by my writers in their fictions orient the reader's gaze towards a range of spaces of South Asian Muslim affiliation and affinity: aesthetic, cultural, historical, political and spiritual. These are located not just within, but beyond and between the independent states of India and Pakistan which much of the subcontinent's postcolonial anglophone writing has attempted to map. In applying the theories of Benedict Anderson (1991) to the work of Amitav Ghosh, Anshuman Mondal emphasises how modern, postcolonial nation states are simultaneously 'imaginary' and 'real' (Mondal 2007: 88). They are 'mental construct[s]' which exist within an often disparate (and widely dispersed) national community's 'psychic' realms (88). But they are also geographically and temporally anchored. Likewise, the spaces of South Asian Muslim affiliation and affinity my writers depict as important to contemporary international/transnational faith communities correspond to specific regions of our Earth, which might be surrounded by borders. They relate to sites of particular historical and strategic significance in which Islamic cultures have flourished, and Muslims found a "Dar al Islam" – a physical and spiritual home.

The fictions I examine are set in diverse locations such as America, England, Japan, Pakistan and Afghanistan. They take place in time periods which include the reign of the Mughals, but also encompass the ceding of British imperial power in India, Partition, the Cold War and the contemporary moment of today's "war on terror". For their protagonists, close encounters with cultural others which occur within these places may result in the surprising discovery of unsought spiritual or aesthetic affinities, a sense of universalism, and a shared humanity. The act of seeking spaces of contemporary 'Muslim' affiliation, meanwhile, may lead not only to imaginary realms of seeming spiritual or historical belonging (such as a sacred, mirage-like "Arabia"), but also to physical conflict zones (the training camp on the Afghanistan–Pakistan border), where cultivated allegiances terminate in disjunction and alienation, even violence and death.

Writing of postcolonial British Pakistani Muslims, Werbner (2002: 3–4) reflects that if 'diasporas are transnational communities of co-responsibility', then in order to understand their divergent responses to the attacks of September 11, and destabilise the now commonplace 'clash of civilizations' thesis, 'we need to disclose where their identifications, the centres of their subjective universe, lie'. In the post-9/11 context, authors who attempt to map in English, and by means of a mainstream, literary fiction, the widely dispersed spaces with which diasporic and transnational South Asian Muslims identify, might be understood to contribute to such an act of public disclosure. However, these internationally focused novels do more than present ripostes to popular Western conceptions of a monolithic Islamic identity, which cast global Muslims as a people torn between a culture of Western modernity and the un-culture of barbarism; potential, if not actual, affiliates to a global umma with 'bloody borders' (Huntington 1992: 13). Rather, they offer subtle attempts to revise both Western imperialist and political Islamist maps of the Muslim world which would attempt to identify a single 'centre' or focus for Islamic subjectivity and identity. The diverse cultural, spiritual and political affiliations and spontaneous, imaginative affinities which Rushdie, Hamid, Aslam and Shamsie explore in the process illuminate the co-responsibilities with which contemporary Muslim individuals and communities contend and coexist. They reconfigure Muslim being and belonging in today's global world as complex, challenging, and always multidimensional.

I have hinted at how the works examined in this book might collectively be viewed, and at the role that the events of September 11 have played in their making. Considering "9/11" as a watershed moment, it could be argued that they contribute to a pan-Islamic attempt to respond in some measure and in English to the reductive and polarising perceptions of Muslims and Islam produced after the attacks on the World Trade Centre, and in the hostile climate of the ensuing "war on terror". Given the national origins and affiliations of their authors, these recent novels – like those of other writers, such as Mohammed Hanif and H. M. Naqvi – might also be identified as part of 'new wave' of politically engaged, and highly marketable, anglophone Pakistani fiction (Shah 2009: n.p.; K. Shamsie 2007a: n.p.).

Other English-language authors published in this period by Western houses include Jamil Ahmad, Musharraf Ali Farooqi, Aamer Hussein, Uzma Aslam Khan, Moni Mohsin, Daniyal Mueenuddin and Ali Sethi. Many of these have won acclaim from Anglo-American prize-awarding organisations but, in comparison with the big-name authors I consider, received somewhat less popular recognition amongst "First World" audiences. A fully differentiated account of how contemporary Pakistani literature engages with the idea of South Asian Islam in the post-9/11 context (and with related feelings of affiliation and affinity) would – ideally – encompass not only the work of such authors, but also novels written in English and published by Pakistani and Indian presses, which have been popular in the region. Possible examples are Bina Shah's *The 786 Cyber Cafe* (2004) and Maha Khan Philips' *Beautiful from This Angle* (2010), with which Western readers will be less familiar. Bearing in mind Aamer Hussein's (2005: 9) assertion of Pakistani vernacular fiction's capacity to 'stage . . . events in the blinding glare of historical awareness (ethnic and religious warfare, migration, resettlement) and social realism', this extended account would also cover novels and short fiction written in Urdu and other regional languages. These could include Mirza Athar Baig's (2009) *Sifar Se Aik Tak*, Tahir Aslam Gora's *Rung Mahal* (2013) or Nilofar Iqbal's (2013) collection *Surkh Dhabbay*, which might operate further to provincialise and historicise Western concerns about shifting Islamic identities, and centre indigenous ones. Critics and reviewers in Pakistan have praised such literature for coming closer to contemporary concerns and interests, both local and diasporic.

Anglophone novels by South Asian Muslim authors written for and consumed, predominantly, by "First World" audiences are, however, a particular phenomenon in their own right; for that reason I limit my enquiry to four of the most well-known in this book. Composed in the wake not just of 9/11, but the US-led assault on Afghanistan, the 7/7 London bombings and the Mumbai attacks of 2008, their spokesman-like writing may – perhaps problematically – provide Western readers with fresh perspectives on Islamic states and organisations of extreme concern to America, Britain and their allies. Widening the lens, the selected writers' literary fictions must also be seen as the transnational, diasporic and cosmopolitan descendants of a South Asian Muslim cultural tradition indebted to twentieth-century authors published in Urdu and English, from Ahmed Ali and Saadat Hasan Manto to Qurratulain Hyder, Anita Desai and Agha Shahid Ali, and expressive of an aesthetics, history and politics which remains distinct from – though it is influenced by – that represented in Arab Muslim and White, Western narrative traditions. Finally, my chosen novels might be considered as works of "world literature", written from a perspective informed by their authors' South Asian and Islamic heritages, and engaging, in English, with global themes.

In seeking to define 'world literature', David Damrosch (2003: 9) suggests that it may be understood as offering 'multiple *windows on the world*'. 'A crucial feature', in his opinion, is that it 'resolves always into a *variety* of worlds'; hence 'every single work...is the locus of negotiation between two different cultures' (9, 14). The anglophone fictions I analyse here, published between 2002 and 2009 by houses such as Faber and Faber, Bloomsbury, Penguin and Vintage, and internationally disseminated, are poised in just such a way. They 'open' – or appear to open – 'windows' for largely foreign (Anglo-American) audiences 'into...varied times and places' (10) connected with Muslim South Asia at a moment when Islamic cultural, religious and political struggles in Afghanistan, Pakistan and India have captured the interest of Western readers. Hence they run the risk Damrosch identifies in relation to 'newly visible' world literary 'texts' which are drawn from cultures in which the West has an 'interest' (10). They expose themselves to the possibility of being mistranslated: made to 'fit comfortably with [stereotypical] American images' (of radical Islamism, for example) or – because of their cultural colour – 'sucked up in the Disneyfication of the globe' (10). And yet, implicated as they are in what Franco Moretti (2000: 54–8, 67) describes as an unequal world literary system in which Indian cultures remain marginal, their authors may combine 'local materials' with "foreign" forms to produce novels which are acts not only of compromise but also of variation and transformation.

Critics and writers including Sarah Brouillette (2007a, 2007b) and Kamila Shamsie (2009c) have highlighted the impact of the domination Moretti describes in practical, material terms, and pointed to the difficulties encountered and compromises made by transnational anglophone authors when writing fiction for a largely White, Western majority community far removed from the parts of the world they might depict. Looking critically at Anglo-American publishing's popular adoption and promotion of what she loosely terms 'minority' writing under the banner of 'World', 'International' or 'Global', Shamsie (2009c: 110) highlights the need to interrogate the hierarchies obscured by such terms and related categorisations. For, as she observes, such labels usually describe work produced by migrant writers whose voices remain under-represented, and yet who must ensure their books appeal to "majority", "First World" readerships if they are to sell or receive crucial attention. The terms ("World", etc.) are therefore far less inclusive than they might seem and, when uncritically applied, may result in the privileging of what Brouillette (2007b: 37) has described as an 'ostensibly delocalised, cosmopolitan English-language writing' (in this case one which provides moderate, "good" Muslim perspectives, or Islamicate "exotica"). Another outcome may be the occlusion of work which 'reckon[s] with the realities' not just of a diasporic elite, but of 'local' and 'non-elite lives'. Hence, as Shamsie warns, "world" literary classifications may ensure the perpetuation of the inequalities on which neo-imperial cultural economies are based. Insights like hers function as caveats, and inform my search for a better or more qualified means to describe the kind of literature which transnational South Asian Muslim writers in English including Shamsie (who herself might be categorised as "elite" by her local/vernacular Pakistani counterparts) continue to develop and create.

When, therefore, I describe the world literature Aslam et al. create and shape as "globally oriented", I am seeking not only to make reference to the fact that it draws readers' attention to diverse spheres of Islamic affiliation and affinity which may provide insights into 'other' (Muslim) worlds. I also hope to point to the "global" critical consciousness that these Indian and Pakistani writers bring to bear when creating such texts, which may pre-empt, resist or even prevent what Damrosch (2003: 13–14) describes as the 'refract[ion]' or 'assimilat[ion] of the images they present when they enter (mostly Anglo-American) "world" markets.[9] In this I align myself with critics of world literature such as Peter Morey (2012). He has commented that, despite critics such as Gayatri Spivak's (2003) rejection of the term when discussing contemporary literary and social 'mode[s] of ethical critical engagement with inequalities of power' (Morey 2012: 21), "global" has a particular utility when it comes to describing a kind of literary engagement (world literature) that testifies to the 'negotiated nature of lived experience' in an unbalanced and unequal world.[10] In his usage, 'global' suggests that novels produced by writers such as Aslam, Shamsie and Hamid 'describe subjects and situations which are the result of the logic of globalisation, at the same time thereby criticising, exposing and awakening in the [predominantly Western, Anglophone] reader a new awareness of the costs of that process' (49).

Writing Islam reads the novels of the four transnational South Asian Muslim writers as discrete textual entities, shaped by local, regional specificities, yet 'enmeshed ... in the world' (Said 1983: 35) and hence "global" in terms of their orientation and the political, historical and material contexts of their production. In doing so, it surveys the range of identities and connections their authors map for globally implicated South Asian Muslim subjects, and attempts to understand the contribution their writing makes to an emerging category of "world" literature in the third millennium.

Authors, texts and terminology

Born in India and Pakistan, resident at times in and between Manchester, London, New York, Karachi and Lahore, the writers upon whose work this book focuses have at times been described as Anglo-American and British Muslim, in addition to South Asian, Indian or Pakistani. Rushdie, who was born in Bombay immediately prior to Partition, and lived for a time after graduating in Pakistan, was educated in Rugby and Cambridge, and has lived most of his adult life abroad in London and New York. Aslam, born in Gujranwala, Punjab, in the late 1960s, came to the UK with his parents as a teenager, settled in West Yorkshire, studied at Manchester, and now lives in London. Hamid, a Lahori by birth, and Shamsie, a Karachiite, both children of the 1970s, left Pakistan to study in the USA, and have since divided their time between New York, London and the cities of their birth.

The authors' affiliations to different national cultural dispositions – Indian, British, Pakistani and American – in addition to their situatedness within certain (relatively elite) class backgrounds and (globally dominant) linguistic formations have a significant bearing on their work. They influence, for example, the critical perspectives the writers' offer in their novels on the place of religious, communitarian and secular identities within the postcolonial nation state; the value systems upheld by 'home'-based and diasporic societies; conceptions of regional and world history, notions of belonging, attitudes of patriotism, ideas of civil responsibility and so forth. Without negating the significance of nationally specific factors, I treat Rushdie, Hamid, Aslam and Shamsie as situated within a South Asian cultural formation and, for the purposes at hand at least, seek to emphasise this dimension. For, both they and their subjects are part of a modern South Asia whose histories, heritages and hybrid identifications long predate the crude partitioning of the subcontinent into Indian and Pakistani nations, and whose future may hinge, as historians like Rajmohan Gandhi (2014) argue, on the recognition and rehabilitation of the common ties that exist between them.

It is my contention that each of these South Asian anglophone authors has either intensified their focus on the Indian subcontinent, its troubled borderlands and diverse Muslim peoples, in the wake of 9/11, or could be considered to have returned their literary attentions to the region following that moment. While Rushdie's *Fury* (2001), for example, narrowed the focus to contemporary New York and the world of an insular, Americanised cosmopolitan, his first post-9/11 novel, *Shalimar the Clown* (2005c), expands out into global spheres, its action split between metropolitan cities but centring the fatal fallout from a ruptured relationship originally forged in Kashmir, a subcontinental conflict zone. His later work, *The Enchantress of Florence* (2008a), looks back to an earlier period of Islamic cosmopolitanism presided over by the Grand Mughal, Akbar. The action of Hamid's first book, *Moth Smoke* (2000c), is confined to Lahore in the stifling summer of 1998, overshadowed by nuclear tests.

The "windows" it offers onto a corrupt outside world are increasingly obscured by its protagonist's heroin haze. His second novel, *The Reluctant Fundamentalist* (2007b), uses an encounter in Lahore between the "fundamentalist" and his American interlocutor as a framing device, but – like *Shalimar* – is intercontinental in narrative sweep. Its Pakistani Muslim antagonist proffers insights into his life in the USA, and the awakening of his global political consciousness after 9/11. Aslam's *The Wasted Vigil* (2008) and Shamsie's *Burnt Shadows* (2009b) feature characters from disparate parts of the globe, and Afghanistan and Pakistan as substantial geographical settings.[11] They seem to consolidate a shift in the authors' post-9/11 fiction away from narratives set purely in Pakistan or among the diaspora and towards direct engagement with questions of Islamic faith, politics and identity arising in contemporary zones of international conflict located increasingly close to "home".

When, therefore, I refer to the four mobile writers of multiple national, institutional and cultural affiliations and their work as "South Asian" in this study, I am seeking to draw attention to the ways in which their fiction reflects the impact of recent geopolitical events on parts of South Asia and South Asian Muslim subjects, and to explore the complex relationship their representations of these may bear to the authors' ethnic identities. Abdulrazak Gurnah (2007: 3) suggests that whatever Rushdie's desires to the contrary, he can never quite succeed in his aim, expressed in *Shame* (1983), 'to write "the East" out of him and found new origins'. *Writing Islam* considers what happens when "Eastern" (South Asian, Muslim) identities are suddenly re-politicised, and explores the effect this may have on the production and reception of the world literary text.

Terry Eagleton (1996: 7) has observed that 'in much that is classified as literature, the truth value and practical relevance of what is said *is* considered important to the overall effect'. Yet ' "value" is a transitive term', as he goes on to point out, 'it means whatever is valued by certain people in specific situations, according to particular criteria and in the light of given purposes' (10). It is my argument that, in the decade of the "war on terror", pressure has been placed upon transnational and diasporic writers of South Asian (and particularly Pakistani) Muslim origin to 'disclose' to Western readers 'where their identifications, the centres of their subjective universe lie' (Werbner 2002: 3), either directly or through their characters. This is a period in which governments and the media have been fascinated with identifying ' "voices from within" Muslim communities' (Morey and Yaqin 2011: 15) that may illuminate the workings of 'the Muslim' 'mind' for the general public (Davids 2009: 178). Perhaps consequentially, distinctions between fact and fiction, and between autobiographical and novelistic formats, have become blurred. For, in this anxious moment, as Mondal (2012: 38) notes, 'subjective experience is taken to validate the [literary] text's representation of a social phenomenon ([such as] Islamism)' in the rush to "understand" its attraction, and the writer's 'representation of what he calls [Islam]... is taken to be "true" because he speaks of it from "firsthand" experience'. Such writings have been treated as authoritative not only because of the ways in which they are marketed (as instructive and insightful accounts by "native" informants), but also because of the ways that their authors present themselves (as spokespeople) and construct their narratives formally so as to produce a reality effect.[12]

The transnational South Asian Muslim authors whose works I examine remain conscious of the ways in which – on account of their heritage, craft and class status – they may be assumed to be "implicated" (or may strategically implicate themselves) in the complex cultural and (geo)political contexts about which they write. Yet, as their non-fiction commentary clearly demonstrates, each feels a strong obligation to use his or her position to somehow "set the record straight" for Western readers when it comes to Muslim-related matters in general, and South Asian Islam in particular. In my book, I draw on assertions made in interviews, essays and other paratexts to suggest that this commitment informs the perspectives of affiliation and affinity which are offered in their fiction.[13] The novels which Rushdie, Hamid, Aslam and Shamsie have produced in the years since 9/11 have ranged in form from (satirical) thrillers to dramatic monologues, cross-continental romances and polyphonic historical sagas. Although their plotlines are facilitated by some improbable coincidences, and their prose is ornamented at times with poetic allusions, dreams and flights of fancy, each novel is grounded in social, cultural and political realities, whether contemporary or historical. Each takes place in an actually existing location, at a precise point (or points) in time, and centres on complex (Muslim) characters whose lives are punctuated by real events. These include the creation of Pakistan, the

Soviet- and American-led invasions of Afghanistan, the collapse of the Twin Towers and true cases of "honour" crimes in British Muslim communities. All of these "factual" elements encourage the reader to accept the perspectives the fictions present as "true" – or plausible as reimaginings of what might well have passed in these particular contexts.

These novels are also quite specifically constructed and framed so as to create reality effects. *Shalimar* compresses over 50 years of Kashmiri history and features a caricatured and demonic "Islamist" as its central antagonist. But its drama is pinned to specific dates of significance to the region, and peppered with "authentic" Kashmiri, Urdu and Arabic vocabulary and allusions to religious and cultural traditions; meanwhile, the novel is fronted by a dedication to Rushdie's Kashmiri grandparents, which hints at the genealogical credentials he brings to his highly authored account. Hamid's *The Reluctant Fundamentalist* contains no such legend. But it is introduced by a narrator whose voice precisely mimics the tones of certain foreign-educated Pakistanis; it encourages the listener/interlocutor to respond to its peculiarly polite and provocative Muslim protagonist *as if he were* real.[14] Aslam (2008: front pages) ushers in his Afghanistan-set epic *Vigil* with a reflection from President Carter's National Security Advisor on the Taliban's role in shaping world history and an excerpt from a fifteenth-century Afghan poet. A disclaimer at the book's close underlines its incorporation of 'real event[s]' (435). Thus Aslam seems to invite world readers to interpret his lyrical, psychological fiction as history rewritten: as a perceptive comment on the current situation in Central Asia, backed by regional connections and intensive research. Shamsie (2002b, 2009b), too, inserts lists of works consulted and for further reading into her meticulously researched global fictions. These perhaps encourage readers to interpret her novels not as definitive, "authoritative" revisions, but rather as decentred interventions into the wider geopolitical discourses with which they engage: as alternative insights into the impacts of colonialism and the postcolonial fallout, neo-imperialism and globalisation on migrant Asian, Muslim citizens.

In identifying Rushdie, Hamid, Aslam and Shamsie as "Muslim", I take my cue from Amin Malak's (2004: 3) study of novels by authors for whom 'Islam retains an identity-shaping valence'. Malak uses this term in preference to "Islamic" to refer to the writers and the narratives he examines, thereby emphasising their cultural (but not necessarily their theological) rootedness in the civilisation of Islam (5). As he explains,

> *Muslim*...denotes the *person* who espouses the religion of Islam or is shaped by its cultural impact, irrespective of being secular, agnostic, or practicing believer... *Muslim narratives* suggests the works produced by the person who believes firmly in the faith of Islam; and/or, via an inclusivist extension, by the person who voluntarily and knowingly refers to herself...as a 'Muslim' when given a selection of identitarian choices; and/or, by yet another generous extension, by the *person* who is rooted formatively and emotionally in the culture and civilization of Islam. (5–7)

It is by the last proposed 'extension' that Malak feels able to defend the inclusion in his study of *The Satanic Verses* (1988). This is a book which, despite its secular author's rejection of religious and cultural 'absolutism' (Rushdie 1991: 394), may function to reinforce stereo-types and thus to facilitate the transformation of what Malak (2004: 110) terms the 'literary product' into a hot-property commercial 'item' attractive to 'anti-Muslim consumers' as a result of its irrev-erent perspectives on the Prophet and Islam. The same accusation, though to a lesser degree, might be lodged at some of the works explored in the later sections of my book. Aslam's *Maps* (2004a) is a novel which the *New York Times* reviewer Akash Kapur (2005: n.p.) considered to be 'infused with an anger that is occasionally overdone, yielding passages that read like an assault on the religion from which all the characters' unhappiness seems to originate'.

Yet while Malak seems anxious to justify the incorporation of the narratives of controversial secular "Muslim" writers such as Rushdie in his book, I see the consideration of the fictions of such ambiva-lent authors as important to mine. Indeed, both their critical and at times anti-Islamic voices, and those narratives which seek to repro-duce the 'inquisitorial, condemnatory' Islamic ones which Malak (2004: 155) might place beyond the pale of Muslim literary tradi-tion, seem a crucial component of any study which seeks to explore a range of depictions of Muslims after 9/11. As I will argue, Rushdie, Hamid, Aslam and Shamsie's recent fictions and related non-fiction texts demonstrate very different attempts to contest in literature what Robert Spencer (2010a) might term official 'fundamentalist', in the sense of unquestioned, dogmatic, essentialist or undemocratic, narratives in relation to Islam generated on either side of the imagined East/West divide. Some of these may, if read in isolation, prove insensitive or unpalatable to certain readers (although Spencer would suggest that the best of them stage dialogues in themselves). Yet, considered together, all may contribute to a vital literary and hence discursive project of (re)orienting South Asian Muslims in texts published in the West in the wake of the "war on terror".

From *Shalimar* to *Burnt Shadows*

In the ensuing chapters, I explore the hypothesis that there has been a shift towards a more politically engaged form of English-language fiction amongst South Asian Muslim (and predominantly Pakistani) writers in the years since 9/11, in part in response to media and market pressures – to a demand for explanatory stories and authentic spokespeople – but also a result of the individual authors' desire to rewrite this Islamic "East" with which, in the contemporary climate, they are assumed to have an intimate connection.

In my next chapter, I consider the work of Salman Rushdie, who comes from an older generation of Indian English writers praised and criticised for their cosmopolitan, migrant, postcolonial and "Third World" perspectives. He is perhaps better known 'as a tongue-in-cheek chronicler of modern India [and] facetious gadfly to Islamic orthodoxies' (Huggan 2001: 86) than as a subtle or sympathetic commentator on "home" events. I suggest that he has responded to the pressure 'to find a way of writing after 11 September 2001' (Rushdie 2002: 436) by refocusing his attention on Islam in its South Asian contexts. I examine, in conjunction with the statements he makes in his essay collection *Step Across This Line* (2002), the two ostensibly very different novels he has produced since then, *Shalimar the Clown* (2005c) and *The Enchantress of Florence* (2008a), which both seek to provide reasons for contemporary Islamic terror and excavate earlier histories of cosmopolitan Muslim civilisation on the Indian subcontinent.[15] Yet I stress that while Rushdie's name has become 'entwined with the literary representation of Islam' (Malak 2004: 91) since the publication of *The Satanic Verses* (1988), he remains a problematic "Muslim" spokesperson with regard to contemporary Islam.

I argue that his post-9/11 fictions tend to fall back on fairly simplistic domestic explanations for individual engagements with political Islam; caricature as fanatics the Islamists whose origins and motivations they might seek to deconstruct; cling on to nostalgic notions of a tolerant, pan-Indian spirituality; and leave unmapped more complex experiences and acts of faith (Rushdie 2005c: 116–17; 2008a: 390). They thus provide a contrast with the more acute, uncomfortable and local perspectives offered by a younger generation of transnational Pakistani writers including Hamid and Shamsie on the attitudes, affiliations and affinities of contemporary South Asian Muslims. Rushdie's recent fictions also seem to lack in their secular scepticism the intricate insights into Islamic history and culture – in particular its aesthetic and spiritual appeal – offered by Aslam and Shamsie in their later novels.

In the third chapter, I go on to consider how in *The Reluctant Fundamentalist* (2007b) Hamid stages a singular, studied and provocative act of "writing back" to Western fictions of Muslim affiliation and identity after 9/11.[16] This book's distinctive monological style sets it apart from the other often polyphonic "world" fictions which form the basis of this study; it resembles more closely the real-life confessional memoirs of former Islamists. At a time of heightened interest in stories told from the '*inside*' (Husain 2007, Preface), Hamid proffers a Pakistani Muslim Other's seemingly instructive tale of a young life lived in corporate America's dark domains, one with obvious parallels to his own, whose authority – ironically, tantalisingly – remains impossible to verify.

Hamid's slippery monologue plays directly with the Western interlocutor and reader. Its Pakistani narrator second-guesses his foreign listener's responses to the "native" life he puts on view, and presents an "official" (but not necessarily trustworthy) interpretation in its stead – one which may serve further to obscure the face of the "fundamentalist" whose true identity the reader seeks. By contrast, Aslam's and Shamsie's third-person narratives describe rather than dramatically create moments of interpersonal tension, uncertainty and unease, as seen from multiple perspectives. They present alternative frameworks for understanding terror, faith and "other" ways of seeing the world in the war on terror's wake, rather than narrating their inability to address these issues.

The fourth chapter considers the first two novels produced by the British-based Pakistani writer Aslam after 9/11: *Maps* (2004a) and *Vigil* (2008). In this period, his fictions turn from depicting the tensions between members of a "close-knit" Pakistani community in a multicultural English town, to sketching the bonds forged by international strangers whose lives collide in a war-torn Afghan village. The chapter asks how far they present alternative conceptions of Muslim affiliation and affinity in zones of inter-faith contact and conflict. It acknowledges the partial and still-circumscribed nature of the Muslim modernities the diasporic Aslam places on display and suggests that he nostalgically promotes a fragile secular, aesthetic, Sufistic Islam while – like Rushdie – surveying other cultural manifestations and theological interpretations of the faith with suspicion. Further, it argues that despite Aslam's commitment to portraying the 'historical dimension...psychology...and...complexity of the social and cultural situation' (King 2009: 474) responsible for producing the conditions where peoples appear to clash, his fiction reinforces the idea that the followers of a fundamental and political Islam and those who adhere to the liberal, democratic principles of the West are ultimately irreconcilable. Whereas in Hamid's faux-confessional narrative the chameleon-like Changez confounds the novel's title by eluding definite classification, Aslam's characters collapse back into the essentialising 'good' and 'bad' Muslim categories of Mamood Mamdani's (2004: 17–18) 'Culture Talk', even as the writer attempts to unpick them.[17] I go on to suggest that Aslam's post-9/11 fiction fails to rise to the greater challenge of using world literature formally and thematically to question the individual's responsibility to comprehend the emotional and spiritual needs, and to confront the geopolitical conditions, that may result in a turn towards a radical Islam, and the apparent "clash" which he bemoans.

The fifth chapter examines Kamila Shamsie's novels *Kartography* (2002b), *Broken Verses* (2005a) and *Burnt Shadows* (2009b). It asks how she responds in these fictions to the pronouncements of a White, Western, male establishment in 9/11's wake; to Rushdie's ambiguous legacies; and to those diasporic writers such as Aslam, who have followed him. In doing so, it notes certain resemblances in terms of trope and treatment: Shamsie's novels and short fiction include figures like Hamid's Changez: moody Pakistani males out of love with a securitised and suspicious West; they feature sensual scenes akin to those of Aslam, where Muslim characters explore their humanity through communing with a range of Islamic and "pagan" religious artefacts; and they entertain with witty, mocking passages in which Rushdie-esque mullahs are synecdochically reduced to "beards". However, I contend that Shamsie, aware of the commercial potency of such "exotic" symbols and tropes, consciously deploys these and other colourful, multicultural and romantic elements to engage the reader in her always more complex fiction. As a result, she avoids duplicating Hamid's deft but elliptical monological affront on Western conceptions of Islamic identity, Aslam's melancholic retreat into a pan-religious aesthetic or Rushdie's (2002: 436) trivialisation of religious leaders otherwise 'unimaginable' to him.

This penultimate chapter argues that, by mapping a range of global 'Muslim' experiences of cross-cultural alienation and interconnection seen from Western, non-Western and feminine perspectives, Shamsie complicates the reader's understanding of contemporary South and Central Asian Muslim identities as enacted within the social and political parameters of Pakistan, Afghanistan and America. She uses a fiction of colliding worlds to stage moments of inter-cultural encounter in which the protagonist and "reader" is urged to interrogate the power relationships that underpin assumptions about Islamic identity, "frame" interpretations of suspect behaviour and dictate a hostile response. The actor in this conflict zone must take responsibility for both her own and her country's role in creating and maintaining the Islamic figure of fear. For, in Shamsie's networked fiction, the South Asian, Islamic "terrorist" is neither a super-powered, otherworldly intruder motivated by a personal vendetta; nor is he a privileged, postcolonial fictional cipher, able to baffle his reader with a barrage of words. Rather, he is an ordinary, often mistaken, and marginal figure, caught up in global politics as he struggles to find a way (to be at) "home".

Ultimately I argue that the novels examined in *Writing Islam* may be read as attempts to respond in writing to the fears, preconceptions and curiosities about Islamic identities which have dominated Western discourses over the course of the post-9/11 decade. They are produced by South Asian authors with disparate attitudes to "Islam", which have been shaped in particular regional, transnational and diasporic contexts. And these writers have widely diverging appreciations of the bearing that the faith has (had) on contemporary and historic Muslim identities. Some strive more simply to reveal where the centres of their suspect South Asian, Muslim characters' subjective universes may lie: to "map" their identifications forensically, so that they might be "known" by the reader and categorised, thus perhaps reinforcing more limited and prejudicial (Western) perspectives. Others approach the act of disclosure more subtly, indicating (ironically) the impossibility of pinpointing a particular space of Islamic affiliation or affinity which may govern their protagonists' hearts and minds. However, I propose that it is those authors who use their novels less to expand understandings about Muslims' intra- and inter-cultural connectivity than to turn the tables, questioning the ethics of exposing ordinary Muslims' personal identifications to public scrutiny, who present the most radical, literary challenge to world readers.[18] For these global fictions contain within them critiques of the dominant political and cultural forces which require nominally Muslim subjects' Islamic affiliations and affinities to be disclosed. Challenging the Amis-Hitchens consensus, these novels in a variety of ways prompt Western readers to reconsider their own prejudices about Islam and expectations about the "insights" Muslim fiction in English may unfold.

2

Enchanted Realms, Sceptical Perspectives – Salman Rushdie after 9/11

2.1 Salman Toor

Introduction

Rushdie's two post-9/11 novels: the transnational thriller *Shalimar the Clown* (2005c) and the continent-connecting historical romance *The Enchantress of Florence* (2008a), are two ostensibly very different works in which the author endeavours to provide his readers with reasons for contemporary Islamic terror, and to excavate earlier histories of cosmopolitan Muslim civilisation in India. These fictions feature a range of idiosyncratic affinities felt by Muslim protagonists for individuals from Islamic and other religious backgrounds, which are dramatised in scenes of both harmonious multicultural coexistence and robust inter-faith debate. In this sense, they continue in part to reflect the 'mosaic of diverse cultural identifications' (Nasta 2002: 147) experienced by Rushdie as a privileged, cosmopolitan intellectual, and cultivated by the hybrid and migrant characters featured in many of his more diasporic fictions.

Yet it is my argument, as this chapter will demonstrate, that the specifically Islamic networks or "affiliations" which *Shalimar* and *The Enchantress* also describe are, by contrast, considerably more limited. In these third-millennium novels, the pursuit of a more orthodox or "fundamental" Muslim connection invariably results not in a healthy, heterogeneous and 'anti-essentialist' realisation of a multicultural self (Nasta 2002: 149), but an aggressive and monomaniacal erasure of any preceding allegiance or identity which might obscure an Islamist's nihilistic understanding of "truth".

Rushdie today: Writer and pundit

Salman Rushdie is today an established if controversial figure within English literary circles. In the course of a career that spans almost four decades he has won fame and notoriety both on and off the page, not only for his many novels – most notably *Midnight's Children* (1981), which in 2008 was awarded the Best of the Booker, and the inflammatory *The Satanic Verses* (1988), which incurred the Valentine's day fatwa in 1989 – but his political and cultural punditry, colourful personal life, and seeming institutionalisation. Whether volunteered or invited, the opinions Rushdie has aired and the actions he has undertaken in the glare of an increasingly global public spotlight have never failed to cause a stir, particularly when they have related to

"Muslim" matters. His (2005b: 19) criticism of Tony Blair's knight-
ing of the Muslim Council of Britain's Secretary General as 'the
acceptable face of "moderate" ... Islam', ridicule of the Archbishop of
Canterbury's "inane" suggestions about the incorporation of sharia
into UK law (Rushdie 2008b: n.p.) and acceptance of a Birthday
Honour in a move perhaps 'calculated to goad Muslims' (Hoyle 2007:
3), provide examples.

Over the course of the last decade Rushdie has perhaps modified
the stance he initially took in support of the Bush and Blair governments' responses to the World Trade Centre attacks and their
subsequent 'War on Terror' (Gurnah 2007: 7), evident in essays like
'February 2002: Anti-Americanism', published in the *New York Times*
and anthologised in *Step Across This Line* (Rushdie 2002: 398–400).
However, a brief sample of his latest newspaper interviews and
comment would serve to confirm Robert Spencer's (2010b: 260–1)
opinion that the savage censure Rushdie has provided of a fundamentalist Islam in such pieces remains unmatched by his critique of
Western universalism and hegemony.

When asked, for example, by *The Guardian*'s Susannah Rustin to
offer his opinion on the French law on secularity and conspicuous
religious symbols which was passed in 2004, popularly discussed as a
ban on headscarves, Rushdie refused to 'defend the veil' in the interest of championing women's rights (Rushdie 2010b: n.p.). Apparently
still seeking to promote a vision of female "freedom" largely based
around the loose notion that this equates to the uncensored wear-
ing of 'short skirts' (2002: 393), he took the opportunity to accuse
'women in the West who use [the veil] as a badge of identity' of
acting in 'false consciousness' (2010b). His negation of the possibility that such politically conscious females may be something more
than misguided says more about the limits of Rushdie's secular liberal
imagination than it does about their ignorance or disingenuousness.

In the same interview, speaking in relation to the controversial and
much-misreported proposals to build a Muslim community centre
in lower Manhattan two blocks away from the Ground Zero site,
Rushdie made the following comment: 'I'm not a big fan of mosques,
I'm not a great fan of mullahs ... [But] of course people should have a
place to be able to observe their religion.' This statement seems more
conciliatory. Yet its author's primary interest seems not to endorse
the centre's (Muslim) users' right to express their faith affiliations

freely, but to ensure that the entire site can 'go back just to being part of New York', with Muslims departing quietly to pursue their faith-related activities in a space nominally approved and sanctioned by Western liberals, but barely visible to American eyes. It is consistent with his view that religion should be confined to the private sphere.

Rushdie's interview with Rustin was ostensibly convened to discuss *Luka and the Fire of Life* (Rushdie 2010a), the author and father's new 'novel for teenagers', a book which she proposes it is 'hard not to see...as a rebranding exercise...a deliberate step...towards something lighter, slighter and much more personal' than its ambitious, topical precedents (Rustin 2010: n.p.). Rushdie's latest story collection may appear apolitical, but it seems inevitable with such a writer that the conversation which takes place around it will be easily sidetracked onto more controversial and political matters.

Decades after Iran's Ayatollah Khomeini pronounced his death sentence, then, it certainly seems that Rushdie remains committed to cultivating the role of 'a political figure and very public writer' in relation to Islam (Rushdie 2002: 432). Indeed his interest in exploring Islam on the subcontinent seems to have been freshly renewed, in the wake of both the 9/11 attacks on New York and the communal violence sparked by perceived acts of Islamic terror in South Asia in the months that followed them (401). He may criticise Western and, specifically, American news media for narrowing the parameters of what it is permissible to say, particularly post-9/11 (Rushdie 2005a: n.p.). Yet the author repeatedly adopts the mantle of pundit. Rushdie uses the "global" opportunities afforded by his international status to emphasise the Indian Muslim aspect of his identity as he seeks to legitimise his claim to speak with authority about how minority Islamic communities should behave in relation to other faiths and cultures.

In his essay 'November 2001: Not about Islam?', Rushdie (2002: 394) focuses on the primitive spectre of hordes of Muslim men amassed on the 'Pakistan–Afghanistan frontier, answering some mullah's call to jihad', in order to emphasise the (to him, clear) connection between 'terror' and a 'belief' in Islam. Later in the same essay he reminds the reader of the critical perspectives he offered of Pakistani Muslims' self-exonerating anti-Americanism in his 1983 novel *Shame*. In 'Not about Islam', Rushdie (2002: 396) goes on to state, 'I wanted then to ask a question which is no less important

now: suppose we say...that we are to blame for our own failings?'
The expatriate author's use of the collective pronoun "we" points to
the kinship he would claim to possess with the Muslims of South
Asia. This is an affinity Rushdie foregrounds even as he seeks from
a Westernised perspective to censor the attitudes of the people who
hail from what he describes, in his contemporaneous 'Lectures on
Human Values', as the subcontinent's 'blinkered monoculture' (430).

It should be noted that critics such as Spencer (2010b: 262) have
recently seen fit to draw a distinction between Rushdie's 'literary' and
'political output', arguing that his early and controversial novel *The
Satanic Verses* offers, by contrast, 'an attack on [a] kind of Islam, not
Islam per se'. Spencer cites Rushdie's interest in 'heterodox Islamic
traditions', such as Sufism, and the emphasis he places in the novel
on 'doubt, discussion, criticism and interpretation', as evidence of its
author's commitment to portraying an alternative and more humane
Islam in opposition to aggressive Islamisms (262).[1]

Rushdie's two post-9/11 novels redirect the reader's attentions
towards Muslims in "native" South Asian (as opposed to migrant,
diasporic) contexts, and would certainly seem to bear witness to a
subtle but arguably significant shift not only in critical but in literary-
fictional focus. This is a shift back in time and geographical location
to the civilised, multi-faith and majority-Muslim societies of pre-
Partition and Mughal India, recalled and recreated from the figures
of Rushdie's childhood memory and remnants of historical nostalgia.
Yet it is one whose visions are ever overshadowed by Rushdie's (2002:
430–1) impressions of a closely related but 'utterly alien' Pakistan,
which he visited as a reluctant adolescent, and by this country's "barbaric" Central Asian Islamic and Middle Eastern Muslim brothers.[2]

Rushdie's tendency to satirise rather than to attempt realistically
to represent religious "fundamentalisms", particularly of an Islamic
persuasion, can of course be traced to earlier works such as *Shame*
(1983) and *The Satanic Verses* (1988). These energetic, entertaining
fictions feature apparently devout Muslim characters – a dangerously
obsessive local Maulana driven wild by his shoestring necklace of
shame (Rushdie 1983: 43); a saintly, seer-like, silver-haired girl on her
deadly mission to Mecca (1988: 473–6) – many of whom may best
be described as deluded and disorientated in their respective relationships to the divine. However, it is their controversial "Muslim"
creator's continuance and consolidation of these types in the globally

distributed fictions he has produced since the launch of the "war on terror" – and hence in relation to a discourse dominated by popular misconceptions about an Islamic "axis of evil", clash of civilisations and meltdown of metropolitan multiculture – which is of greatest relevance to this book.

Some literary critics and theorists have dismissed Rushdie in recent years for his lack of political engagement, pointing to his failure as a 'migrant' writer to continue to 'rebuke' or 'challenge' the fundamental (and unequal) values of a Western society which, since the fatwa, has provided him with shelter (Eagleton 2007b: n.p.). In Terry Eagleton's opinion, Rushdie is 'a man who moved from being a remorseless satirist of the West [in Thatcher's 1980s] to cheering on its criminal adventures in Iraq and Afghanistan' in the age of Bush and Blair; one whose literary output no longer retains the radical perspectives of 'the left'. While not overlooking the limitations of Rushdie's recent punditry, other critics have sought rather to refocus attention on the dissenting and sceptical perspectives provided in his earlier novels, such as *The Satanic Verses*, which exposes both the apparent bigotry of the "character" of Muhammad and the inequality of Britain under 'Mrs. Torture' (Rushdie 1988: 266). They argue that what might be termed the anti-fundamentalist or "a-theistic" position adopted by the novelist in relation to any voice of authority, political, cultural or religious, remains particularly vital at a time when the survival of our world is threatened not only by the proponents of global jihad but also by global capitalism (Spencer 2010b).

Bradley and Tate (2010), however, in their study of *The New Atheist Novel*, suggest that Rushdie's most recent fictions, like those of other British men of letters, including Amis, Ian McEwan and Philip Pullman, 'too often end up bearing witness to the sheer poverty of our public discourse on religion' (111). In their opinion, these writers are more likely to 'dramatize...a return to some pre-rational religious dogmatism' or 'fetishiz[e]...liberal enlightenment values' than 'attempt to move beyond the Manichean clash of religious and secular fundamentalisms epitomised by 9/11...offering more complex and variegated pictures of the multi-faith world beyond' (109). Yet *The New Atheist Novel*'s authors also emphasise the important role the novel has to play in the current climate in providing a means by which readers can sensitively and seriously engage with alternative and undogmatic modes of 'religiously-inflected seeing and being' (109). The creators of such 'post-atheist' literary texts, they argue, must write despite personal doubt 'as if [they] believed in the possibility of religious experience as something irreducible to the standard categories available to science and method' (85).

The post-9/11 fictions

Shalimar the Clown

Shalimar the Clown (2005c), which appeared in the UK less than two months after the 7/7 bombings, was Rushdie's first work of fiction since his pre-9/11 *Fury* (2001). The earlier novel, set in New York, imagined America at the decadent height of a hubristic 'golden age', troubled by a malaise linked to a growing consciousness of the less privileged and exploited world's oncoming wrath or 'fury' (Rushdie 2001: 114). Like *Fury*, *Shalimar*'s narrative spans continents – namely the Indian subcontinent, Europe and North America – but a single geographical space is located at its story's heart. In this case the space is a South Asian one: the disputed Muslim-majority state of Kashmir, which Rushdie has described as being of particular interest:

> Because I am more than half Kashmiri myself, because I have loved the place all my life, and because I have spent most of that life listening to successive Indian and Pakistani governments... mouthing the self-serving hypocrisies of power while ordinary Kashmiris suffered. (2002: 305)

It provides both the idyllic setting for the novel's inter-faith romance, and – when love fails – the site of Shalimar's terroristic turn.

Shalimar compresses and selectively embellishes over 50 years of political Kashmiri history, from the moments immediately prior to the cessation of British rule and Partition of India to the ongoing conflicts of the twentieth century, focusing on the incursion of communalism into the idealised space of the predominantly Muslim Valley of Kashmir. When the subcontinent was partitioned and granted independence in August 1947, the feudal Hindu ruler of Jammu and Kashmir, Maharaja Hari Singh, was undecided as to whether to join Congress-led India or the newly established Muslim nation of Pakistan. He eventually signed a treaty of accession with

India following the invasion, in October, of Pakistani tribesmen from the North-West Frontier. War broke out between the two nations, and was ended by a ceasefire initiated in 1949 and overseen by the United Nations Security Council, which also adopted a resolution that a plebiscite should be held once hostilities had ceased to decide the question of the state's accession. But troops were not evacuated, and Kashmir was partitioned for practical purposes between Pakistan, which administered "Azad" (Free) Jammu and Kashmir and the Northern Areas, and India, which controlled the state of Jammu and Kashmir, including the 'prized valley' (Schofield 2000: xi). War broke out again in 1965, but the 1949 ceasefire line (renamed the "Line of Control" in 1972) 'remained the de facto border' (xi). By 1989, a protest movement against the Indian administration among the valley's Muslim population had gathered momentum. This was, according to Victoria Schofield, 'both an armed struggle and a political rejection of their continuing allegiance to the Indian Union' (xiii). But, as she also notes, it 'lack[ed an] obvious unanimity of objective', and was resisted by other inhabitants of the state, such as the Ladhaki Buddhists, Kargil's Shia Muslims and the Hindus and Sikhs of Jammu, while the Pakistani government 'was only too happy to support the movement "morally and diplomatically" ', and 'unofficially ... to assist in reviving the spirit of the 1947 "jihad"' among the "Islamist" insurgents', hoping that it might thus 'achieve militarily what it had failed to gain through negotiation' (xiv). The conflict continues in the twenty-first century and, following the 9/11 attacks, Pakistan's involvement in fostering terrorism in the region has come increasingly under the international spotlight.

At the level of global politics, Rushdie may be understood to use his multiply located "world" novel to explore the ties that connect and bind the oppositional and archetypal figures of the powerful, covetous American and the embittered Kashmiri jihadi. Yet the link traced between their different worlds in Rushdie's ostensible 'fiction of intrigue' (a fiction born of imperial contexts which, according to Siddiqi (2008: 1), 'foregrounds a threat to the [Western hegemonic] social and political order') appears on examination more personal and cultural than religious and political, based as it is on human bonds of love, sex and "honour".

Shalimar's drama revolves around the fallout from a love affair that flares in the early 1960s between two Kashmiri teenagers who are born in 1947, at the dawn of Partition. Raised in the idyllic multi-faith community of Pachigam, the tightrope walker Noman ("Shalimar"), son of the village *sarpanch*, falls for a dancer named Boonyi, the pandit's green-eyed daughter. Their romance unfortunately flares at a time when sectarian differences in the disputed valley are becoming increasingly exaggerated, and communal violence is escalating. But when their sexual liaison is exposed, the villagers decide – despite some consternation – to support the Hindu–Muslim match in the spirit of '*Kashmiriyat*', or of national, social and cultural solidarity (Rushdie 2005c: 110).[3]

Tensions increase in 1965 with the appearance of a foreign 'iron mullah', Bulbul Fakh, in the neighbouring town of Shirmal; the local people shelter the firebrand preacher and build him a mosque. He denounces the pluralist Pachigam as an enemy to the "true faith". But things only truly fall apart with the arrival of the Alsatian Resistance hero turned US Ambassador Max Ophuls, drawn to the "issue" of Kashmir by a sense of a common cause. He seduces (or is seduced by) Boonyi, installs her in Delhi, then abandons her – first to gluttony and narcotics, then, when the scandal of their affair breaks, to the clutches of his envious wife. She abducts the resulting child, "Kashmira", and raises her in America as "India". Bent on revenge, Shalimar retrains as an Islamic terrorist; Boonyi, broken, returns home to wait for death.

The Kashmiri tale central to Rushdie's continent-spanning novel unfolds largely in extended flashback, framed by the story of Max's assassination in Los Angeles in 1991. Max, now America's chief of counterterrorism, is knifed to death in the book's opening pages by his Kashmiri driver "Shalimar" in a seeming act of Islamic terror. After this, the narrative leaps back to paradisiacal, pre-Partition Kashmir to tell the story of Boonyi and Noman's births and fatal love. It goes on to encompass Nazi-occupied Strasbourg, Islamist training camps in Pakistan and the California of the migrant elite. It ends there, in America, with India/Kashmira's Manichean struggle to defeat Shalimar, her vengeful stepfather.

The instances of Muslim or Islamic connection featured in this complex narrative are largely split between feelings of a broadly spiritual and cultural affinity on the one hand, and more radical religious and political affiliations on the other. The affinitive connections seem largely to be local and benign – a sympathy felt for a popular

Sufi saint long revered in Kashmir or favourite figure from Mughal literature, for instance. The affiliations, however, appear more dangerous in persuasion; they are typified by the commitments of the delinquent, deranged or politically enraged to an 'un-Kashmiri and un-Indian' hard-line Islam (Rushdie 2005c: 122).[4]

The first of these senses of connection – affinity – is perhaps exemplified by the spontaneous flood of feelings of what we could term "psychical or spiritual attraction" experienced by Shalimar's father Abdullah on entering the Mughal pleasure gardens where his acting troupe is to perform the 'traditional *Ram Leela'* and *'Budshah, the tale of a Muslim sultan'*, in service of Kashmir's maharaja (71). Abdullah's emotions are intensified partly as a result of a pre-existing sense of kinship with the gardens' founder, the Mughal emperor Jehangir, whom the Muslim headman deems superior to Kashmir's current Hindu ruler; and partly as a result of his substantial imaginative and auto-suggestive abilities as a professional actor-manager (78–9). For the dreamy and nostalgic Abdullah, the draw of the garden is predominantly aesthetic and secular. He is entranced by the 'water music' that plays from its 'liquid terraces', and hypnotised by the 'horticulturalist monarch['s] ... love-song' to the earth (78).

Such feelings of affinity may lead the gentle, moderate village headman wistfully to fantasise about deposing Hari Singh and reinstating Jehangir's glorious past:

> The present maharaja was no Mughal emperor, but Abdullah's imagination could easily change that ... [He] closed his eyes and conjured up the long-dead creator of this wonderland ... he felt himself being transformed into that dead king ... the Encompasser of the Earth, and [he felt] the languorous sensuality of power. (78)

But for Rushdie's comic character, the impulse toward or desire to embody an Islamic potentate remains benign: Rushdie gives the reader no reason to anticipate that Abdullah's indolent daydream of becoming Jehangir will translate into any insurgent action. Yet the author hints that his protagonist's nostalgic, aesthetic connection may nevertheless pose a threat, not to global civilisations or international relations, but to local civilian ones, at a time when Kashmiris – made nervous by rumours that 'looting, raping' armies of *kabailis* (Pashtun tribesmen) have crossed into Kashmir from the new-made

Pakistan – are beginning to wonder: 'maybe we are too different after all' (85, 87). The negative implications of Abdullah's dreamy pursuit of his affinitive aspirations is registered in Rushdie's narrative by the *sarpanch*'s level-headed wife, Firdaus, who interrupts her husband's delusional ventriloquising of the Mughal emperor in his philosophical death throes to return Abdullah to the demands of the narrative present:

> She grabbed her husband roughly...she shouted, deliberately making her words as harsh as possible. 'This garden has a big effect on small men. They start believing they are giants...If you want to prepare to play a king...think about Zain-ul-abidin in the first play. Think about Lord Ram in the second.' (79)

Firdaus may simply wish her husband to refocus on the task in hand – the night's coming performance. But her words also seem to betray a fear that Abdullah's fixation on this Muslim aspect of their syncretic Kashmiri heritage may contribute to tensions within the region's multi-faith community, for which their acting troupe has always striven to provide a balanced portrayal of Muslims and Hindus alike. In the fractious post-Partition climate *Shalimar* describes, symptoms of sentimental experiences of religio-cultural affinity must be suppressed in order to lessen the risk of causing cultural offence.

Other benign-seeming Muslim connections charted by *Shalimar* include a spiritual affinity or feeling of 'fond[ness]' on the part of the residents of Pachigam for a range of historic Sufi saints or *pirs* and living seers, ranging from the fourteenth-century saint Hazrat Bulbul Shah, fabled for introducing Islam to Kashmir and for unfreezing the waters of the Jhelum, to Khwaja Abdul Hakim, a 'doctor and Sufistic philosopher', who ministers in the twentieth to the bodily and spiritual needs of Pachigam and Shirmal's diverse populations (82, 115). The doctor momentarily appears in the narrative to preside over the lovers' nativity in the Shalimar gardens. He fails to find a medical remedy from amongst his impressively heterogeneous skill set, which encompasses the practices of West and East, to save Boonyi's mother; she dies in childbirth. Yet the learned doctor is nevertheless able to offer the grieving Pyarelal Kaul some philosophical consolation, drawn from the teachings of Sufi mysticism but equally accessible in the religiously 'blurred' Kashmiri context, to the Hindu *pandit* (83).

The *khwaja*'s gentle dialogue with Pyarelal on the bitterness of his beloved wife's untimely departure: 'the question of death...proposes itself, does it not, panditji, every day...[But] you have a beautiful daughter...The question of death is also the question of life, panditji' – lulls both parties into a sentimental sense of accord, like the 'Sufi hymns' which, harmoniously alternating with the 'Hindu *bhajans*', soothe the jangling nerves of the guests at Shalimar and Boonyi's carefully orchestrated multi-faith wedding (83–4, 113). He is a figure of 'sectarian ambiguity' whose practices may present 'a compendium of everything of which Islamic puritans most disapprove' (Dalrymple 2009: 114–15); yet the *khwaja* also appears to represent, in Rushdie's idyllic vision of pre-conflict Kashmir, 'everything that was best about the valley...its tolerance, its merging of faiths', which made a nonsense of 'austere monotheism' (Rushdie 2005c: 83).

The Sufistic sensibilities dramatised in *Shalimar* seem to resemble those of the author's Kashmiri grandfather, also a doctor. Rushdie dedicates the novel to him, and remembers the old man with respect and affection. In an interview he gave to Johann Hari soon after the book was published, Rushdie (2006: n.p.) is reported to have described his ancestor as simultaneously devout, rational and enlightened; a 'model of tolerance' happy to engage in conversation, even disputation, when faced with his teasing grandson's religious doubt. Hari (2006: n.p.) emphasises the distinction drawn by Rushdie between this elder man's 'mild, mystical' Kashmiri Islam, akin in Rushdie's opinion to that practised today by India's pluralist and 'secular-minded' Muslims, and the 'austere' brand of fundamental Arab Islam introduced to the valley in the 1960s. In Hari's crude terms, 'the Kashmir of Salman's grandfather stands for [Rushdie] as an alternate Islam, a radically different way of being Muslim to the Khomeinist and Bin Ladenite head-choppers'. Rushdie depicts "Islamic" affinities largely peaceable in character in *Shalimar*'s opening stages.[5] But it is the stricter affiliations of precisely such radically "other" Muslims – Islamist insurgents and fundamentalist fanatics – that he strains to represent as his novel turns from Kashmiri romance to global jihadist thriller.

In the narrative, the residents of Pachigam retain their 'fond' attitude toward – or affinity for – the centuries-old saints and scholars associated with Sufi mysticism even as the foreign-leaning Islamic preachers who enter the valley threaten to usurp or drive them into

extinction (Rushdie 2005c: 115, 87). Rushdie portrays the inquis-
itive native Kashmiri community's openness towards such Sufistic
figures as harmless in itself. Yet his novel illustrates the potential of
such instinctive and intense emotions – like Abdullah's fixation on
the Mughal aesthete Jehangir – to lead the villagers into more sinister realms, particularly if exploited. The 'iron mullah' whom, it is
rumoured, was 'miraculously born' of abandoned Indian 'war met-
als', and who poses on arrival as the reincarnation of the saint Bulbul
Shah, ostensibly stays in Shirmal at its populace's behest: 'many
ears' are curious to hear his message, we are told (115–16). When
articulated in his harsh, alien tones, the familiar *azaan* or summons
to prayer is transformed into a 'call to arms', a means of drawing
the variously enthralled, obedient and opportunistic Kashmiris into
pan-Islamic insurgent networks (123). It is to the Maulana's sectarian cause of 'resistance and revenge', preached from his pulpit, that
Shalimar and several of the valley's dissatisfied youths subsequently
become affiliates (115).[6]

In his unyielding, metallic quality, the iron mullah resembles other
militant religious "fanatics" portrayed in Rushdie's earlier fiction,
such as the hard-line Hindu nationalist Sammy Hazaré, also known
as the 'Tin-man', who appears in *The Moor's Last Sigh* (Rushdie 1995:
301). However, Sammy, a Christian Maharashtrian convert, is to some
extent humanised. We learn, for example, that he joins Fielding's fundamentalist 'crew' for 'regionalist rather than religious reasons', yet
that the somewhat unhinged individual has become 'half-man, half-
can', less as a result of a radical political commitment and more on
account of his obsession with bomb-making (311–12).

Rushdie (2005c) uses the scrap-metal legend in his critical Kashmiri
narrative to emphasise a causal link between aggressive Indian military intervention in the region and the rise of this radical new
brand of Islamic preacher which is its direct legacy, born out of
and fostered in opposition to it. The foreignness of Fakh's ideology
and bearing are repeatedly emphasised: the occupying Indian army
Colonel, Hammirdev Kachhwaha, for example, scornful of the 'mir-
acle' theory, suspects him to be 'a pro-Pak communalist' (120). This
patriotic Hindu deems the infiltrating Muslim outsider a hypocrite
'who dare[s] preach about [Indian] enemies within the state' when,
having sown the seeds of communal discord, he is in fact the 'incarnation of that foe' (120). Yet the motivation and affiliation of the

much-mocked but impassive mullah, silent in relation to his past and place of religious instruction, remain unknown, and the faceless Fakh an all the more disquieting figure as a result (117).

Later it is confirmed that the Maulana takes his religious cue and culture from hard-line 'Islamist-jihadists', whose ideological commitment to an aggressive and austere form of the faith is motivated by the religiously rooted but political 'desire to crush the infidel' (262, 264–5). His 'seductive tongue' gains potency from emotive allusions to the 'immorality' and 'evil' of godless, idolatrous '*kafirs*' (125). This belligerent, moralistic, and ideological discourse clashes with the tolerant language deployed by Hindu and Muslim Kashmiri villagers, yet resonates with that we might popularly associate with an absolute, Saudi Arabian and Wahhabi-inflected Islam, and with its global jihadist proponents (116, 120, 122, 125 and 264).

The youthful affiliates turned Islamic militants featured in *Shalimar* include, in addition to Shalimar: Anees Noman, his depressive brother; the delinquent Gegroo boys; and Abdulrajak, the diminutive 'Filipino revolutionary' who attempts to befriend Shalimar at a training camp (269). All are associated with Fakh's fearsome new interpretation of the faith, yet differ slightly in their affiliative motivations. Anees, who is abducted one night by the local liberation front commander and 'asked if he would like to learn to make bombs', is portrayed as a morbid and melancholic character; he assents because he finds some cause for optimism in the promise that at least this way 'life was likely to be short' (106). The Gegroo boys are more maliciously self-seeking, while the seemingly polite and orderly Abdulrajak 'shine[s] with some sort of crazy internal light', fuelled by a peculiar religio-political fervour which borders on insanity (268).

Rushdie's lack of patience with 'superstitious madmen' (Hari 2006) of an Islamic fundamentalist kind seems particularly evident where the Far Eastern Muslim is concerned. The more rational arguments Abdulrajak might articulate for joining radical Saudi- and Pakistani-funded organisations for national liberation are undermined by his broken Hindi. His dialogue amounts only to unenlightening expressions of allegiance and action, such as 'Man of God inspire. Man of war do' (Rushdie 2005c: 269). The "factual" information the omniscient narrator supplies to contextualise Abdulrajak's impassioned speech offer only a textbook-style explanation for the impoverished and persecuted Filipino's route to radicalisation:

> The luminous little man...had accepted U.S. arms and backing
> but loathed the United States because American soldiers had his-
> torically backed the settlement of Catholics...against the wishes
> of the local Muslims. The Christians controlled the economy and
> the Muslims were kept poor. (269)

Hence, where Rushdie's Filipino Islamic revolutionary is permitted
to speak it is in stumbling syllables and for comic, if chilling, effect.
The character cannot himself convey in any sophisticated fashion
what sparks his fanatical zeal, nor what personal and political circumstances drive him to make the absolute commitment to kill a
hated American and so link his 'story' to Shalimar's (269).

Abdulrajak and the iron mullah's commitments to a partial, pro-
Muslim God may be understood both as somewhat insanely devout,
and as politically strategic. But the "Islamic" opinions and alignments of the bored and bullish brothers Gegroo, 'a trio of disaffected
layabout[s]...looking for trouble' are more simply cynical and self-
serving (126). The boys' "turn" to Fakh in 1965 is precipitated purely
by their anticipation of a father's rightful wrath over their rape of
his daughter; the hell-fire preacher's exclusively male mosque (we are
informed that 'no provision had been made for ladies') is the only
Shirmali space which will grant them asylum (119). Similarly, their
attempt, on return to Shirmal in 1988, to impose the 'Islamic decen-
cies' promoted by their 'holy' employer, the fictional 'Lashkar-e-Pak',
is attributable to no higher cause than their desire to avenge themselves on the father of the girl they defiled and the compatriots whose
principles they violated in the process (126–9, 286–7).

Rushdie's (2002: 395) characterisation of the misogynistic Gegroos
seems partly consistent with his assertion in his *New York Times*
column 'November 2001: Not about Islam?' that:

> For a vast number of "believing" Muslim men, "Islam" stands, in
> a jumbled...way...for a cluster of customs, opinions and preju-
> dices that include [amongst other things]...the sequestration or
> near-sequestration of "their" women, the sermons delivered by
> their mullah of choice, [and] a loathing of modern society in
> general, riddled as it is with music, godlessness and sex.

Yet it is also inconsistent. In the essay quoted above, Rushdie
firmly links the majority of Muslim men's apparently illiberal and

anti-modern behaviour to a muddle-headed commitment to some superstitious 'mulch of "belief" ' promoted and exploited by the political proponents of an Islamist ideology (395). But in *Shalimar*, the Gegroo boys, thuggish although not stupid, are seen cleverly to exploit the insurgent movement for their own venal ends. The young men's aggressive and stereotypically "Islamist" behaviour – torching the village's television tent, terrifying its unveiled women – thus interpreted, is therefore *not* so much "about Islam" (Rushdie 2005c: 285–7). Rather, it seems to be more about the dangerous egotism of three young swaggering, self-styled cowboys and their need publicly to demonstrate that no man can insult them and escape censure, thus perhaps adhering to a bloody code of 'honour' which, though popularly associated with Muslim culture is not, as Tillion (1966, back cover) has demonstrated, an 'aberration specific to Islam'.

Like the Gegroos, Rushdie's 'terrorist' central protagonist, Shalimar, burns with a desire to avenge his 'honour', which drives him towards political Islam (Rushdie 2005c: 258). Turned comic-book fashion towards the dark side by Boonyi's betrayal, this suddenly sinister clown affiliates to the Kashmiri liberation front, and thence to the 'worldwide Islamist-jihadist' movement, in order to exploit the *umma*'s military education programme, arsenal, and global networks for his own sadistic gain (264). As he informs a leader of the local militia, 'I need to learn a new trade... For now... I'll kill anyone you want me to... but... one of these days I want the American ambassador at my mercy' (252). Realigning himself with the separatists, the former beneficiary of Kashmiri pluralism now describes Muslim Pakistan, whose weapons fuel the insurgency, as an ally; he talks of national 'freedom' gained through trust in a 'common God', 'faith' and 'a higher allegiance' (259). As an affiliate to the cause of global jihad, he submits his body to the rigours of training at the Pakistani Inter-Services Intelligence-backed FC-22 camp (264–8). Under the tutelage of the iron mullah, Shalimar surrenders his mind for reprogramming with an international religio-martial 'ideology', for which the only 'permitted' textbooks are 'training manuals' and 'the Holy Qur'an' (265). Yet despite his protestations to the contrary, Shalimar remains driven, fundamentally, not by a desire to 'turn' – in his brother's words – into 'some kind of fire-eater for God', but by a jealous husband's urge to destroy the man who stole his love (259). In this sense his commitment differs from that of the devout, fanatical Islamists characterised by Rushdie both in this fiction and elsewhere, to waging 'holy' war against Western and Jewish 'infidels' or even 'fellow Islamists', for solely sacred or political ends (Rushdie 2002: 395).

Rushdie's (2005c) portrayal of his eponymous protagonist's ultimately disingenuous affiliation is not lacking in some complexity. The absolutist Shalimar, turned from love to hate, is certainly attracted by radical Islam for its own sake. In the training camp, he half listens to the preacher's uncompromising lessons about 'God's work' and 'truth', the latter of which is presented to new recruits as a replacement parent, sibling or life-partner:

> Everything they thought they knew about the nature of reality . . . was wrong, the iron mullah said. That was the first thing for the true warrior to understand. *Yes, Shalimar the clown thought, everything I thought . . . was a mistake . . .* In the world of truth . . . there was no room for weakness, argument, or half-measures . . . Only the truth can be your father now, but through the truth you will be the fathers of history. – *Only the truth can be my father . . .* Only the truth can be your wife. (265–6)

Shalimar willingly accepts the iron mullah's liturgy as a substitute for the other, earlier, Kashmiri lore about the nature of man, good and evil, laid open to him in youth by his Hindu *pandit* father-in-law (91–2). He hopes that by subscribing to the mullah's more exacting dictates he may sever his ties to the painful, shameful past and yet, at the same time, that his cultivation of a hard-line Islamic affiliation may provide a means to fulfil a violent pre-existing need for vengeance. So when Shalimar rises and tears off his 'garments', crying: 'I cleanse myself of everything except the struggle [to expel 'the infidel']! . . . Take me or kill me now!' he does so with a cheating heart and double tongue (267–8). He may 'almost believe . . . [in] his own performance . . . that he was no longer what he was and could indeed leave the past behind', but Rushdie's sceptical clown remains conscious of his inability to commit himself disinterestedly to this new cause, given his overriding urge to pursue a personal vendetta (268).

Despite such attempts to furnish them with greater texture, Rushdie's representations of the connections and motivations of Kashmir's fictional Islamists are crude in comparison, say, to those pertaining to the strict Muslim reformists and Islamic insurgents described in *Curfewed Night*, Basharat Peer's (2010a) first-hand account of the Kashmiri conflict. For example, Peer ascribes the attractiveness of a stricter form of Islam introduced in the late 1980s to educated individuals from amongst his village's lower middle classes not to locals' awe and curiosity about 'blood-and-thunder preachers' (Rushdie 2005c: 115), but rather to their interest in its focus on social reform:

> They [the Salafist group] revolted against the way Islam had been practised over centuries in Kashmir...They wanted to shear the local traditions...saving the peasants from the mumbo-jumbo and exploitation of the priestly class – the *moulvis* and *pirs*, the Muslim Brahmans. (Peer 2010a: 167)

In Peer's account, the young men who join the anti-Indian liberation movements do so partly out of boyish envy for the glamorous insurgent's Pakistan-gifted Kalashnikov, 'green military uniform and...[the] badge on the chest that said: JKLF!', and partly because they find themselves caught in the relentless tide of 'death, fear and anger' which was sweeping with the escalating conflict through the valley of Kashmir, but not for the venal reasons Rushdie attributes to the bad-boy villains of his piece (23–4). As 'wild...men, fanatics, [and] aliens' (Rushdie 2005c: 130), *Shalimar's* fundamentalist affiliates ultimately reinforce rather than expand the range of the now familiar type of the mad, 'bad', dangerous Muslim (Mamdani 2004). In his 1995 novel, *The Moor's Last Sigh*, Rushdie characterised Hindu nationalists as being driven by 'engines stranger' and fed by 'darker', more personal 'fuel' than that of '*the nation, the god*' (Rushdie 1995: 312). In the hands of the same author, the post-9/11 "world" fiction becomes largely a vehicle for stripping the cold-blooded "Islamic" assassin-antagonist not only of any real religious and ideological motivation, but of any political one, too.

Further, it becomes a means instead of dressing the wronged, embittered, Muslim subject's anti-American behaviour in the primitive garb of misogynistic "honour" (Rushdie 2005c: 258). The result is the deflection of responsibility for contemporary acts of religious extremism and, in this instance, "Islamic" terror, onto the aggrieved and aggressive Muslim male whose rage may be concurrent with a turbulent era, but whose propensity to evil seems inherently his own. Responsibility is perhaps also partly deflected onto the patriarchal culture from which Shalimar hails, which permits the pursuit of his bid for vengeance.

In his essay on contemporary fiction and terror, Robert Eaglestone (2010: 366–7) suggests that *Shalimar* lacks a 'sense of the world of the Islamist' and points to an inability on the part of the novelist to 'get to grips' with 'the Islamist "truth" ' to which individuals such as Shalimar are ostensibly converted. Indeed, the 'sulfurous' Maulana's railing disquisition against the materialist enemy and his self-interested values, which immediately precedes Shalimar's dramatic 'revision' of his 'screwed up' 'worldview' and supposed avowal of hard-line Islamist principles, is comprised predominantly of nihilist platitudes (Rushdie 2005c: 264–5). Bulbul Fakh asserts:

> The infidel holds that the picture of the world he draws is a picture we must all recognize. We say that his picture means nothing to us... The infidel speaks of universal truth. We know that the universe is an illusion and that truth lies beyond... The infidel believes the world is his. But we shall.... cast him into darkness and live in Paradise and rejoice as he plunges into the fire. (267)

Shalimar 'scream[s] in assent': 'without the struggle I am nothing!' Yet what the Mullah's "struggle" is – save a bloody-minded rejection of Western capitalist attitudes and values, expressed in the most generic of terms – remains, like the preacher's identity, almost entirely obscure (268). The complexities not only of this particular type of radical and political Muslim affiliation ("Islamism"), about which the West continues to be anxious, but also of other more profound experiences of spiritual connection, seem to be relegated in Rushdie's elliptic if not reductive world fiction to a space firmly 'outside [the author's] world-view' (Eaglestone 2010: 367), equating, in that novelist's own terms, to the realms of 'spiritual fakery and mumbo-jumbo charlatanism' (Rushdie 2005c: 48).

Despite the fact that it discriminates to some extent between different forms, expressions and uses of the faith – Sufi versus Salafi, religious versus secular, private versus political – *Shalimar* is a work that could arguably be considered part of a wave of "new atheist" fiction, in which 'Islam [and Islamic extremism in particular] comes to embody the irrationality, immorality and violence of religion in general' (Bradley and Tate 2010: 5). It is interesting, then, that several of the novel's characters, Hindu and Muslim, can be seen to attempt in different ways to disconnect themselves altogether from the shifting influences of what could be termed the God-like 'shadow planets' of (religious) ideology, tradition and superstition (Rushdie 2005c: 48). Such heavenly bodies, diabolical and divine, are exemplified in *Shalimar* by the Hindu 'dragon planets' Rahu, the 'exaggerator' and 'intensifier' and Ketu, the 'suppressor' of human instincts (48). These spiritual entities, like other addictive secular gods (such as stimulants and narcotics), 'grab' and govern man's understanding of his own morality, freedom and ability to think and act for himself, whether for good or for ill (46). Rushdie's suspicion of them is well documented in his previous fiction and prose.[7] In *Shalimar* his Kashmiri characters, from the obese and opium-addicted Boonyi to the disaffected "Islamist" Shalimar, variously try to break with these simultaneously seductive and dangerous influences in order to regain control of their own destinies and, ultimately, realise their desires – the woman for her husband's earthly love; the man for vengeance on his unfaithful wife.

For Shalimar, the process of 'let[ting] go' in order to achieve self-determination entails the severance of the two contradictory vows which he makes to Ketu and Rahu: to let his adulterous wife live; and to annihilate her along with her lover (226, 237). He must rescind the first in order to realise the second, but disassociate himself entirely from both if he is to forge on the basis of self-abnegation the new Islamist ties which will grant him access to the fundamentalist networks he exploits then betrays (267–8, 271). In the end the selfish Shalimar jettisons the "holy" cause for a secular satisfaction more sublime – a husband's bloody, brutal revenge for his wife's infidelity, dressed in the guise of jihadi terrorism. It is this individual motivation, not his lawyer's captivating ' "sorcerer's" or "Manchurian" defence' (that Shalimar's 'free will was subverted by mind-control techniques'; that he was 'programmed to kill' at Hamas-style 'brainwashing centres'), which the Los Angeles court that sentences him recognises (383–4). The realisation of individual desires, and hence the achievement of selfhood, seems in Rushdie's sceptical fiction to preclude the possibility of a pure or total commitment to any external governing authority. Bradley and Tate (2010: 99) have referred to Rushdie as perhaps 'the most intensely theological of contemporary British novelists'. The theme of 'the quarrel [with and] over

God': of the individual's desire to cut his ties with – or "disaffiliate" from – a supernatural being and organised religion; and the impact of their demise, disestablishment or death on society, is something that Rushdie continues to pursue alongside more aesthetic and 'enchanted' experiences of South Asian spiritual affinity in his later novel, *The Enchantress* (Rushdie 2008a: 440).

The Enchantress of Florence

Set at the time of the sixteenth-century Mughal Emperor Akbar, Rushdie's next book, *The Enchantress* (2008a), is focused in part on the Grand Mughal's cosmopolitan court and in part on the Florence of Niccolò Machiavelli and the Medici. It incorporates characters whose fortunes carry them across continents, dramatises their foreign encounters and invites the reader to draw comparisons between India and Italy's two rich and contemporaneous cultures, but largely keeps distinct the European and South Asian civilisations which it depicts. Rushdie uses in *The Enchantress* the bare bones of what might popularly be considered "world" fiction – transnational protagonists, "exotic" locations and a plot that features intercultural exchange – to create a historical fantasy rooted in India and its Mughal heritage.

In this sense, Rushdie's second novel of the third millennium differs from those of his younger contemporaries Hamid, Aslam and Shamsie. Though they remain interested in the earlier and often hybrid histories of Muslim countries, these authors have consistently chosen more modern Islamic peoples, cultures and conflicts as the subjects for their recent fiction, particularly those of late twentieth- and early twenty-first-century Pakistan and Afghanistan. Their post-9/11 novels therefore present a more obvious and direct creative challenge to contemporary media (mis)representations of South Asian Muslims. Yet it seems important to note that *The Enchantress*, Rushdie's post-7/7 novel, appeared at a time of heightened anxiety in Britain over multiculturalism's apparent failure, rising religious intolerance and perceived 'ethnic segregation' (Phillips 2005: n.p.). It explored in the midst of such misgivings the cosmopolitan nature of an earlier Islamic civilisation or 'middle nation' (Nederveen Pieterse 2007: 160), which might be upheld as a model of pluralism and openness.

In turning back to this time, Rushdie perhaps took up in *The Enchantress* the threads he loosened in *The Moor's Last Sigh* (1995).

In this novel the eponymous Indian protagonist, part-descendent of a Moorish Sultan, laments the communal riots that tear through Bombay in the early 1990s after Hindu militants destroy the Babri Masjid, and sets his sights on the lost paradise of Al-Andalus. This medieval Muslim homeland is epitomised in the novel by the mirage-like image of Granada's intricate Alhambra, a fourteenth-century feat of Islamic architecture constructed on European soil and today preserved by UNESCO as a "World Heritage Site" (Rushdie 1995: 433). The secular, unaffiliated and yet unforgettably 'Moorish' narrator, a man 'full of theses, [with] never a church door to nail them to' (3), lauds this space as a 'masterpiece' of cultural complexity and harmonious integration;

> Palace of interlocking forms and secret wisdom, ... monument to a lost possibility that nevertheless has gone on standing ... [and] testament to ... our need for flowing together, for putting an end to frontiers, for the dropping of the boundaries of the self. (433)

This rose-tinted vision of an earlier, 'golden' civilisation and a wistful desire to reawaken its 'sleepers' haunts Rushdie's late-twentieth-century narrative, its concluding pages in particular (227, 433). But while his ever-elaborate and magical fiction conjures up in colourful detail an ornate Andalusian façade, it ultimately leaves its Moorish protagonist and readers alike lingering on the threshold of the Alhambra's 'noble courts' (433). Over a decade later, in *The Enchantress*, Rushdie invites us to enter and explore these Islamic palaces' rich interiors and culture, not in a modern European or South Asian setting but in an historic 'Hindustani' one (433).

At the time of *The Enchantress*'s publication, critics characterised its creator as a 'walking political symbol, peculiarly liberated by his new book', a novel which they deemed to be 'resolutely not of this world' (Muir 2008: 6). While ancestral ties linked the modern, hybrid Indian protagonist of Rushdie's 1995 novel to the era of Arab-Islamic dominance in Iberia, inviting readers to compare this earlier time of apparent religious pluralism and tolerance with the extremism and intolerance of the present day, Rushdie's 2008 work is set entirely in the past. As a result this post-9/11 fiction – like Tariq Ali's *A Sultan in Palermo* (2005), which was written at the time of the Iraq war, and redirects our attention to an era of Arab presence, cohabitation and cross-cultural exchange in medieval Europe – can perhaps be expected to provide only an indirect corrective to, or comment on, simplistic Muslim stereotypes by means of a lesson in cultural history.[8] Yet Rushdie's focus on the Mughal court and emperor brought to life by *The Enchantress* indicates a 'willingness' on the part of its author not just to acknowledge but also to 'think through' the 'more humane elements' of Islamic traditions which Spencer (2010b: 261), in his reconsideration of *The Satanic Verses*, describes as necessary to a twenty-first-century literary project of undermining Huntington's 1992 'clash of civilisations' thesis. It also demonstrates a desire to engage to some extent with the 'darkness' (Rushdie 1995: 303) and confusion with which times of 'cultural admixture' have today been associated.

Rushdie observes in his essay on the *Baburnama*, published in *Step Across This Line*, that the events which followed 11 September 2001 have had an impact on the way in which we "read" and represent the historical Muslims described in such texts; 'who', he asks, 'then, was Babur – scholar or barbarian, nature-loving poet or terror-inspiring warlord?' (2002: 191). He highlights the fact that, depending on one's political persuasion, it is equally possible to stress the destructive and iconoclastic aspects of Grand Mughal regimes as their 'polytheistic inclusiveness' (191). *The Enchantress* was written not only at a moment of multicultural misgivings, but also at a time when Rushdie's contemporaries amongst the British literary and "New Atheist" elite were at pains to question the intolerance of an apparently illiberal and yet 'mainstream' Islam (McEwan 2007: n.p.). This was a moment when, conversely, scholars of Indian and Pakistani Muslim origin like the historian Ayesha Jalal (2008) were at pains to offer more complex historical perspectives on the fluctuation of religious discourse within South Asian Islam, including the relationship of the religion's 'outer husk' to Muslims' 'inner faith' (K. Shamsie 2008: n.p.). Rushdie's choice of the debating chambers of Akbar's doubtful cosmopolitan court as a setting for *The Enchantress* cannot be deemed apolitical if considered within this compositional context.[9]

The Enchantress opens in late-sixteenth-century India with a European traveller's approach to the Mughal capital of Fatehpur Sikri. He wishes to tell its founder Akbar a tale that connects a Florentine adventurer called Argalia to the Emperor's great-great-aunt, Qara Köz, a princess long forgotten by his family. Meanwhile Akbar, increasingly dissatisfied with orthodox religion and his inherited Islamic faith, has constructed a 'Tent of New Worship' for theological debate, where 'the adoration of the divine was re-imagined as an intellectual wrestling match in which no holds were barred' (Rushdie 2008a: 97). The European, who calls himself the 'Mogor dell' Amore', is judged a fraud and placed on trial by Akbar's advisors (81). Yet Akbar is intrigued by the younger man's outlandish but well-reasoned arguments and claim to be the Emperor's uncle. He permits the stranger, who now says his name is Niccolo Vespucci, to entertain him Scheherazade-like with the story that reveals their genealogical connection, and so authenticates the Mogor's Mughal heritage.

The novel moves between Akbar's struggles to remain interested in 'questions of kingship' (such as who should succeed him: his legitimate, fundamentalist son, or the free-thinking Italian) as he broods over the 'question of Man', the enchantments of 'Woman', and the Mogor's captivating ancestral tale (177). This starts in Renaissance Italy, traverses Central Asia, and concludes in the Americas. It charts Argalia's enforced conversion to Islam in the services of the Ottoman Sultan, encounter in Herat with Qara Köz, and their escape to Florence where her magic bewitches locals.

The Mogor asserts that after Argalia's death, the adventurer's cousin, Ago Vespucci, sailed for "India" with Qara and her maidservant, but disembarked in the New World; here the princess gave birth to a yellow-haired child, whom the stranger claims to be. Yet Akbar's royal mind cannot quite encompass such a tall tale of stopped time, commingling races and new worlds. Vespucci, rejected, vanishes from the city and Fatehpur Sikri mysteriously self-destructs, forcing Akbar's migration. The Emperor 'solves' the riddle of the Mogor's ancestry for himself: Vespucci is not the child of the enchantress, Qara, but the son of her mirror-like maidservant. Thus ends the deception of "nephew" and "uncle", although the world-weary Akbar remains conscious of the provisional nature of any (dis)enchantment.

The Enchantress, like its predecessor *Shalimar*, revisits in a historic Hindustani setting some of the mystic and philosophical aspects of Islamic traditions which Rushdie touches upon in his earlier fictions. One might infer therefore that its author is – and the more sympathetic of his creations are – still 'sentimentally devoted to a gentler [and indigenised, Indian] Islam' (Brennan, quoted in Spencer 2010b:

262). Yet by the start of Rushdie's latest novel the potency of this Islam, at least for characters such as Akbar, is beginning to fade or to be diluted by other "enchantments". *The Enchantress* is an altogether more philosophical and fantastical fiction than *Shalimar.* Rushdie seems more interested in pursuing in it a project he began in *The Satanic Verses* of making the novel a means to establish and maintain the 'contestability of [all] doctrines and practices that trace themselves to some sort of unchallengeable origin' (Spencer 2010b: 254). Akbar's multicultural and multiply "enchanted" Mughal city provides an ideal context for this. In the India of *The Enchantress*, where worlds, faiths and thought-systems collide, "Muslim" affiliations and affinities, and indeed all feelings of religious connection, are contextualised by those of other believers. They are also rendered problematic as a result of a wider theological debate – that which Rushdie's (2008a: 440) Akbar terms the 'quarrel over God'.

We are briefly informed at the novel's outset that Akbar, seeking some strong, heroic being to be his 'hammer and [his] anvil, [his]...beauty and...truth', his infallible prop and support, 'had trusted the mystic Chishti whose tomb stood in the courtyard of the Friday Mosque, but Chishti was dead' (72–3). Having swiftly spelt the death sentence of the unfortunate Sufi mystic, the playful writer then trivialises Akbar's feelings of affinity for him. Rushdie hastens to inform us that the questing emperor simultaneously 'trusted dogs, music, poetry...and a wife he had created out of nothing', as well as 'beauty, painting, and the wisdom of his forbears': secular deities and seeming surrogates for the sterner Gods one might associate with more orderly, orthodox and monotheistic expressions of religious faith (73).

Looking to Muslim connections which are more historical and aesthetic than spiritual, *The Enchantress* maps in greater detail the Mughal and Hindustani emperor's ancestral linkage via his grandfather Babur and 'Iron' forbears Timur-e-Lang and Chinggis Qan, with whose 'murderous' associations he would prefer to break, to the rich cultural and linguistic heritages of Central and North-East Asian dynasties (42). Akbar draws solace from the peaceful teachings of his childhood tutor, a Persian Mir, and finds a great affinity, for example, with the heroes of Persian epic such as the legendary Hamza, the widely travelled uncle of the Prophet Muhammad. Yet it is the artistry of the Indian masters who paint such figures into teeming life and, with them, 'Mughal Hindustan' and the soul of its emperor, that most captivates him (148).[10]

It is apparent here that while he will acknowledge in his fiction the weight of the Baburian legacy on the sensitive Akbar's psyche, Rushdie is keen to emphasise Akbar's feelings of difference from these overbearing forebears. He stresses the emperor's sense of having an 'other' and more potent South Asian Muslim identity, and hence of being '*Hindustani*' (41–2) – unlike his Timurid ancestor who, as Rushdie (2002: 193) has noted elsewhere, found India lacking in 'charm'. Despite his own not insubstantial tyrannies, the aggression Babur's cultivated Mughal grandson associates with the marauding hordes of his '*Mongol*' ancestors is altogether too harsh for him (Rushdie 2008a: 42).

In addition to mapping the emperor-protagonist's Central Asian and Islamic inheritance, *The Enchantress* makes frequent reference to his attraction to the artistic, philosophical and imperial practices of other faiths and cultures; of 'people...not his', and yet for whom he feels a powerful 'sense of kinship' (176). For Rushdie's god-like Grand Mughal, himself a great 'Enchanter', has a prodigious appetite for bewitchments sourced from outside the perhaps comforting but limited circles of his family's Islamic faith and culture, whether in the beguiling form of exotic women, or fresh intoxicating thoughts (53, 102). His interest in these is emphasised in the narrative by his enthusiasm for creating new architectural spaces such as Fatehpur Sikri in which 'religion, region, rank and tribe' can collide (53). Within these are situated new forums like the 'Tent of the New Worship', where expansive metaphysical discussions may take place (97).

Examples of the non-Muslim art and ideas that capture Akbar's imagination range from the inspirational songs of the Hindu composer Tansen and imaginary heavens of the rival Rana of Cooch Naheen, to the apocryphal tales of the enigmatic European stranger and 'megalomaniac fantasies' of his charming authoritarian contemporary Elizabeth I (43–4, 53, 92). Here faith is perhaps best understood as the willingness to permit oneself to believe or trust in the potential reality (or realisability) of a delightful deception or a powerful dream. Its artefacts and instruments are talismans or wishing bones: props in a fantastic act of self-delusion. This works in reverse, too: the Scots pirate Lord Hauksbank, who briefly features as Argalia's dupe, carries with him a collection of 'objects of virtue' to keep his traveller's soul anchored (17, 19). These include an illuminated miniature copy of the Holy Qur'an which the superstitious Scottish 'milord' stores alongside other treasures – a pagan goddess's silk handkerchief, a locket containing the image of England's faerie queen – each of which commands equal reverence (19–20).

Rushdie's exploration of the attraction of the enlightened if somewhat susceptible Akbar towards eclectic, alternative and mind-opening 'enchantments' drawn from 'the guardians of the unseen realms...palmists, astrologers, soothsayers, mystics and assorted divines' (403) seems largely light-hearted and expansive. Yet his treatment of what Kamila Shamsie (2007a: n.p.) might describe as the 'landmine' connections – the radical Islamic beliefs felt and affiliations forged by the novel's less eclectic or privileged cosmopolitan characters, of lurid fascination to Western world readers today – is, by contrast, more darkly cynical and reductive.

The Enchantress offers miniature sketches of child soldiers, troubled sons and 'holy' men, all variously deployed in a clash of empires, and obviously intended as negative reflections on contemporary Islamist affiliations (Rushdie 2008a: 226). It covers, for example, the alignment – troubling for Akbar – of his son, Prince Salim (who would later become the Emperor Jehangir), with 'puritanical' types such as the religious thinker Badauni (98–101); and the forced conversion of children to Islam in the training camps of the Ottoman Sultan (225–6). The 'surly' Salim's "turn" towards Islam is not a maturing adolescent's considered assertion of a reclaimed Muslim identity, but a predictable and easily manipulable act of teenage rebellion (98). To the foreign, Florentine observer, Akbar's bored, 'petulant', extreme son is a pawn in the hands of a humourless and austere religious thinker, and a potentially 'dangerous' weapon to be deployed in the power games of court; to his guilty and nervous father, he is a weak 'puppet' confused by the multiple spiritual and secular influences, puritan and profane, to which he has been exposed, and which he mimics (101). While Akbar warms to the visiting Argalia or 'Mogor dell' Amore' (indeed, he even considers adopting him), he becomes distant from his 'diehard' son, the mass of whose contradictions he – assuming a lack of affinity, or common comprehension – makes little effort to unravel (101).

The depiction provided later in the novel by Argalia's brainwashed 'memory palace' of the indoctrination of abducted children at the Ottoman 'prison camp[s]' in the Balkan city of Usküb likewise emphasises the lack of agency of the Christian initiates captured from the wide-ranging geographical region encompassed by the Caucuses (225). Forced to forget their filial loyalties and to convert to Islam by a wizard-like dervish of the Bektashi Sufi order, and trained as a fighting force, these alpha boys, crack recruits, newly dressed and named, are transformed into terrifying 'instruments of the Sultan's will' (225). Rushdie describes this disabling and deforming process as the placing not only of the enslaved child's physical being, but of his entire 'soul ... under new management' (226). In this instance, the 'angry' children are unwilling affiliates; their parrot-like mimicry of Arabic doctrines, unlike that of the perhaps equally ignorant but more empowered Prince Salim, is 'frightened' and resentful (226). Yet the result is perhaps the same: the forging of new kin-like bonds amongst those committed to a common political or imperial cause, which replace the natural ties of blood, and curtail individual freedoms (230). In *The Enchantress*, the face of fundamental Islamic affiliation seems as sullen, closed and joyless as the wine-flushed visage of the Grand Mughal, sceptical entertainer of multiple enchantments, is open and cheerful.

It would appear important to note here that Akbar is profoundly disturbed and depressed by the behaviour of other strict adherents to religious faith, such as the observant Brahmin girls, who would rather sacrifice their lives than compromise their Hindu beliefs and practices by serving a Muslim king. He remains inclined to interpret their drastic actions as ones of aggression: 'these girls died because they preferred division to unity, their gods to ours, and hatred to love' (247). Earlier in the narrative, the Mughal emperor, adopting the majestic plural, informs his Italian visitor Argalia that despite his 'affection' for the 'supernatural entities' of polytheistic religions, 'Yet we must be what we are. The million gods are not our gods; the austere religion of our father will always be ours, just as the carpenter's creed is yours' (175–6).[11] Rushdie's magical fiction explores through the eyes of the resolvedly Muslim and yet resolutely sceptical Akbar the wonders and terrors of an imaginative 'world beyond religion' situated outside the bounds prescribed by the 'comforting circularity' of inherited faith (53, 103).

Given the pressing need for a countering of the lack of complexity and nuance offered by contemporary representations of the claims of religious authorities, Rushdie's interest in depicting an alternative kind of enchantment is of course desirable. Yet, in giving an almost superior weight to non-spiritual forms of enchantment, he conveniently sidesteps a serious examination of incidences of feelings of affiliation and affinity experienced from *within* the ever-porous boundaries of any particular religious faith, and specifically Islam. This, and his failure in *Shalimar* and *The Enchantress* to represent more than what might be described as the familiar faces of a more extreme, devout or fundamental Islamic faith, is what, I will go on to argue, sets these fictions apart from the novels produced after 9/11 by a younger generation of Pakistani Muslim writers, Aslam and Shamsie in particular.

Areas left unmapped

This book contends that, in an apparently secular age, world literary works by authors of Muslim backgrounds may describe deep-felt spiritual connections and attachments which have popularly been trivialised as superstitious or irrational, yet which remain central to their characters' sense of selfhood. Further, it suggests that by expressing in their fiction 'Islamic subjectivities and cultural epistemologies' which the reader may incorporate into his or her understanding of a 'world of equal differences' (Majid 2000: vii), they may contribute to a process of 'demystifying and de-alienating Islam and Muslims' (Malak 2004: 11). This is something that remains of central importance in the context of the present day, when the word 'Islam' and the mention of Muslims continues, in Shamsie's words, 'to exert a magnetic field... pulling in a host of words of which the most thickly clustered is "Terror" and, hard on its heels... Offence' (K. Shamsie 2009d: 1).

Rushdie attempts to explore not only a variety of types of Islam, but also a variety of types of faith in *Shalimar* and *The Enchantress*, Yet the result is not only that Muslim stereotypes such as those propagated by writers like Martin Amis are reinforced, but also that those more complex, nebulous (and potentially controversial) spiritual convictions, political commitments and historical-cultural connections which may underlie contemporary South Asian (and Pakistani as opposed to Indian) experiences of affinity or affiliation for Islam are largely left unmapped. The next chapter explores how his younger contemporary, Mohsin Hamid, seeks to redress this imbalance in a fiction which features a Pakistani Muslim protagonist whom its author deems is anything but 'stereotypically Muslim' (Hamid 2008b: 46).

3
'A Devilishly Difficult Ball' – Mohsin Hamid's *The Reluctant Fundamentalist*

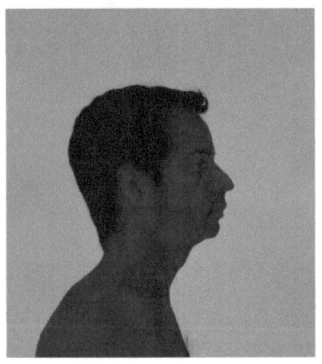

3.1 Ali Kazim

Introduction

The transnational Pakistani novelist Mohsin Hamid (2013a: 15) recently observed that his fiction 'has what might be called a real-istic narrative – there is no magic, no aliens – but the frame...it uses isn't realism. It is something else...play'. He went on to explain his reasons for staging his noirish post-9/11 thriller, *The Reluctant Fundamentalist* (2007), as a game:

> My project was...to try to show...how feelings already present inside a reader – fear, anger, suspicion, loyalty – could colour a narrative...I wanted the novel to be a kind of mirror, to let readers see how they are reading, and, therefore, how they are living and how they are deciding their politics.

This subtle, opaque and equivocal portrayal of a young Pakistani man's flirtations with "fundamentalism" offers many leading hints but no verifiable clues as to his "real" Islamist proclivities. Yet it forces its expectant anglophone readers to sit in judgement over its Muslim narrator's supposed "confession", making them players in a literary game of misrecognition (and recognition), the rules of which Hamid dictates.

This chapter examines in detail the ambiguous personal affiliations and peregrinations of *The Reluctant Fundamentalist*'s author, and the dubious and ultimately unknowable affiliations of its playful protagonist, Changez. It asks how Hamid's novel has been decoded, both as a result of assumptions about the autobiographical contents of this fictional confession, and of the prejudicial and psychological misreadings that it invites and partly engenders. Last, it considers his later formal experiments, which continue to encourage the participation and play with the expectations of their co-creating readers. At its best, Hamid's ludic fiction reflects and refracts stereotypical images of a Pakistani Muslim nation still framed by fears about Islamist affiliations in the English-speaking world. This chapter's final section asks whether his post-*Fundamentalist* short fictions present new, productive developments, or simply dead ends.

Hamid's ambiguous affiliations

The cosmopolitan Hamid is a Princeton graduate who has worked in New York and London as a management consultant. He was born in Lahore, raised partly in California and resident for nearly a decade in the UK. However, he has subsequently – and publicly – elected to return to live in his home city in Pakistan's Punjab. Hamid's fictions are rooted in Pakistan, and provide windows onto national and transnational subjects whose trajectories seem aptly topical in an early twenty-first-century context. In *Moth Smoke* (2000c), an unemployed Lahori banker becomes addicted to narcotics while his country teeters on the brink of nuclear war; in *The Reluctant Fundamentalist* (2007b) a jaded Pakistani expat, Lahore-returned, seems poised to deliver to his American listener a contemporary tale of a turn to terror. In this novel, which was shortlisted for the Man Booker Prize and is an international bestseller, Hamid performs a sly and skilful act of "writing back" to contemporary Anglo-American fictions of Islamic identitarian issues and interconnections. The soliloquent form and affected narrative voice he deploys make the novel stand out starkly from the other many-voiced, third-person fictions (for example those by Aslam and Shamsie) I consider in *Writing Islam*'s subsequent chapters. In terms of genre, as a supposed confessional narrative, it perhaps resembles more closely the real-life confessional memoirs of former Islamists like Ed Husain (2007). Both *Moth Smoke* and *The Reluctant Fundamentalist* have drawn international attention, and provided Hamid with a reputation as a subtle master of chilling, urbane thrillers, and (for some) a vivid portraitist of young, contemporary Pakistani life.[1] However, Hamid is best known for the latter novel, in which the apparently eponymous Pakistani Muslim protagonist reflects on the period of his youth he spent in America before the scales fell from his eyes. That this novel has received the lion's share of the attention is perhaps unsurprising given the prevailing climate of fear and suspicion that has surrounded Pakistani and Muslim matters. However, as I will go on to argue, the novel, and its reception, is by no means unproblematic.

When it comes to his own faith, Hamid (2003c: n.p.) has described himself as a 'secular, liberal, progressive man' for whom 'Islam' forms a significant but by no means sole 'component' of his identity. He acknowledges that its importance to him has increased and his sympathy for fellow Muslims grown since the attacks of 11 September 2001. But he rejects the 'simplistic and dangerous notion' that Muslims of diverse backgrounds, including himself, can be 'disassociated from their ethnic, cultural, political and personal characteristics and meaningfully grouped together for any positive purpose', whether that be "anti-terror" interrogations or global jihad (2003c). Instead, he is keen to assert the 'diversity' of his beliefs and tastes, political and cultural. In doing so he seeks to delink them from the adjective "Muslim", and simultaneously to emphasise their similarity to those of 'millions of my fellow large-city dwellers around the world'. He asserts:

> I believe in democracy ... I believe that religion should influence laws only through universal ballots, not through the will of a clerical elite ... There is nothing particularly Muslim about these beliefs ... I like many types of music, ranging from the blues to qawwali. I like the novels of the Japanese Haruki Murakami and the Egyptian Naguib Mahfouz. I like cricket. I like dogs. I like to

dance... Surely, shared values and shared tastes... are components of identity that... should not be brushed aside. (2003c)

Hamid crafts this studiously neutral public profile in a period in which measures such as racial profiling; the disproportionate stopping and searching of Asian youths; the surveillance and disruption of Muslim communities; and ' "good character" tests', have been justified as expedient for identifying potential suspects in the "war on terror" (Brown 2010: 173–5). As Morey and Yaqin (2011: 106–11) note, when a connection is assumed to exist – as it has been after the attacks of 9/11 and 7/7 – between culture and political activity, and religion 'elevated' as the key component of cultural identity, the hitherto private matters of faith and culture become issues of public concern. The need visibly to demonstrate allegiance to a government-sanctioned set of "good" (British) social, moral, political and economic values and version of 'good [Muslim] faith' is urgent (Brown 2010: 181; Morey and Yaqin 2011: 111). The irony in Hamid's case is that even as he attempts to distance himself from this 'good Muslim' discourse, giving a flavour of his eclectic, global and not specifically Islamic mix of preferences, he in fact arguably inscribes himself within it as the kind of 'Normal Muslim' for whom:

Religious beliefs and observance come into the equation but [who, ultimately] is willing... to orient [themselves] in relation to a presumed consensus around individualism and the market... [And for whom] religion has not trumped material aspiration and, as securitizing discourse so often insists, turned them into fanatical separatists or jihadists. (Brown 2010: 180)

As Morey and Yaqin (2011: 111) point out, for the Muslim citizen and subject in the West, there is 'always an element of self-stereotyping involved in answering the call to authenticity'.[2]

Geographically, Hamid prefers to say that he lives "between" the city of his birth, Lahore, and other metropolitan centres, including London and New York (http://www.mohsinhamid.com/about.html, n.d.). In doing so he draws attention to his international mobility and, again, to the breadth of his cosmopolitan connections and sympathies. He lays claim to being a citizen of the world ('a law abiding, productive inhabitant of whatever city I currently choose to call my home'), disinclined to discriminate between faiths. Thus Hamid (2003c) reserves the right not just to state an aesthetic preference

for an aspect of non-Muslim culture, but to extend political support to the populations of majority-Muslim regions like Kashmir and
Palestine as they struggle for statehood. Yet Hamid (2000b: n.p.) is
also strongly committed to remaining resident at least for part of the
time in his native Pakistan and to preserving his "Pakistani" identity, despite the fact that doing so may at times have threatened to
inhibit his freedom to roam. And, interestingly, the Pakistan to which
he cleaves is one relieved of its global Islamic role, no 'beacon to
the world's Muslims' or 'sword-arm' to an aggressive umma, but a
collapsed state kept on 'life-support by international lenders' and in
desperate need of the means to stand alone (Hamid 2000a: n.p.).

In his self-positioning the Pakistan-born writer therefore differs
considerably from more senior diasporic and "atheistic" authors of
South Asian origin, such as Salman Rushdie (whose work I discussed
in Chapter 2) and Hanif Kureishi. Despite selective claims and incumbent requirements that they speak as subcontinental authorities,
these authors have remained physically and politically located on
what they would want to perceive as the side of cultural openness,
liberality and reason when it comes to Pakistan and Islam (see, for
example, Kureishi 2004; 203–6; Rushdie 2002: 430–1; Suroor 2011).

Publications such as Muneeza Shamsie's (2011) special edition of
the *Journal of Postcolonial Writing, Beyond Geography: Literature, Politics
and Violence in Pakistan* and *Granta 112: Pakistan* (Granta 2010) have
sought to showcase Pakistan's diversity and dynamism as expressed
through its literature. In these journals and magazine special issues,
Hamid's writing has been grouped alongside that of other Pakistani
English-language novelists of Muslim background such as Nadeem
Aslam, Mohammed Hanif, Uzma Aslam Khan and Kamila Shamsie.
The common denominator when it comes to these authors is the fact
that they were mostly born and raised in Pakistan during the 1970s
and 1980s, studied for degrees at American and British universities in
the late 1990s and early 2000s, and remained resident abroad for significant periods in their early careers. Though differing significantly
in treatment, scope and focus, their novels and non-fiction testify
to their consciousness of having been affected personally, politically
and professionally by their experiences. These include having grown
up in times overshadowed by Zia's Islamization, the Afghan–Soviet
War, localised ethnic conflict and nuclear standoffs with India, and
having come into maturity at the time of the 9/11 attacks (see, for
example, Hamid 2006: n.p.).

Such "new" Pakistani authors demonstrate a 'hunger', in Uzma Aslam Khan's (2010: n.p.) words, to understand their place amidst their home country's 'chaotic layers', give voice to what they see and perhaps shape how they are seen. They remain quite acutely aware of the apparent expectations of foreign markets when it comes to literature about Pakistan. They are conscious that they possess the dubious privilege of being local 'custodians' and 'beneficiaries' of a global 'brand' whose commercial success depends on its replication either of 'Paisley designs' and 'bridal wear', or of 'bombs/minarets' and 'burkhas', misappropriated metonyms for Islamic terror (Hamid et al. 2010: n.p.). Yet they retain a conviction that none of these things should be placed 'out of bounds' to them as writers, either as a result of censorship or self-censorship: neither the 'mosquito nets', 'the extended families', the sexually abusive mullahs or the Guantanamo detainees (Aslam 2010b: n.p.).

In 'Where to Begin', Aslam (2010b) identifies the task of the contemporary Pakistani English author as being to flesh the 'tourist clichés' with 'human warmth, longing and complexity' and, conversely, to accentuate characters' universality by stripping away the specifics of their lives and making them stand alone as bare humans. Jamil Ahmad, a former Pakistani civil servant and "new" but older addition to the group, whose work was also included in the *Granta 112* anthology, implied in his fiction that Pakistani writers and journalists should continue to prioritise local causes, lives and deaths, 'expos[ing] the wrong being done outside their front door' before seeking other, wider human dignities to expound and protect (Ahmad 2011: 34). Although differently inflected, the requirements these authors have outlined are essentially similar. They gesture towards a contemporary Pakistani English writing aesthetic in appeal, and ethical and political in scope, which speaks out where others remain silent. Encompassing Islamic geographies and affiliations which continue to engender international concern, this literature is global in reach. But it introduces locally nuanced perspectives of the geopolitical spaces it describes, thereby unsettling Western ways of seeing and exposing the legitimacy, humanity and ambiguous quotidian reality of South Asian Muslim ones.

Hamid seems almost to write to these requirements, as this passage published in *New York Times Magazine* on 30 September 2001 illustrates:

> My family waits, like many...watching battle plans being dis-
> cussed on television, ex-guerrillas being interviewed about the
> Afghan terrain, radical figures threatening bloodshed if Pakistan
> helps America. Meanwhile the long summer has come to an end
> in Islamabad. The city is green and bougainvilleas are blooming.
> Fresh pomegranates are arriving from nearby orchards, along with
> grapes and apples. The fruit, which rarely makes the news, still
> makes people smile.
>
> (Hamid 2001a: n.p.)

In this paragraph, Hamid subtly reconfigures our impressions of
Pakistan and its people. He juxtaposes the exotic fruits the Western
reader might anticipate consuming in a Central Asian country
(pomegranates) with those also familiar in European climes (grapes,
apples). He demonstrates that there are more than two sides to every
story, balancing Afghan radicals who oppose Pakistani cooperation
with the Americans with former rebels prepared to assist them. He
situates his onlooking family, potential voyeurs and victims, caught
somewhere in between. Last, he restores the capital city of an Islamic
country so often described in terms of decline in its national – and, in
this context, rejuvenating – green; he paints the faces of its citizens
not with grim visages of despair, but with quiet smiles which might
offer a modest sign of hope. The resulting impression is of a diverse
nation, where ordinary people are affected by the pull of different
tides but retain an ability to swim against them.

The post-9/11 context has intensified the requirement for the
kind of Pakistani writing which can command the English-speaking
world's attention without pandering to what it wants to hear; which
strives not only to demystify or rewrite its orientalised images, but
also to make it recognise the impact of its neo-imperialistic attitudes
and policies on the theatres of the East. Hamid's consciousness of this
is acute, as his article 'The Usual Ally' demonstrates. This appeared
in *TIME Magazine* on 1 October 2001, when Pakistan was about to
be dragged into the front line of the escalating "war on terror", and
in it he draws attention to America's convenient blindness to the
humanity of peoples it does not know:

> In America, the murky, unknown places of the world are blank
> screens: stories of evil can be projected on them with as little

difficulty as stories of good … Americans must consider the consequences of projecting a war film onto what is not a blank screen at all.

(Hamid 2001b: n.p.)

Hamid repeatedly seeks in his writing to populate the screen he describes with diverse images of ordinary Muslim lives which are neither wholly bad nor wholly good, forcing Western readers to recognise the potentially devastating impact of belligerent acts of erasure.

Perhaps out of a desire to demonstrate his allegiance to an alternative vision of Pakistan at a time when the country remained under threat, Hamid in 2008 joined his contemporary Mohammed Hanif in rather publicly announcing his relocation to Pakistan after several years spent abroad (although in practice and as noted above, Hamid continues to spend significant amounts of time away from Lahore). Like Hanif (2008b), he made his case for the move in a comment piece in *The Guardian*, stating that despite the fact that he had 'thrived' in the UK, his 'heart remained stubbornly Pakistani' and, furthermore,

> I never believed in the role Pakistan plays as a villain on news shows. The Pakistan I knew was the out-of-character Pakistan … without its … plastic fangs. These are troubled times … But there is reason to be hopeful … When it comes to where we think Pakistan is heading, we are voting with our feet.
>
> (Hamid 2009a: n.p.)

Their articles differ in tone – Hanif's tends towards cynicism; Hamid's seems more optimistic – but what both writers have in common is a confidence that they may at least discover a 'new [social] texture' on their respective returns to Karachi and Lahore (Hanif 2008b: n.p.).

These authors' relocations to twenty-first-century Pakistan should therefore not simply be seen as the wistful attempts of expatriate writers to realise an outdated myth of return, although they are in part driven by emotional yearnings – Hanif (2008b) longs for Karachi's sea breezes, while Hamid (2009a) still feels Lahore's powerful 'grip'. Rather, they are pragmatic and ethical ventures: as disillusioned British residents they seek to escape deteriorating race relations and rising living costs; as committed returnees they feel a 'duty' to show solidarity with their compatriots, to be present at and bear witness to the birth of 'a more equitable and tolerant Pakistan' (Hamid 2009a; Hanif 2008b).

Hamid (2006: n.p.) in particular has made repeated reference to the fact that his relationship with New York – once his 'most passionate' metropolitan 'affair' – has changed in recent years. His articles in British and American magazines and broadsheets document in some detail the negative impact of the events of 11 September on him, and on his compatriots' New York-based lives, leading to feelings of fear, anxiety, even paranoia, and precipitating their departure (Hamid 2001a, 2003a, 2006). They indicate his frustration with the way in which the Pakistani and Muslim components of his 'transcontinental mongrel' identity have been aggressively thrust upon him – and subsequently held against him – in the persecutory post-9/11 climate of the West, and in particular the US (2003b: n.p., 2003c).

Frequently figured in amorous terms, New York becomes 'the girl I will always lust for but who left me exhausted' (Hamid 2003b). The jilted articles Hamid published in the years immediately following the World Trade Centre attacks are impassioned, informative and yet also plaintive, frustrated and at times patronising in tone. They reflect his disappointment as a civilised, compassionate, secular Muslim with his experience of 'democracy' in Bush's US, his total disinclination to embrace Bin Laden and his desire to re-educate his woefully ignorant listeners about the reality of contemporary Islamic perspectives vis-à-vis the West (Hamid 2003a, 2003c).[3] In their tone and style, the author's non-fiction writing appears consonant with some of the positions put forward by Changez, the protagonist of his 2007 novel, *The Reluctant Fundamentalist* (2007b). This book has been interpreted in some quarters as a novelistic attempt to offer an authentic window onto a terrorist mindset, and has provoked some interesting autobiographical and pathological readings of its author and subject as a result.

Moth Smoke and *The Reluctant Fundamentalist*: Contemporary readings

Hamid's debut novel *Moth Smoke* (2000c) was well reviewed when it first was published in 2000 and has reportedly achieved a kind of 'cult status' in India and Pakistan (Elliott 2011: 9) Yet in comparison with the international bestseller that succeeded it, this early novel has attracted relatively little academic or popular attention in Anglo-American or "world" literary circuits at least, perhaps, until the early 2010s.[4] Set in late-1990s Lahore, *Moth Smoke* presents from a range of narrative perspectives a complex portrait of Daru, a young male middle-class protagonist. Daru loses his banking job, falls out with his privileged and America-returned best friend Ozi, and descends into a life of drugs and crime in a Pakistan beset with crisis: in the throes of economic meltdown, financially reliant on narcotics and locked in a potentially nuclear conflict with India. Like Mueenuddin's more recent collection of short fiction *In Other Rooms, Other Wonders* (2009) and perhaps Hanif's darkly comic *Our Lady of Alice Bhatti* (2011), this early work gives a powerful sense of the difficulties its central characters face in the course of their daily lives as a result of social inequalities and systemic corruption which may be the legacies of a feudal and colonial past, but are articulated in new forms by their twenty-first-century inheritors.

Moth Smoke encompasses narrative strands and themes which may chime with the concerns international audiences have had in relation to nuclear-armed Pakistan and the conflicting loyalties of its increasingly transnational Muslim subjects after 9/11. But these were less visible to publishers and readers prior to the World Trade Centre attacks. When reviewing *Moth Smoke* for the *Los Angeles Times*, Jonathan Levi (2000: n.p.) observed that its New York-based author had 'created a hip page-turner about the mysterious country that both created the sophisticated Benazir Bhutto and hanged her father'. But it was not until May 2011 that Rachel Aspden suggested in her re-reading that the novel also 'provides the context for [a] clash of cultures' in its 'portrait of a country violently divided against itself' (Aspden 2011: n.p.). That clash, between the corrupt and complacent foreign-educated and advantageously connected rich, and their increasingly impoverished and resentful Pakistan-remaining brothers, is partly figured in the characters of the expatriate Ozi and his sinking peer, Daru.

Hamid (2000c: 11, 74) "frames" the upwardly mobile and moneyed Ozi as the Pajero-driving, Black Label-drinking, Switzerland-visiting, New York-returned son of a 'frequently investigated but as yet unincarcerated Federal Secretary' who specialises 'it's said, in overpaying

foreign companies for equipment and pocketing their kickbacks'.
His embittered and rapidly socially descending boyhood companion, Daru, is a parentless PhD dropout (having studied micro-credit
at Punjab University, he has switched to banking in the hope of
earning a living) whom Ozi's father advises to downscale his ambi-
tions from 'large multinational' to local car-dealer when his firm
gives him the sack (75). If Ozi attempts, in Hamid's ironic, "ethno-
graphic" fiction, to realise in Pakistan 'The utopian vision of Over
There or Amreeka' which 'promises escape from the almost unbearable drudgery of the tribe's struggle to subsist', then Daru tries for
his part to reveal that the facade of living the American dream is
one maintained with little enthusiasm by a bored and compromised
transnational Lahori elite (79). Yet, despite his disillusionment with
it, Hamid's 'brilliant' and aspirant middle-class protagonist covets the
privileges and cultivates the company of the 'crowd' he holds in contempt, even seeks to re-establish a long-lost 'bond of boyhood trust
and affection' with Ozi (36, 79, 89). That is, until he becomes this
society's scapegoat. For, Daru's trial for the hit-and-run murder of a
child which Ozi "inconveniently" commits ultimately provides the
frame for Hamid's inconclusive narrative. Through the characters of
Daru and Ozi, then, *Moth Smoke* perpetuates a discomfiting divide
between the dispensable, locally situated middle-class Pakistani subject (who *is* nevertheless culpable, if not for this, then for other
disquieting crimes visited on its lesser citizens) and his elite, cosmopolitan cousin, figured as an 'overgrown child...who gets away
with everything' (96, 244).

Hamid's first novel also presents an experiment in form, whereby
the role-playing reader is required to stand in judgement over the
protagonist, to become his defender or detractor, to determine his
guilt or "innocence", thus adopting a position Hamid would go on
to critique in *The Reluctant Fundamentalist*. As he explained in an
interview:

> *Moth Smoke* is about this young guy,...who is being tried for
> a crime [killing a child]...A number of people tell their sto-
> ries...The idea was to encourage the reader to form an opinion
> about what's going on, to make a judgement on the central char-
> acter, what he's being tried for, who he is. In a way my second
> novel tries to do the same thing.
>
> (Hamid 2008b: 45)

The second time, in *The Reluctant Fundamentalist*, the form almost replays as farce. Gone are the multiple conflicting portraits through which we must diligently search for the truth about the shadow of the man who stands in the dock, however tempted we may be to place our 'faith in [his] promises' or believe his 'fantasy [of] being framed' (Hamid 2000c: 235). In their place we have a dramatic monologue which Hamid (2008b: 45) has described as a 'one-man-play', performed by the erudite, anglophone Pakistani, Changez, to a silent American listener. There is no firm accusation, no second witness nor any concrete evidence that can tie the protagonist to a tangible offence. There are, however, plenty of references to the fact that he keeps 'intimidating' company and puts the listener 'ill at ease' (2007b: 123). As with Daru's story, Changez's narrative will remain incomplete if some conclusion about what kind of man he is, and what he is capable of, cannot be supplied. But the difference here, in *The Reluctant Fundamentalist*, is that when this judgement is made it will be indicative not of the reader's having weighed the evidence with an open and impartial mind. Rather, it will point to his or her residual 'preconceptions and prejudices and fears' about this clever Pakistani protagonist and the thoughts he articulates in his polite, familiar and 'vaguely menacing' British-sounding voice (Hamid 2008b: 46).

Moth Smoke was reissued by Penguin in April 2011 (Hamid 2000d). It may have attracted greater interest at that time a result of the status its author had accrued since 2000 as a commentator on Pakistani affairs, spokesman for the perspectives of the region's people and ' "pin-up boy" for Pakistani-English literature' (Elliott 2011: 9). However, although its title may have become more familiar to readers of literary fiction in the second decade of the third millennium, it does not necessarily seem to follow that the complex affinities and affiliations which it maps are more than superficially "known".

Hamid's appearance alongside the political scientists Francis Fukuyama and Anatol Lieven, and Bangladeshi novelist Tahmima Anam, on BBC Radio 4's topical discussion programme *Start the Week* (2011) hosted by Andrew Marr shortly after the killing of Osama Bin Laden in May 2011, seems a case in point.[5] Hamid's task was ostensibly to explore for listeners 'what it means to be middle class in Pakistan'. Marr (*Start the Week* 2011) supposed the recently republished *Moth Smoke* might be deemed to describe 'from the inside' the world mapped by Lieven in his historical survey, *Pakistan: A Hard*

Country (2011).[6] The conversation touched on themes that included the lack of provision made by the Pakistani state for ordinary citizens, and the support provided by non-governmental social structures in its stead. However, these were not discussed in relation to *Moth Smoke*'s specific narrative content or characters. Instead, Hamid cited in the course of the programme examples of instances in which such networks had been activated which would be familiar to listeners with a more general interest in news and current affairs, such as the 2010 floods in Punjab and Sindh. He offered a single, largely positive reading of the social structures which came to the aid of Pakistanis who were severely affected in this time of crisis. This differed considerably from the ambivalent and multi-perspectival portraits he presented to readers in *Moth Smoke*.

During the course of the programme, Hamid succeeded in modifying some of Marr's more simplistic descriptions of the Pakistani social structures discussed with formulations of his own. For example, the broadcaster's clannish 'family' and 'kinship groups', concerned to close ranks and protect their members, became in Hamid's reformulation sophisticated and 'powerful patronage networks' providing a 'safety net' for those in need (*Start the Week* 2011). But in the main the interviewer set the agenda, selecting the topics and choosing the controversial terms of debate which might spark and frame ensuing conversations.[7] Following the discussion of the popular response to the floods, he swiftly steered the conversation onto other, pre-ordained topics deemed of relevance to a consideration of the modern Pakistani state. These were, primarily, 'Pakistani paranoia' (a term proffered by Marr in the guise of agent provocateur) about the Indian "enemy" across the border, and questions of Islamic identity, centred around choices of dress, drink, drugs and language (*Start the Week* 2011).

Start the Week is a *cultural* discussion programme, yet this edition, ironically, provided little space for a consideration of how Hamid's *literary* portrayals might extend the parameters of current debate around aspects of quotidian Pakistani culture often configured as problematic in the West. An examination of Hamid's depiction of the poverty of career prospects available to home-grown graduates disinclined to toe the line of Pakistan's ever-evolving elites might, for example, encourage the reader to revise their understanding of the extent to which this apparently close-knit and nepotistic culture actually supports its members. The more complex positions and less absolute attitudes to which *Moth Smoke* in particular strives to give life remained if not exactly overlooked then certainly under-explored, as a result of a need to contain them within a fairly narrow journalistic agenda which privileges sound bites and simple images even as it expresses a desire to get beyond them.

Distinctive in its tone and style, *The Reluctant Fundamentalist* is perhaps the best known and most unsettling literary intervention into the discourse around South Asian Islamic extremism to have been produced after the attacks of 9/11. It has been shortlisted for several prizes, including the 2007 Man Booker Prize for Fiction and the 2008 Commonwealth Writers Prize (Eurasia Region), and in 2008 it won the South Bank Show Annual Award for Literature. The novel has proved arresting to readers on account both of its seeming promise to deliver some sensational-sounding content and of its slippery narrative form.

The Reluctant Fundamentalist presents in the shape of a dramatic monologue the story of the high-flying Pakistani executive Changez's love affair with New York and disenchantment with the "fundamentalist" capitalism of the West. The novel opens at a cafe in the Old Anarkali district of his native Lahore several years after the 9/11 attacks, where he appears to be entertaining a silent American visitor with the story of his turning away from America. Changez talks of his Princeton education and of how he came first to acquire and then to part with his prestigious job as a financial analyst, his ambiguous 'love' Erica and adoptive city of New York; he describes the circumstances surrounding his relocation to Lahore, where he becomes a university lecturer (Hamid 2007b: 18). The protagonist details in particular his unexpectedly joyful reaction to the attacks on the World Trade Centre, the sense of solidarity he felt with the beleaguered Afghan tribesmen whom America targeted in their bloody wake, and his reluctance to serve as a 'janissary' to a modern-day empire that privileged 'maximum productivity' and 'maximum return' over any humane agenda (41, 132, 173).

In the latter part of the novel, as the Old Anarkali market empties and shadows fall on the heart of Old Lahore, Changez makes reference to what he did to 'stop' the inhumanity of his formerly beloved America, grown dangerously defensive in the years since the 9/11 attacks (190). However, the actions he has taken in this regard remain, crucially, in doubt. The Pakistani protagonist's concluding commentary as he escorts the American back to his gated hotel reflects both the increasingly uncomfortable state of Changez's 'guest', and his host's anxiety to reassure this man that, despite playing 'Kurtz' to his 'Marlow', he in fact poses no threat (208). The outcome of this dubious Pakistani–American encounter, like the extent and nature of Changez's "reluctant fundamentalism", remains unclear: at the end of the novel the Pakistani tour guide, lecturer and 'potential terrorist' offers a handshake to his American confessor and receives a glimpse of something metal beneath his jacket in its stead (209). Hamid's reader is left to draw his own conclusions as to which of the characters is the victim and which the assassin here; whether the reasons for their meeting could perhaps have been benign; and who exactly must be misled or misread in order for this work of fiction to find foundation.

Fictional in content and confessional in tone, Hamid's artful dramatic monologue mimics in ostensible subject and style such "factual" Muslim memoirs as Husain's (2007) *The Islamist*, which critics have praised for opening their eyes to the realities of Islamic fundamentalism.[8] Yet, unlike Husain's ' "refusenik" ' recantation (Morey and Yaqin 2011: 94), Hamid's playful novel maps "fundamentalist" affiliations entertained by its secular Muslim subject which might surprise the reader, and in cleverly elusive fashion refuses to speak of others which may be deemed more (stereo-)typical.

Encoded in Changez's narrative is a warning that any literal interpretation of his apparent confession – and, by extension, Hamid's fictional text – as an insightful and authentic act of post-9/11 Muslim spokesmanship could serve to 'implicate' the reader and interpreter at least as much as its narrator and author (Hamid 2007b: 80).[9] Any nod of assent, either when Changez ventures to suggest that the American may not be 'entirely *surprised*' to hear him admit to some initial sense of pleasure at the World Trade Centre's destruction, or when he hazards a guess that his guest may have felt comparable 'joy' when the US launched retributive attacks on the Muslim world, will ensnare the "world" reader (84, 86). It will appear to confirm their prejudice and pre-existing hostility. It seems crucial that attention be paid to this propensity to politically determined suppositions at a time when there is a tendency amongst Western commentators and even governments to assume that highly authored individual accounts of encounters with Islamic extremism can provide 'illuminating' and 'instructive' insights into young male Muslim minds which may contribute to their 'decod[ing]' (Mondal 2012: 37; Morey 2011: 138–9).

Ironically, many readers of *The Reluctant Fundamentalist* seem to have fallen into the same trap as that set by Changez for his fictive interlocutor. They have found in his autobiographical account the confession they are perhaps 'set…up' to seek about his sinister embracement of Islamist terror, and overlooked his other Muslim affiliations and non-religious connections (Morey 2011: 138). When reflecting on *The Reluctant Fundamentalist*'s reception in the months following its publication in March 2007, Hamid has remarked on his readers' tendency to conflate the novel's cosmopolitan protagonist with the character's creator (Hamid, 2007c: n.p.). On occasion aspects of Changez's behaviour – typically, his confession that he '*smiled*' when he saw the Twin Towers collapse – have led to emotional exchanges with Hamid's readers (Hamid 2007b: 83). While Hamid has said that he 'wouldn't call the[se] confrontations', he acknowledges that people were 'angry or upset' and required him to provide 'an explanation' for his character's seemingly callous reactions to an act of international terror which had a devastating impact on America (2007c). The author and his protagonist's biographies are not dissimilar: both are young, articulate Pakistani men born in Lahore, educated at Princeton and employed in corporate New York; both have fallen in and out of love with that city and subsequently emigrated from America. Crucially, both may also be thought to fit the 'well-educated, upwardly and geographically mobile, migrant constituency' which Bart Moore-Gilbert observes is 'consonant with the profiles of the real-life 9/11 attackers' (2012: 193). What is interesting with regard to the reader responses is the assumption that perhaps because of these correlations they have a shared point of view to communicate, and that this is "real" or "representative": that Hamid, via Changez, gives voice to the thoughts of a certain type of Islamic "fundamentalist" which he at least partially supports.

In the years since *The Reluctant Fundamentalist*'s publication, some attention has begun to be paid to this oblique novel's capacity both to engender and to undermine such straightforward readerly assumptions. John Mullan (2011: n.p.), for example, has remarked on a tendency amongst *The Guardian*'s Book Club audience to take the novel's contents literally, assuming an autobiographical overlap between the Princeton-educated author and his erudite creation, and interpreting his seemingly prescient fiction as a 'thesis' with the potential to illuminate 'attitudes and beliefs that might shape political events'. Morey (2011: 139) has gone on to analyse how Hamid's intimate account, while 'subtly parodying successful quasi-autobiographical texts', forces its reader into a new and unsettling relation with its fictional "fundamentalist" narrator, making it impossible to link his 'political awakening' to the 'default positions attributed to Islamic radicals'.[10]

Likewise, Bart Moore-Gilbert has pointed to the fact that it is difficult to trace ' "Islamic fundamentalism" as habitually conceived in Western public discourse' at all in Hamid's slippery novel, for Changez's predominantly cultural "Muslim" affiliations and affinities are sparsely represented. However, this critic would still use Hamid's text to identify 'loc[i] of opposition to (American-led) globalization', and is keen to emphasise that Changez's resistance is 'linked to the long tradition of leftist pursuit of social and political justice' and in sympathy with a 'rainbow coalition' of anti-imperial antagonists (Moore-Gilbert 2012: 194–5). While he acknowledges that to emphasise the secular, leftist aspects of Changez's supposed "fundamentalism" is to 'risk *re*-presenting resistance...in terms which can be more or less comfortably "recognised" by the liberal metropolitan reader', Moore-Gilbert nevertheless focuses mainly on analysing information which may help us discern 'whether Changez is, indeed, a "fundamentalist" and, if so, of what kind': sociopathic, rational, or morally conflicted (195–7). Reading the lack of resolution offered in relation to Changez's "fundamentalist" affiliation as testament to the fact that it may not be possible adequately to represent or recognise 'in the current climate of vexed relations between the West and certain Muslim formations', his essay leaves unexplored the alternative explanations for the novel's intriguing ellipses which this chapter seeks to foreground (197).

Mullan and Morey have perhaps placed greater emphasis on *The Reluctant Fundamentalist*'s ludic qualities. Mullan (2011), for example, framed his survey of audience responses which point to a shared conviction of the reality of the 'attitudes and beliefs' described in the text, with his own critical observations. These foreground the novel's fictive elements – the provocative ambiguity of the narrative first person; Changez's chameleon-like capacity to change "fundamentally" when scrutinised in different lights – and would seem to dissuade the sophisticated reader from taking any single interpretation of Changez's fundamentalist associations as read.

Morey (2011: 140–1) also draws attention to the ways in which this symbolic and allegorical novel's 'constant attention to fiction-making' not only makes a mockery of any attempt to fix the allegiances – Islamic or otherwise – of its deterritorialised and unreliable narrator, but disorients the reader with alarming effect. Morey's argument is that by 'making the text a site of struggle for ... different versions' of events or experiential truths, Hamid forces readers to detach themselves from habitual, culturally conditioned modes of perception. Thus freed, they may see into the 'spaces' the writer constructs for being and believing 'between [the] conflicting interests and positions' typically associated with East and West (138). The implication is that 'deterritorialised literature' can make us realise the constructedness of the essentialising shorthand used to describe (Muslim) protagonists in the wake of the "war on terror" (138). Such writing may perhaps therefore force its readers to confront their responsibilities as players in a potentially deadly game of framing others' identities, as Hamid (2013a: 15) – retrospectively – has hinted that he hopes it might. Literary tricks and effects – such as Hamid's recruitment of the shifty Changez in place of a "trustworthy" narrator, and his clever fashioning of a faux confessional narrative – are essential to the process of laying bare the artificiality of the text and the character positions which Hamid invites us to construct and deconstruct.[11]

Hamid (2011a, n.p.) has remarked that as a child he was captivated by the role-playing *Choose Your Own Adventure* series of puzzle books, and as a maturing writer has come to 'wonder if the power of the novel ... [is] rooted in the enormous degree of co-creation it requires on the part of its audience'. He is intrigued by the notion that it is incumbent on the reader who listens in to the 'half-conversation' of a dramatic monologue to 'supply its missing context'. Perhaps coerced, certainly invited, to engage in an act of co-writing, the reader creates – in Hamid's words – a version of the book which reflects his or

her 'individual inclinations and world views' as much (if not more)
than those of its characters.

His tone may seem disinterested here, his motivations benign, but
in a post-7/7 world where, as Tony Blair declared, 'the rules of the
game have changed' (quoted in Wintour, 2005: n.p.) and it appears
to be open season with regard to the treatment of Muslim subjects,
Hamid creates a novel which 'plays' a mischievous even malicious
'kind of game' with the Western reader – one which that reader can
never win (Hamid 2009b: 225). Brazenly foregrounding the likelihood that *The Reluctant Fundamentalist* is in fact a 'confession that
implicates its audience' (Hamid 2007b: 80), the author asks the reader
to meet the challenge of 'responding to [the Pakistani protagonist's]
manipulation' (2009b: 225). But he must do so in a 'vacuum', devoid
of any external referent, forming a character judgement of the protagonist – either as a 'random chap' or a 'terrorist' – based on his instincts
(225). The reader has no way of knowing whether he or she gets it
right: Hamid cuts the ending short, and Changez's 'true' nature –
if indeed this can be thought to exist – is never disclosed. Furthermore, any "fundamentalist" identity the protagonist may propose
is undermined by the fact that he may be misleading the American
who listens to his one-sided conversation. As he repeatedly reminds
his audience: 'there is no reason why this incident would be more
likely to be false than any of the others I have related to you'
(Hamid, 2007b: 172–3). The monster, martyr, mimic or middleman
apparently embodied by Hamid's "Changez", but given flesh by the
apostrophised Western interlocutor and reader, will – in this sceptical
reading of the text – only ever 'implicate... its audience', reflecting
the kind of transnational Pakistani Muslim they anticipate seeing or
want to see (80).

Hamid uses his central protagonist to complicate the idea of South
Asian Muslim affiliation by avoiding a commitment to any identities
available to him. The "fundamentalist" of his novel's title remains
unrepresented; like an empty signifier, Changez floats free. His are
potential rather than *actual* affiliations; it is not possible to determine
whether Changez is responsible for an act of Islamic terror, or to
what extent he subscribes to a radical Islamist's agenda. Hamid simply opens up the possibility of his being an affiliate of a jihadist's
global umma; it is the reader who decides to what extent he indeed
subscribes.

Changez as psychological case study

I am going to insist that this [*The Reluctant Fundamentalist*] is fiction and whatever learned members of the audience determine about the psychosis of the characters involved, they have nothing to do with me.

(Hamid 2009b: 225)

Hamid attempts to emphasise his novel's fictive qualities. But his intimate portrait of a Pakistani Muslim subject remains susceptible to being interpreted as an incomplete and literal confession of a fundamentalist turn, rather an intentional and highly literary cipher, in a period when commentators have suggested that testimonial accounts of Islamic radicalisation should be 'prescribed like medicine' (Wakefield 2007: n.p.).[12]

This is a problem perhaps compounded by the contemporaneousness of *The Reluctant Fundamentalist*'s publication with books which purported to offer authentic insights into the world as seen from a radical Muslim perspective. Examples include *The Islamist: Why I Joined Radical Islam in Britain, What I Saw Inside and Why I Left*, a memoir by Ed Husain (2007), and *Terrorist*, a thriller by John Updike (2006). Both of these – like Hamid's novel – were published by Penguin.[13] In the former work Husain (2007, 'Preface'), a reformed British Muslim extremist who now works as an "expert" on international threats from Islamist radicalisation and terror, claims he will take the reader on a journey behind the scenes of 'today's Islam' as he saw it first-hand. Husain endeavours to answer the kind of questions he imagines non-Muslim American and British readers have harboured since the 9/11 and 7/7 attacks.

But what Husain purports to "know" about the impulses and emotions that inform a young Muslim's turn towards violent extremism, fiction writers place in doubt. Hamid's novel leaves the details of what Changez may or may not know about the operations of a terrorist cell unclear, and the question of how far he either fabricates or withholds an insider's perspective on radicalisation remains unanswered. Yet at a time when 'the possibility that [an] extraordinary personal story ... can help to answer ... pressing questions about the ... Muslim community' (Bunting 2007: n.p.) has been central to its appeal, Hamid's ambiguous account of Changez's fundamentalist affiliations seems to have piqued audiences' curiosity rather than acted as a deterrent. *The Reluctant Fundamentalist* remains susceptible to some equally intriguing diagnostic readings.

One such reading is offered by the psychoanalyst M. Fakhry Davids in his 2009 essay 'The Impact of Islamophobia' (2009), which had its first outing at a conference on psychoanalysis, fascism and fundamentalism in November 2008. His aim in the paper is to explore 'what light ... psychoanalysis [can] shed on what goes on in the mind when the Muslim is vilified as the enemy of the public good', a racist trend which he argues has intensified in the period following the attacks of 9/11 and 7/7 (178). Specifically, he seeks to understand the role Islamophobia has played in making a 'radically anti-Western Islam' attractive to Muslim adolescents in the West at a time when, in his view, fundamentalism has been 'inscribed' as Islam's 'problematic heart' (178, 191). He takes as case studies three young male Muslims attracted by fundamentalist interpretations of Islam and examines their struggles to integrate the Muslim aspects of their identity with those of their Western selves. The first is "Ahmed", a British Muslim of Pakistani background who attended Davids' psychoanalytic practice in late 2001 or early 2002 presenting anxiety about his former militant connections; the second the ex-Islamist Ed Husain – or at least his authorial persona as portrayed in his intimate memoir; and the third a fictive creation, the seemingly eponymous protagonist of Hamid's *The Reluctant Fundamentalist*.

Following Frantz Fanon's theories about 'violent resistance' (189), Davids reads as 'normal' the trajectories traced by the now apparently reformed and reintegrated Ahmed and Husain. They gravitate away from the Afghan training camps and tutelage of *Hizb-ut-Tahrir*, which attracted them in their rebellious adolescence, and towards modified and less militant forms of Islam, community roles and university courses by the time of their early twenties. Yet Davids seems profoundly disturbed by Changez's "case". For Changez's behaviour fails to fit this developmental pattern: in Davids' reading, he first appears to suppress his Pakistani Muslim identity in order to pursue a career as a management consultant in New York, then actively embraces Islamic fundamentalism on relocation to Lahore (188–9). The language and tone the psychoanalyst uses to describe this seemingly total transferral of allegiance is one of deep concern. Davids describes Changez's severance of his New York ties as destructive rather than liberating, and reads his shift towards a more political consciousness as a 'descent', not as a progression. He considers the metropolitan Pakistani's crisis of confidence in American capitalism to have ushered in a 'catastrophic breakdown of the personality' from which the protagonist seems unlikely to recover (189). Meanwhile, Changez's story is haunted by 'the prospect of the violent return of the repressed', meaning – in this instance – the Muslim Pakistani subject's dangerously "fundamental" Islamic side.

In Davids' opinion, the two British Muslims, "Ahmed" and Husain, benefitted from having been raised in a society 'that tolerated a fundamentalist voice within' (189). This gave them scope, he argues, to play out their 'fundamentalist' fantasies – to look into what he terms Islam's 'problematic heart', realise its fissures, and find a way of remaining Muslim in the West (191). He fears that Changez, whom he observes was not so fortunate as to be born into such a liberal society, has adopted a 'narrower interpretation' of Islam which, unexorcised and unintegrated, will 'constitute a danger' not only to the young man's individual psyche but also to non-Muslim peoples as a whole (181, 189).[14]

The problem with Davids' deployment of Hamid's novel as a tool for analysing the situation and psychological condition of actually existing Muslims living in contemporary Western societies is that it relies on the unstated assumption that the author, presumably because of his cultural and religious background, creates in the fictional Changez a textbook example of a real-life 'problem' (188). Davids does not challenge Hamid's credentials as a commentator on Muslim issues, or question the author's capacity to speak with any genuine empathy or authority about the militant radicalisation of a single expatriate Pakistani Muslim youth (let alone all such individuals). Nor does he enquire into the extent to which the novel's protagonist may be intended to be representative of a particular (stereo-)type. And although Davids acknowledges that the details of what exactly Changez's 'reluctant fundamentalism' entails remain 'unclear', and concedes that 'we assume' (rather than *know*) the nature of the mindset into which Changez enters, the psychoanalyst leaves unconsidered the author's reason for omitting them (189).

In short, Davids fails to ask the kinds of questions which philosopher Gregory Currie (2011: 14–15), who is interested in the interplay between psychology and literature, has suggested should be raised by readers who value creative writing for the insights it appears to offer into the workings of the mind – into 'moral thinking and acting', for example, or the causes of human behaviour. Currie lists these questions as follows:

> Is the practice of fiction one we can reasonably expect to give us the insight we hope for? Are serious fiction writers well equipped to give us that insight?...[And] is what I'm supposed to be learning consistent with or supported by the best science? (14)

The philosopher maintains that such a reader should remain conscious that a literary work is 'an exercise in pretence', and that the beliefs and perspectives its creator presents as reliable may not correspond with any external reality they have experienced or taken time to research (15). Currie also reminds us of the fallibility of our perceptions when it comes to interpreting human behaviour, whether as creative writers or as readers.

Ultimately, Davids' assessment of Changez may reveal more about what the professional psychoanalyst wants to read or believes he is reading concerning an expatriate Pakistani Muslim's response to Islamophobia in the post-9/11 West than it does the mentality of Hamid's fictional and ambiguously 'fundamentalist' subject. Noting trends and diagnosing psychosocial problems based on literal readings of contemporary novels by transnational Muslim writers in English would therefore seem at best a hazardous business.

Dead ends? Hamid's recent short fiction

'The (Former) General in His Labyrinth' (2008d), 'A Beheading' (2010) and 'Terminator: Attack of the Drone' (2011d), three works of short fiction which Hamid has produced since *The Reluctant Fundamentalist*, suggest a continuing desire on the part of the author to engage with presumed reader expectations for an international "brand" of contemporary Pakistani (Muslim) writing by means of experiments in literary form. These tales' bold titles, like that of Hamid's second novel, seem to promise to deliver characters and narrative content in accordance with "world" requirements – in these instances portraits of decadent despots, deadly bombardments and gruesome scenarios that may 'scare the shit' out of readers (Hamid et al. 2010: n.p.).

'The (Former) General in His Labyrinth' is a work of digital fiction which makes the reader an active participant in a story-making game. 'A Beheading' is a fragment of dramatic monologue which appears to 'function' like *The Reluctant Fundamentalist* 'as a thriller which mirrors the pre-existing thrill in the audience and reader' (Hamid 2009b: 226). Both are designed to entertain. But despite their postmodern reflexivity and game-playing, these shorter works lack the inbuilt framing devices which are crucial to the ironic process of using fiction first to place and then de-face the apparent trademark characteristics and affiliations of the bearers of the Pakistani brand.

Hamid wrote his interactive story, 'The (Former) General in His Labyrinth' (2008d), for Penguin's digital fiction project, which was produced in collaboration with alternative reality game designers Six to Start, and ran for six weeks in March and April 2008 (*We Tell Stories*, 2008). Interactive readers are ascribed the task of navigating the courses of action available to the failing president and '(Former) General' of a country with nuclear capacity. They adopt the guise of the General himself, who is surely a fictive echo of the now former, and then current President, General Pervez Musharraf. At the click of an arrow we may choose to occupy ourselves with some important business, entering ornate marble hallways to proceed to meetings or enter our TV studio to record a political speech. Alternatively, noting that we have a long night ahead of us, we may prefer to sit back and be entertained by our private secretary, Shaan Azad, who maintains there are 'always at least two ways to tell a story'. While the story's game-like format provides us as readers with the apparent freedom to choose the direction we wish the story to take, in reality our options are limited: we must select from a prescribed set of quickly exhausted options and then either abandon the hope of concluding the narrative, or retrace our steps back to the start. Caught in the limited loops available in the rather lacklustre and lethargic (Former) General's labyrinth, we have ample opportunity to reflect on his and "our" current choices, but no capacity independent of him to generate alternative actions or initiate any change.

If we read the story allegorically, it offers more than an ironic comment on Pakistan's contemporary political situation, led by an increasingly isolated president who, by mid-2008, had 'outlasted his welcome' (Ali 2008: 255), been electorally defeated and was under threat of impeachment. It playfully provides the interactive worldwide player with an opportunity actively to embody the shuffling figure of the (Former) General Musharraf, to eavesdrop on his thoughts and – by exhausting a circumscribed set of options – to realise both his inability and his disinclination to act to alter the status quo. The General is 'unable', in Hamid's (2008c: n.p.) critical words, 'to accept the logical conclusion of the project he had begun: his own departure'. At a stretch it might be argued that the story's format encourages a degree of empathy on the part of the interactive "reader" with the plight of Pakistan's beleaguered leader, some of whose initiatives Hamid once respected; or that it even functions to implicate the role-player by making him temporarily responsible for Musharraf's (in)decisions. Yet Hamid uses the second person narrative mode when addressing the General/gamer ('you...'), thus encouraging a more objective attitude on the part of his global, anglophone audiences towards the autocratic Pakistani persona he invites them to adopt. And he limits the range of preprogrammed actions available to those of a dictatorial stereotype. As a result, 'The (Former) General' simply presents an amusing diversion, a wry and comic insight into the imagined dilemmas of a slightly exotic and ineffective modern autocrat.

'A Beheading' (Hamid 2010), published in *Granta 112*, but written prior to Hamid's return to Lahore, is a fragment of a dramatic, monological account, this time in horror-story mode, of a writer's nightmarish abduction by shadowy intruders. It speaks to the rational but also 'pernicious' fears to which Hamid gives voice in his commentary about the vulnerability of Pakistan-based writers, artists and other individuals who are critical of the country's powerful political, judicial, military and religious authorities (Hamid 2011c: n.p.; Haque 2011: n.p.). Hamid claims in his newspaper essay 'Silencing Pakistan' that 'A Beheading', in which the anticipated 'blood-bath' (Hamid 2009b: 227) is delayed but not denied, was fashioned out of a desire on his part to investigate his feelings of fear and intimidation – 'doom' and 'terror' – about being an outspoken Pakistani writer prior to his relocation to Lahore (Hamid 2011c). The implication in his essay is that perhaps, by publicly confronting his demons, he will encourage his free-thinking compatriots to follow suit and exorcise their own, speaking out about their state of 'insecurity', rather than letting it force them into self-censorship or silence.

The point of the story is that it 'mirrors' not just an assumed 'preexisting thrill in the audience and reader', but also the author himself

(Hamid 2009b: 226). Yet the fictional (and formal) experiment which is the outcome of Hamid's having permitted his imagination temporarily to fall prey to 'a fear that gives rise to self-censorship' (Hamid 2011c), does not stand as a complex creative expression of the author's paranoid psychic state. Rather, devoid of this literary context, it appears in an edition like *Granta 112* as a 'horror' story which plays to exactly the kind of misperceptions about what is "typical" in Pakistan which Hamid has criticised the global media for amplifying in his commentary and – in fictions like *The Reluctant Fundamentalist* – endeavoured to undermine (Hamid, quoted in Haque 2011).

'A Beheading' may perhaps be a necessary by-product of what the transnational Pakistani writer has described as the 'divided man's conversation with himself' (Hamid 2007a). One suspects, however, that like 'The (Former) General' it does more to indulge nightmarish fantasies about a Pakistan governed by inept autocrats and infiltrated by terrifying Islamic militants than to develop Hamid's earlier stated project of 'reintroduc[ing] complexity into a world that, for reasons of space and economy, is desperately trying to minimize it' (Hamid 2008a: 118–19).

'Terminator: Attack of the Drone' (2011d), the dystopian fiction Hamid wrote for *The Guardian Review Book of Short Stories*, is perhaps his most interesting attempt to use creative writing to "reintroduce complexity" to international depictions of Pakistan since *The Reluctant Fundamentalist*. The story is set in what initially seems to be a burnt-out, post-apocalyptic landscape, a science fiction or fantasy space almost devoid of animal and human life. Against this backdrop, a plucky young boy, one of a handful of human survivors of a continuing onslaught from a mechanical race, narrates the story of a night he spends 'huntin' his nemesis in a strange and drawling accent (2011d: n.p.). A few clues are gradually introduced which may convey a sense of a real cultural, geographical and historical context. We learn that the narrator's friend is called 'Omar' and another boy, 'Yousuf', has vanished. The region they live in is prone to earthquakes, abandoned Kalashnikovs are easy pickings, hidden caves provide a safe space and firing at unmanned aerial vehicles is a deadly kind of game.

Using form to alienate and disorient the reader, Hamid makes him fall back on his knowledge of prior texts and intertexts. These may include dystopian visions of broken worlds conveyed in fractured prose, disturbing works of science fiction (filmic and literary) where alien and artificially intelligent life threatens to colonise and ultimately eradicate humanity, even perhaps frontier narratives or Western films. Reading the juvenile narrator's experience of multiple US drone attacks through these pre-existing fictional lenses, perhaps we can begin to realise the magnitude of their impact on his vision of everyday life: how they shape and warp his impressions of reality; and how he understands and counters the threat these enemies pose. Experiments in form such as these, which attempt to use unexpected aspects of genre fiction to make the reader reconfigure reality and read it in different modes, undoubtedly serve a purpose at a time when it is all too easy to fall back on clichéd and stereotypical ways of reading, particularly in relation to young, male Muslim subjects. But while they encourage small shifts in viewpoint, perhaps tricking the participating reader into seeing contemporary Pakistani "horror" stories through "other" eyes, they lack the 'devilish' and 'difficult' ludic edge which distinguishes *The Reluctant Fundamentalist* (2007b: 80). Ultimately, Hamid's surreal, nightmarish forays in short and virtual fictions fail to build in any substantial way on the very real challenge that his disconcerting post-9/11 novel presents to its highly implicated, co-creating Anglo-American audiences and their prejudicial perspectives. They may suggest new directions but lead, literally and metaphorically, to dead ends.

Beyond the constructed confessional

The Reluctant Fundamentalist vigorously exposes the constructedness of the confessional Muslim narrative as presented to hypothetical Western readers who are disoriented in oriental lands. It encourages them to adopt a sceptical position not only vis-à-vis the Pakistani Muslim suspect they encounter in their midst, but also with regard to the "suspect" aspect of his or her Islamic identity. In doing so, it leaves unmapped those components of contemporary radical Muslim affiliations, spiritual and political, which the secular, Western world finds most troubling. Hamid's arch fictive account of his Pakistani protagonist's American encounter and his subsequent comments about how Changez's "adventures" may be replayed by the always creative reader combine to undermine any novelistic attempt to "frame" or to "speak for" "authentic" South Asian Muslim subjects. One suspects this is as much the result of the author's discomfort with the role of 'representative' Pakistani Muslim writer as his desire to push the bounds of contemporary fiction (Hamid 2011b). In this he contrasts with his contemporary, Nadeem Aslam (2010b), who, as we will see, uses his literary output to illuminate precisely those 'area[s] of darkness' in the lives of his Pakistani and Afghan Muslim protagonists which Hamid's novel would render obscure, and unfailingly frames the insights he presents as "real".

4
Re-culturing Islam – Nadeem Aslam's Mausoleum Fiction

4.1 Imran Qureshi

Introduction

In Nadeem Aslam's *The Wasted Vigil* (2008), set in twenty-first century Afghanistan, an English doctor who has converted to Islam attempts to salve the wounds of a young Islamist. Aslam makes us party to the elder character's thoughts as he exits the disused perfume factory where the boy, Casa, has been sheltering; Marcus muses:

> The world is apricot light and blue shadows. In sura 27, Solomon laughs on hearing the conversation of two ants – a rare example of humour in the Koran – and there is a third-century Buddhist version of that tale with two butterflies instead of ants. It's no point sharing with the boy the delightful essential idea that tales can travel, or that two sets of people oceans apart can dream up similar sacred myths. (231)

And yet throughout Aslam's narrative, Marcus, a man with a seemingly encyclopedic knowledge of Western science, world literature, art and cosmopolitan Muslim history, tries to do just this: to expose Casa to alternative aspects of Islam's written, oral and visual culture, which may transform his understanding of the 'tales' told by the Qur'an, and help him trace his own features in fragments of Afghanistan's multi-faith heritage. But, as in the passage above, the Englishman also strategically withholds certain narratives, deeming them too delicate or dangerous to discuss with the volatile young Islamist.

Focusing on the two novels Aslam produced in the first decade of the new millennium, *Maps* (2004a) and *Vigil* (2008), this chapter examines how the British Pakistani author's ecumenical fictions make manifest the pre-Islamic Buddhist, Persian and Sufi mystic and aesthetic heritages of South and Central Asian Islam. It contends that his post-9/11 novels recast those regions' resident and diasporic Muslim peoples – child soldiers, perfume-makers and migrant housewives alike – as both susceptible to influences which present an alternative to an austere scripturalist Islam, and deeply, sensually human. Significantly, it argues that his novels stage moments where Muslim characters of different doctrinal and sectarian backgrounds are provided with a fleeting chance to identify commonalities of perspective through a mutual contemplation of this art. And it notes that the moments of affinity they dramatise seem impossible to sustain.

In writing these fictions Aslam appears to be absorbed in a precarious ethical, humanitarian and artistic venture which may be described as "re-culturing" Islam.[1] It could be argued that *Maps* and *Vigil*, which are replete with images of burqas 'studded with fireflies' (2008: 227), Mughal miniatures and bejewelled calligraphic texts, simply pander to Orientalist tastes. But their author seems less interested in inviting occidental readers' delectation or 'doing PR' (Aslam 2011a: 140) for some palatably "moderate" version of the faith, than in repopulating contemporary imaginations with unorthodox stories of Islam for the sake of rehabilitating and restoring its ordinary South Asian Muslim adherents' own (self-)image. This seems particularly important at a time when that faith has been steadily "un-cultured" both by the barbarising discourses of the West, as Steven Salaita (2008: 1–2) notes, and by the brutal actions of the Afghan and Pakistani Taliban.

Anthropologist Shaila Bhatti (2010) acknowledges, in 'What can Museums do for Pakistan?', the educative power of artefacts which point to a heterodox South Asian Muslim cultural history and the significance of the buildings which house them. She also remains attuned to the irony of the fact that such diverse aesthetic objects are exhibited in institutions where they are abstracted from their origins and hard for the majority of people to access. Conscious of museum spaces' 'cultural value and positioning' in Pakistan's 'current socio-political climate', Bhatti is interested in investigating 'the contributions that they make to its society and towards constituting a sense of identity, history and heritage of the nation for its citizens and global travellers' (27). She seeks to highlight their capacity to project an image of this Muslim nation as something other than a 'terrorist civilization' – a place where a 'marble Hanuman' or a Gandhara Buddha may perhaps also find a home (28, 31).[2]

The two novels by Nadeem Aslam which are examined in this chapter, *Maps* (2004a) and *Vigil* (2008), seem to aspire to museum status. They preserve and conserve within their pages both "muse"-inspired and secular arts, and also present spaces of scientific, historic and cultural interest where deep understandings of individual Muslim connections to one another and to the wider world may be nurtured and sustained. Yet those characters who would distribute their cultural knowledge more widely among the Pakistani and Afghan communities which Aslam depicts are invariably thwarted. As a result, his "museum" fictions fall short of this implicit aim. I argue that they may better be characterised as "mausoleum" fictions: stately literary edifices in which the artefacts treasured by (largely European or Western-educated) curators of heterodox Islamic tradition are carefully interred, moribund symbols of an earlier time of tolerance for whose resurrection Aslam keeps "vigil", yet retains little hope.

'All the colours?' Aslam's Islamic spectrum

Aslam was born in the Punjab town of Gujranwala in 1966, raised in Huddersfield from the age of 14 and educated at Manchester University. This diasporic writer describes himself as 'not [having] lived a very cosmopolitan life' because his foreign travel was limited prior to his becoming an established writer (Aslam 2006: 67). He continues to cultivate a more retiring and ascetic profile than the transnational Hamid, Rushdie and Shamsie (see, for example Rees 2004: n.p.; Malik 2013: n.p.). Yet, as the "unbelieving" son of a Marxist filmmaker and poet, and of a mother whose background was orthodox Sunni, Aslam is nevertheless keen to portray the family from which he hails as so diversely comprised that it contains a world of ideas in miniature. Made up of 'communists and rightwingers, religious nuts and atheists', it displays 'all the colours' which Aslam (2011a: 151) believes the writer needs to convey 'the very different ways [of being] Muslim' – something he attempts to do in different ways in his first two "9/11" novels, *Maps* (2004a) and *Vigil* (2008).

   Aslam's intense and richly detailed fiction is deeply embedded in a modern, cultured and anarchic globe which encompasses and frames the Pakistani, British and Muslim worlds that Aslam, on account of his heritage, feels he most intimately knows. It is influenced, according to Aslam (2010b: n.p.), by Urdu before American, European or other "world" literature; inflected with memories of being raised in Zia's "Islamised" Pakistan and coming of age in Thatcher's Britain; and shaped by British Asian politics. It gains urgency after 9/11 as a result of an internalised obligation to raise "moderate" concerns about the situation of globally implicated Muslims in "multicultural"

Middle England or in a benighted Afghanistan which the Taliban has drastically "un-cultured".

Aslam's youthful encounters with the beliefs and practices of orthodox adherents to a 'strict unsmiling' faith seem not just to have given him insight into the different hues of Muslimness that may populate his fictive spectrum (2006: 66). They have also heavily shaded his impressions of a certain kind of Islam and Islamic character type. Particular memories, actual and inherited, resurface in various guises in Aslam's fiction and non-fiction, such as the essay 'God and Me', which was published in an edition of *Granta* magazine devoted to exploring through literature 'the varieties of religious belief and their personal, social and political effects' (*Granta* 2006: back cover). The author's highly personal contribution is punctuated by recollections of clerics beating the terrified boys who attended his Qur'an class when they forgot the incomprehensible words of Arabic which they were meant to learn by rote. His oppressively religious uncle looms large. Aslam recalls the austere man smashing his "idolatrous" toys and threatening to thrash his mother for listening to devotional music – a pre-Talibani figure of Islamist menace as seen through the adult author's eyes. The 'loud chanting of the Qur'an' in alien Arabic also made a strong impression (Aslam 2006: 67). Aslam recalls it occurring not only at designated prayer times but, with increasing frequency, throughout the day on Pakistani radio and television as Zia's Islamisation policy took hold: an intimidating soundtrack to the steady imposition of Saudi-style ' "Islamic" values', of which public executions were one traumatic result (67).

Aslam's recollections in *God's Own Countries* also indicate that it was in these early years that he developed a contradictory love for the aesthetic aspect, but not necessarily the religious content, of South Asian Islamic culture – in the case of the Qur'anic calligraphy, he loves the lettering, but not the letter of God's word.[3] In 'God and Me' Aslam describes his near fetishisation of illuminated copies of the Qur'an, with their intricate geometric designs, 'sinuous calligraphy' and floral motifs, and absolute refusal to put them to their devotional use (67). Confused by this seemingly paradoxical sense of Islamicate affinity, Aslam has more recently sought to understand how a faith founded on 'words of love', 'kindness' and 'longing' has acquired 'brutal' Wahabi overtones (68). For, although he is an unbeliever, Aslam (2010b: n.p., 2011a: 145) is attracted by religion's 'moral' foregrounding of 'love' and 'filial obligation' for 'strangers'.[4] Further, he is interested in making works of art which bring spectators, as witnesses, into shocking proximity with the suffering humanity they place centre stage, engendering compassion (and, perhaps, a sense of elation that verges on the sublime).[5] Aslam's fiction, then, should be understood as profoundly shaped by an enduring personal need to mine the 'workings of [an individual] consciousness' seared by and infused with intense experiences of exposure to Islamic 'religious' practice and to South Asian aesthetic culture. His hope is that undertaking this literary-exploratory act will help him better comprehend his 'place in the wider world', and – by extension – that of the others his work portrays: Muslim, non-Muslim, human (2010b). As a result Aslam's growing opus may offer subtle and complex, although at times misunderstood, interventions into Western neo-conservative and militant Islamist diktats about what beliefs "good" or "bad" global Muslims must accept, the networks with which they connect, and their presumed psychology.

'Mirror-writing': Aslam's realism

Aslam's delicately delineated global novels, set most recently in international conflict zones in Afghanistan and Pakistan, present world readers with a poetic realism through which the pull of metaphysical connections or porous experiences of existence may be expressed, and aesthetic and empathetic sensibilities cultivated. His quiet, mimetic craftsmanship is altogether different from the satirical skill of the quick-witted Rushdie or the hyper-real artifice of Hamid. Aslam's concern about the exploitative and corruptive potential of organised and orthodox religion and his profound belief in the enduring power of art may appear in keeping with that of Rushdie (2002: 59). But the similarly unbelieving younger author's attitude to individual spiritual experience is more yielding.

Where Hamid's fiction presents smoked-glass surfaces, Aslam's novels might be described as "mirror-written". They are crafted with the intention that the Western world reader will see his own visage reflecting back from the character portraits the author produces, recognise in the face of a fictive Muslim other his own 'basic human concerns', and bear "witness" to his story (Aslam 2010b). This seemingly transparent yet highly personal approach to 'honest' realist representation, which Aslam outlines in the essay 'Where to Begin', proceeds on the basis of a Romantic assumption that 'if something is true of [him], then there is every likelihood that it is true of billions of others'. It takes as read that the British-based writer's pre-occupations – 'love', 'loneliness', 'grief?' – which also pervade the consciousnesses of his Pakistani, Afghan, American and European characters, and provide grounds for empathetic connections to be established between author, subject and reader, are actually 'common' to all (2010b).[6] But it leaves unquestioned the epistemologies that may inform just who or what is made the focus of Aslam's 'human concern', or is permitted to prevail as more or less human(e) in his fiction.[7]

All authors will of course write from a particular, situated position, and – like Aslam – universalise certain claims which may be used to bolster a particular (geopolitical) worldview.[8] Yet the pictures the Pakistan-born writer presents in his increasingly geopolitical fictions, from his small-town, Punjab-set debut *Season of the Rainbirds* (1993), to the anonymous Afghan wastelands of the short fiction 'Punnu's Jihad' (2011b), are never of a straightforward clash between 'good', Western(ised) local cultures and 'evil' Islamic ones, or a simplistically inverted variant on that theme. Although painstaking in his portrayal of South Asian Islam's artistic heritage, Aslam, who would distance himself from ideas of 'nationalism' and 'ideology' (2011a: 150), seems uninterested in performing a triumphal act of "writing back" to Western notions of a benighted Islam or oriental decadence. Rather, he appears ethically committed to bringing his readers, disconnected from their habitual identifications and thus deterritorialised, into a new sense- and emotion-led understanding of the feelings of affinity his Muslim characters may experience within and across perceived bounds of faith and culture, and the extent to which the affiliative bonds they make and break may be compatible with these.

Maps presents a rich, ecumenical tapestry of the largely aesthetic South Asian Muslim affinities which disparate diasporic Pakistanis may elect to pursue. It also points to the often cruel curbs that a misguided older generation may impose on them in name of "honour" or loyalty to the "true" faith and culture of their long-distant homelands. Aslam's (2004a: 111) second novel draws attention to the damage one 'dangerous' but domestically limited anti-heroine, the housewife Kaukab, inflicts on her family as a result of her orthodox religious beliefs. In 'turn[ing]' his mind 'towards the war-lord' in his third novel, *Vigil*, which unfolds in Afghanistan, Aslam (2008: Daulat Shah epigraph) seems equally if not more preoccupied with re-educating the Muslim world he believes Islamic scripturalists have "un-cultured", as with expanding the perceptions of the largely white, Western audiences who are his most likely readers. He appears in this global novel to be trying to find an aesthetic means by which an enlightened, 'translocal[ly] committed' (Gilroy 2004: 89) "we" – Muslim and non-Muslim alike – may not only "talk to [Islamist] ter-rorists" but 'win over' Islamic cultures' potential 'murderer[s] with an embrace' (Aslam 2008: 422).

Aslam (2011a: 140) asserts that 'a novel is a democracy'; the 'nov-elist [must] work hard at making… everybody human' and under-standable to his readers – and hence at representing all parties equally – however much this may dissatisfy dominant 'ideologues'. Here he parts company with the likes of the iconoclastic Rushdie and Rushdie's contemporary, Martin Amis, for whom the novel is an entry into a more universalised Western worldview. Amis (2008: 11–20), reeling from the attacks of 9/11, seizes the novel as the last outpost for a secularly "enlightened" literati who may "legislate for mankind" (16). He seeks to defend its 'intransigently… individual' form against incursions from Islam's 'desolate', irrational and dan-gerously dogmatic 'lonely crowd' (16, 19–20).[9] Rushdie, too, uses the novel not only to pull down all 'doctrines and practices into the realm of history where they can be questioned, criticized, con-trasted… even refuted or overhauled' – as Spencer (2010b: 253) notes, but to expose them and their adherents to ridicule so as to discredit them utterly.

Despite their liberal, anti-ideological triumphalism, both ageing *enfants terribles* unfailingly champion the unbeliever over the man of faith, self-inspiration over divine, and individual over collective experiences. Aslam differs fundamentally in that he believes that no one human's fervently held perspective can be dismissed as 'incom-prehensible, nor inconsequential' (2011a: 139), however far-fetched or unpalatable. Not, that is, if a novel is to function as 'a power-ful instrument against injustice', as Aslam (2010b) believes it must, accurately representing the world and legislating for common under-standing as a safeguard against the alienation and radicalisation of disenfranchised elements.

Yet the "truth" of Aslam's fictional representations of Islamic figures of terror, from jihadist militants to immigrant housewives, remains slightly compromised. He is convinced that, as a 'moderate Muslim' deeply affected by the World Trade Center attacks, he must use literature publicly to condemn both Bin Laden's acts of international terror and the 'small scale September 11s' which occur in Muslim communities each day (Aslam 2004b: n.p.). While they point to austere Muslim characters' capacity to feel affinity for heterodox traditions which may shake the foundations of their absolute faith in an exacting Allah, Aslam's fictional depictions of "fundamentalists" seem foreclosed, as if their psychological affiliations to a "fire-and-brimstone" interpretation of Islam and its divinely dictated scripture will always prove unbreakable. It is the iron grip of ideological and scriptural Islam which Aslam foregrounds most consistently in his post-9/11 novels, although he also points to the dangerous zeal of his British Asian and American atheist characters, who never question the compatibility of their anti-Islamic stance with their self-appointed role as 'watchmen on the walls of world freedom' (Aslam 2008: 277). In the end, its affiliates collapse back into the 'bad' Muslim category of Mamdani's (2004: 17–18) 'Culture Talk', or die trying to escape. Aslam's world fiction is weighted subtly but significantly in favour of educated, open-minded, socially responsible and slightly privileged "good" (Muslim) characters, from European converts and Westernised Afghans to secular lovers. These individuals are cognoscent of a heterodox (and unscripted) Islam and able to let sensual, aesthetic, spiritual affinities shape their understanding of faith and inform the paths they take. Caught in a contemporary era of religious extremism and violence where the desire to preserve and cultivate alternative Islamic culture and use it as a bridge to extend their humanity is dangerously out of place, they cut courageous, semi-tragic figures, prepared to risk their lives for the sake of rehabilitating Muslim societies.[10]

Ultimately Aslam's third-millennium novels function as mausoleum fiction. They attempt at every possible instance to recall and commemorate the hybrid and unorthodox traditions of Muslim lands. These function as mementos of a model of moderate Islamic enlightenment, which foregrounds Islam's originary and historic emphasis on the values of self-knowledge, tolerance, compassion, humanity and justice as a possible focal point for rehabilitation and reform.[11]

But Aslam's fictions also suggest that these traditions, and associated art and artefacts must now, for the sake of preservation, be extracted from their South and Central Asian roots and interred, archived or safely concealed from view. Islam *is* revealed as replete with alternative affinitive dimensions – and in this sense "re-cultured" – in Aslam, but as a museum piece which only a literate and largely Western minority can access.

Maps for lost lovers: Prescribed affiliations and elective affinities

> I won't move to Pakistan. What would my life be then? My children in England, me in Pakistan, my soul in Arabia, and my heart –
>
> (Aslam 2004a: 146)

These impassioned words, uttered in a tumult of hurt, frustration, love, guilt and grief by Kaukab, the immigrant Pakistani housewife in Aslam's second novel *Maps*, provided the inspiration for this book's examination of how South Asian Muslim experiences of affiliation and affinity are mapped in contemporary fiction. Plaintive, impassioned, halting, elliptic, they point to the complexity of a single orthodox, exilic protagonist's transnational Islamic ties, and the emotional and intellectual strain their simultaneous tenure places on her consciousness. Earlier in *Maps*, Kaukab tries to calm herself with the image of the world-sculpted Adam, his 'head...made from the soil of the East, his breast...Mecca, his feet from the West' (31). But this speech frames as unlikely the possibility of her being able to feel at home in such a body, or to orient herself in any one direction where her moral "soul" and human "heart" can be at rest. It strikes a mournful keynote common to the experiences of "global" Muslim being and belonging charted in Aslam's novels.

Maps is set in the late 1990s in a northern English town known to its immigrant population as 'Dasht-e-Tanhaii'; that is the 'Wilderness of Solitude' or 'Desert of Loneliness', in Aslam's (2004a: 29) bleak translation. The novel tells the story of what transpires in Dasht-e-Tanhaii's close-knit Pakistani community the year after the unmarried lovers Jugnu and Chanda disappear. It begins with Chanda's brothers' arrest in winter on suspicion of their killing; spans the spring and summer in which her parents employ a pair of illegal immigrants to give false alibis; and ends with their sons' conviction in autumn for a crime of 'wicked[ness]', not 'honour' (348). Events unfold mainly from the perspective of Shamas, Jugnu's brother, an ageing, unbelieving communist exile, amateur poet and Community Relations Council director. In trying to retrace the lovers' last steps he trespasses on the affairs of others. These include a Hindu boy mad with grief for his battered Muslim girlfriend, and an attractive divorcee, Suraya, who seeks a route to reunion with her alcoholic husband and beloved son via a sham marriage to Shamas. Meanwhile the anxieties of Shamas's austere and orthodox Muslim wife Kaukab weigh heavily on the narrative. She struggles to exonerate herself from blame for the lovers' vanishing and re-establish relations with her children: the artist Charag; dutiful, abused Mah-Jabin; and atheist Ujala. Kaukab fails in this, as does Shamas in his affair with Suraya. After a fractious family dinner overshadowed by the murder verdict and a series of devastating revelations about the damage Kaukab's "Islamic" beliefs have done to her family, she attempts suicide. The novel ends with a report of Shamas' unexplained death at 'Scandal Point', the site of his trysts, and with the figure of the boy immigrant. Touched by this news, he prepares himself 'to go out into the world again' and face with his fellow humans the 'calamity' he knows will ensue (369).

The acts of terror Aslam describes in *Maps* mirror those which he understands Islamic fundamentalists daily to inflict not on American "infidels" in foreign lands, but on Muslim families and communities "at home", whose ordinary, lived experiences of Islam are not recognised as legitimate by their Islamist censors. Aslam (2011a: 141) describes his novel as 'the literary equivalent of a Persian miniature'. It demonstrates on a detailed, domestic, diasporic level the dangers of displaced and disenfranchised migrant Muslim characters cleaving "fundamentally" to an extreme (Western) atheistic or (Saudi Arabian) Islamic ideology and an imagined homeland. It contrasts severe pathways carved by atavistic affiliates with those traced by more "moderate", "modern", mobile Muslims who remain open to Sufi mystic interpretations of South Asian Islam and its heterodox Persian and Hindu aesthetic culture while seeking to loosen their ties to stricter religious and cultural traditions. But *Maps* also suggests that positions along an Islamic spectrum – atheist, enlightened moderate, extremist – are never entirely fixed. There is scope in his novel for all subjects to be moved by aspects of the faith-based cultures which they would censor or outlaw: for rigid positions to soften, even if, eventually, tense vigils are resumed at either post. *Maps* also touches on the transformative and healing effects of encounters with unorthodox counterculture on Dasht-e-Tanhaii's "multicultural" community as a whole. Like Shamas's Hiraman-inspired 'artist' these may 'tell...us what we should aim for,...reveal the ideal to us, telling us what's truly worth living for, and dying for, in life' (Aslam 2004a: 168).

Aslam casts the housewife Kaukab as a devout, superstitious South Asian advocate of orthodox Saudi Wahabi Islam, and hence (in his depiction) a domestic demon. She believes in *djinns*, considers 'stoning' a punishment of 'divine origin', and deems the dead lovers 'dirty unclean sinners' (322–3). A conservative cleric's daughter 'born and bred in a mosque' and 'trapped within the cage of permitted thinking', Kaukab is described by her daughter Mah-Jabin as 'the most dangerous animal she'll ever have to confront' (56; 110–11). Kaukab struggles hazardously in *Maps* to reconcile her conservative beliefs and emotions as a dutiful, god-fearing and largely housebound wife and mother in a seemingly godless England where her husband and beloved children have established new roots. But, as Amina Yaqin (2012: 113) notes, 'the book shows that "state multiculturalism" is a meaningless notion for...a rootless underclass who cling to an unforgiving mode of belonging in an alien environment'. Kaukab's ability to "integrate" into mainstream British society is not on trial here. What Aslam's novel instead puts to the test is her capacity to relax her ties of faith sufficiently in order to enter into a more compassionate, "forgiving" way of being with her own migrant Pakistani family: to entertain and even perhaps accommodate the secular, atheistic and cultural Muslim ideas and identities they express beneath the roof of their shared northern English home.

Kaukab remains loyal to a sepia-tinted vision of a paternal Pakistan as 'a country of the pious and the devout...where boundaries are respected', which she knows is not strictly true (Aslam 2004a: 63). She deflects, for example, a wealthy Islamabadi's criticism of Dasht-e-Tanhaii's little Pakistan as home to 'sister-murdering, mosque-going...veil-wearing inbred imbeciles' (312). She turns for guidance to 'holy' diasporic upholders of "Islamic" values, like the 'cleric-ji' who gives her sacred *salt* (libido-quelling bromide) to make adolescent Ujala 'obedient' (304). She directs prayers to Mecca in Arabia's 'sacred land', at whose gate she knocks in dreams; and entrusts her 'soul' to an omniscient, admonitory Allah, who is her sole confidant (99, 145 and 291). Kaukab's deep familial love, capacity for guilt, aesthetic sensibility and powerful imagination make her an understandable if not sympathetic constituent of Aslam's (2011a: 140) novelistic 'democracy'.[12] When the estranged Ujala knocks at her door she 'wants to take his face in her hands, to kiss him'; she is mortified when she discovers the harm she has inadvertently inflicted on her family, lamenting: 'I can't seem to move without bruising anyone, but I don't mean to cause pain' (2004a: 293, 326). And, musing on how her merciful Allah can have had the lovers killed, she experiences flashes of doubt (332).

Tragically, only Aslam's readers are privy to the silent, internal vacillations which humanise Kaukab. Meanwhile, the fundamentalist tenets to which she publicly clings appear as 'moral[ly] cripple[d]' to her judges, filial and legal, as Jugnu and Chanda's "sinful" union is to her (113). These censors cannot comprehend how Kaukab's 'code of honour and shame' can operate concurrently with love (348); she cannot permit sympathy for the lovers to erode her conception of morality (147). Kamila Shamsie (2004: n.p.) observes that *Maps* presents readers with the real face of 'the devoted mother behind the headlines' about "honour" crimes. But, tellingly, when that mother envisages 'her image...in the mirror' she anticipates an encounter with a son-poisoning monster (Aslam 2004a: 308).

The less developed Ujala, an extreme atheist, provides a rebellious Muslim "refusenik" foil to his immigrant mother's fanatical faith and his father's guarded scepticism, countering Kaukab's emotional, exculpatory self-representations with cold, unflattering images. Ujala recasts the religion his mother says gives 'dignity to millions' as irrational and inhumane: 'derang[ing]' of the 'ignorant', impossible to disaffiliate from and unforgivably implicated in 'barbaric' practices like punitive 'amputation' (322–3). He exposes the long-term negative impacts of his mother's faith-inspired attempts to control her children, about which Mah-Jabin stays silent. Ujala will not let his family 'relegate' fundamentalist Muslim housewives like Kaukab to what Aslam (2011a: 140) has elsewhere described as 'an inconsequential category' because they are not 'involved in things considered of consequence' (such as acts of global, anti-Western terror).[13] But, rather than 'invite…contrasting readings', Aslam's fictional British Asian youth reinforces interpretations of his mother and her principles of "shame" and "honour" as problems specific to a monolithic Islam (140). This native-informant's 'superior value judgements' paint the migrant Muslim woman's 'domestic life [as] alien, organized according to creeds spawned thousands of miles away', and reconfirm an 'unbridgeable divide between Islam and the West' as a quotidian reality (Morey and Yaqin 2011: 77).

Yet in striving to make Ujala 'human' and show the 'very ordinary "face" behind [his] words', Aslam perhaps draws the sting from his tail (Aslam 2010b). We catch a glimpse of the character's humanity in a telling "mirror" moment when he peers into a polished spoon at the family dinner table. He has kept a firm hold on this object while trying to trap his mother into revealing her most intolerant views. Now, gazing into it, Ujala sees not a coherent image of his defiant visage, but 'a distorted portrait' reflecting back (2004a: 323). Ujala's twisted features loom large in this instance, but so do his memories of the congenial naturalist Jugnu, the embittered young man's curious, irreverent boyhood mentor. Momentarily, Aslam dilutes Ujala's supposedly principled aversion for Islam with the hint of the partiality of personal grief, and allows a softer, subtler mode of challenging orthodoxy to be illuminated.

Not surprisingly for a novel dedicated to the activist poet Faiz Ahmad Faiz, *Maps'* most sympathetic and humane character is a 60-something socialist non-believer who, despite his perturbation regarding certain traditional Pakistani Muslim practices and beliefs, remains enamoured of aspects of a cultural Islam. Understanding 'that the universe is without saviours' and convinced a 'more just way of organising the world has to be found', Shamas serves Dasht-e-Tanhaii's practical and political needs as the Director of its Community Relations Council (15, 20, 324). But as a poet and romantic whose 'imagination insists that all aspects of life be at its disposal', he embellishes impressions of its 'Desert' with eclectic 'appropriation[s]' from 'supernatural' imagery (82). Most significantly, he tries to bring spiritual 'solace' to himself and the neighbourhood's lonely Hindu, Sikh and Muslim settlers by reconnecting them with a resistant, questing Sufi political aesthetic which prizes the pursuit of selfhood, humanity and love (9).

Aslam's belief in the importance of cultivating self-knowledge as a means to understanding his place in the world, standing against (perceived) oppressions and rediscovering the holy grail of 'love' for oneself and one's fellow humans, must explain the relative credence he gives to broadly Sufistic cultural and aesthetic practices, philosophies and pathways, even as he stresses his consciousness of Sufism's 'corruptions' (2011a: 151).[14] *Maps* exposes, for example, the deviant practices of those holy men who may claim kinship with the "soft" Muslim saints the novel's lovers venerate, but now serve other, more venal masters. They persuade strict Muslim parents to let them beat 'malevolent' *djinns* from their daughter, who loved a Hindu boy; shred the love-poem that 'garland[s]' her grave; and condemn both as 'minions of Satan' (2004a: 185, 194).[15] But such men are depicted as aberrations who have long betrayed the truth-seeking Sufis who tread 'internal path[s] of love of God and people' (Frembgen 2012: 13–14).

As this perhaps demonstrates, a degree of caution should be applied when referring to the "Sufi" dimensions of Aslam's worldview and works. First, as Zahra Sabri (2012: 12, ellipses and italics author's own) warns, to tack this newly trendy adjective onto 'familiar' elements of heterodox South Asian Muslim tradition – '*buzurg . . . mūsiqi . . . shā'irī* (elder . . . music . . . poetry)'– which resurface in contemporary Pakistani culture and loom large in Aslam's fiction, may be to risk obscuring subtler meanings. Second, when heterodox culture is ushered into the "Sūfi" 'mainstream', the blanket of a 'universal concept' is pulled not only over its diverse and divergent features, as Sabri also notes, but its apparent advocates, too – including the atheistic Rushdie and unbelieving Aslam.[16] Yet Aslam's relationship to Sufism is in fact more serious, subtle and substantial than Rushdie's, based less on rose-tinted memories and more on an acute personal affinity for its intoxicating, moth-to-the-flame aesthetic and profound, humane conception of how it may answer to material and existential needs.

As caretaker of the lakeside bookshop the *Safeena*, Shamas has private access to a non-domestic space which becomes a lifeboat for him and for the divorced Suraya in their grief. Here, over twentieth-century Urdu literature from Pakistan's leftist Progressive Writers' Movement, they forge a friendship more intimate than their restrictive community would publicly allow between a husbandless woman and a married man, but which addresses the 'universal' needs Aslam

(2010b) identifies as 'basic human concerns'. He cites the following as examples of 'universal' concerns: *'What is love? What is this loneliness? What can I do with my grief? I made a mistake I don't know how to correct'* (italics in the original). When Suraya recalls a recital by the exiled socialist Wamaq Saleem, a fictional character Aslam modelled on his poet-father who told him to 'write about love', Shamas feels to meet her 'is to meet oneself': to find a kindred soul (Aslam 2004a: dedication, 155). When, in turn, Shamas cites Syed Aabid Ali Aabid's protesting verses: 'I did warn: the prison out there has been expanding slowly, and now its walls have almost reached your own garden', his 'melancholy voice singe[s] her heart' (211, emphasis Aslam's). Shamas cites these verses in answer to his doubts about whether he did enough 'to condemn the pernicious excesses' of Jugnu and Chanda's killers (211). His transparent compassion also touches the scheming Suraya morally, shaming her in her chicanery. Both characters seem to experience in the novel a feeling akin to the mysterious ache of "selfhood" or *khudi*. This is an emotion which the Sufi-influenced philosopher-poet Muhammad Iqbal described as a metaphysical element that drives individuals to free themselves from earthly limits and aspire to loftier goals, the ultimate being affinity with God reached via a recognition of God within: of the divine spark that animates the human (Mir 2006: 30–1). In Aslam's realist fiction, secular trysts informed by this philosophy lead to "mirror" moments in which the face of a lover reflects on the other's humanity.

Maps goes beyond simply charting its central protagonist's personal affinities. It also sanctions through Shamas' indirect, internal dialogue the sense of catharsis, solace and spirit of defiance which he imagines devotional music can instil. In particular, he imagines it filling the hearts of a chorus of minor female characters, repressed by a conservative and patriarchal mainstream and searching for reprieve. In the novel's most lyrical set-piece, the Qawwali singer Nusrat Fateh Ali Khan comes to Dasht-e-Tanhaii to give a concert at the home of some descendants of his patron saint. Shamas functions as a partial, peripheral interpreter of women listeners' 'visible' 'agony', in accordance with Aslam's (2010b) model of witnessing. Locked in the marquee's intimate space, he sees a young woman married to a cousin whose children suffer from genetic defects; she is 'moved to tears' by Nusrat's portrayal of the expiry of Sassi, who dies with her head pressed to a crescent-shaped sign of hope. The weeping girl is, Shamas thinks, 'no doubt, asking the soul of the...poet-saint – whose verses are being sung... – to tell Allah to lessen her burden' while 'women hold her, striving to console' in a collective outpouring of grief (Aslam 2004a: 189). Shamas spies Chanda's parents by a moth-encircled lantern as Nursat sings the passion of the analogous Heer, poisoned by her brothers, family and the mosque's holy men for abandoning an arranged marriage and pursuing union with her beloved. Such empathetic reflections lead to an ethnographically intoned endorsement of Sufism's history of artistic dissent and the sacrificial struggle of its 'pure-hearted' (Iqbal in Mir 2007: 168) followers to realise their right to self-determination and unmediated union with the divine:

> The poet-saints of Islam express[ed] their loathing of power and injustice... [and] – because they advocated a direct communion with Allah, bypassing the mosques – were denounced by the orthodox clerics...Even today the Sufis are referred to as 'the opposition party of Islam'. And always...the vulnerability of women...was used by the poet-saints to portray the intolerance and oppression of their times: in their verses the women rebel and try bravely to...make a new world. And, in every...story they fail. But by striving they become part of the universal story of human hope.
>
> (Aslam 2004a: 191–2)[17]

It is precisely this brief, 'brave' Sufistic lifecycle of unsuccessful striving towards an affinitive light and yet falling victim to the strictures of a Pakistani Muslim community which cannot cut its atavistic ties, and bequeathing to the next generation a legacy of morbid hope, that shapes the narrative arcs *Maps* continues to describe until its closing frame (192). Yet Aslam's characterisation of Shamas as a lonely, romantic fantasist, blind to his lover's pretences and neglectful of his family, slightly undermines the credibility of the escapist, cathartic reading the novel's structure proposes. The idealised lovers Shamas would nurture appear as the pale icons of a marginalised Sufi mindset (or, at least, of the Sufi mindset given prominence by Shamas). These characters are too 'curious...about ways of *living*' – or 'mak[ing] a new world' where they can be one with their beloved – to survive Dasht-e-Tanhaii's arid climate of orthodoxy and superstition (192,

280). Instead, they expend brief, shadowy half-lives almost exclusively in Shamas' mind: they appear in myth, memory, daydream, poetry and as ghostly metaphysical presences. These lovers' 'innocent', world-shunning bids for sublime self-realisation may pattern future utopias, but the reality – as the unbelieving Shamas 'knows' – is that 'the dead will not be resurrected' and the living are 'trapped [on Earth] with each other... and there is no release' (20, 280, 288). Not unless, that is, they can collectively 'confront' their complicity in "honour" crimes, ask 'penetrating' questions about their failures and 'face' each other in the truth's unflattering light (288).

A brief appearance at the family home by the 'Young British Artist' Charag, taught by Jugnu 'to break... the bonds and ties [of] manipulative groups', indicates how a second generation of cultural Muslim disaffiliates from orthodoxy, educated and domiciled beyond Dasht-e-Tanhaii, may bear the burden of engendering self-reflection among the migrant communities who raised them (321). Charag has been inspired in adolescence by the bright shades and exquisite shapes of South Asian fabrics to 'look at Matisse more carefully' (310). In adulthood, he retains a delight in delicate Islamic aesthetics: reviews describe a 'rhapsody in restrained form and colour'; Kaukab admires 'immaculate butterflies' (320). Yet he also brings to his artwork a consciousness enhanced by (European) critical theory that prevents him from 'paint[ing] with handcuffs on' (321). He places taboo personal content – a portrait of himself uncircumcised – in intricate Islamicate frames, creating metaphorical art that questions 'act[s] of violence done... in the name of a religious or social system' (320). Struck by a lakeside encounter with Suraya, who propositions him, then asks if he can 'paint' her shame, Charag is also increasingly aware that he must honour his commitment to try cautiously to 'incorporate' her complex history, and those of myriad immigrant 'others', into his artwork, examining and exploring their sorrows, if not celebrating them as Shamas might (133; 318–19).

Aslam describes as 'special and arresting' his first experiences of visiting galleries 'where the people on the walls staring back at me were the colour of my own skin' – thereby, confronting him with their "human concerns" (2011a: 143). In the end, Kaukab rejects Charag's art, unable to see its 'merit' and deaf to his reasoning: in her opinion, the '*Uncut Self-Portrait*' is a 'wicked' affront to Islam, his concern to record non-relatives' struggles unnecessary (2004a:

318–21). But by briefly opening up space for Charag to sketch his vision for an interrogatory, Islam-inflected art – controversial yet sensitively framed, beautiful but not romanticised – Aslam points to its "real" potential to reflect ambivalent experiences of contemporary diasporic South Asian Muslim affiliation and affinity. These are experiences which Kaukab or Ujala would dismiss as unrepresentative, and Shamas eulogise.

Maps charts a movement towards a responsible, realist fiction which is porous and lyrical. It presents readers with a 'forensic, pseudo-documentary analysis' (Yaqin 2012: 101) of immigrant Pakistani Muslims' polyvalent relationships to inherited, imposed and elective doctrinal beliefs, religious and cultural practices. It attempts to bridge this anthropological divide and soften searing critical perspectives by encouraging readers to see as subjective reality characters' psychological experiences of supernatural enchantment. It also uses lyrical passages to develop deeper emotional understanding of how ideals encapsulated in Islamicate South Asian aesthetics may enhance their impressions of the world and aspirations for a future within it. And, even as it valorises them, it reveals the inadequacy of romantic "Sufi" counter-narratives to account for a sustainable way of "moderate" Muslim life in a domestic climate of Islamic extremism.

The Wasted Vigil: Re-culturing Islam, salvaging art

Vigil remains in poetic realist mode but shifts away from isolated migrant worlds-in-miniature and towards native Afghan Muslims deeply implicated in "global" landscapes and narratives of culture clash. Prefaced by an epigraph from Daulat Shah, the fifteenth-century biographer of Persian poets, it explores how the recognition and re-cultivation of Afghanistan's spiritual and aesthetic connections to Persianate and Gandhara culture may bring emotional release and spiritual solace to isolated Muslim communities ruled by Americans, warlords and Taliban, where freedom of (religious) expression remains severely restricted.[18] It suggests this culture, strategically deployed, could salve the traumatised and corrupted psyches of civilians and militants caught in the crossfire of international forces on the thresholds of their Afghan homes and hence – perhaps – ensure the survival of a dangerously 'thread[ed]' 'world' (432).

Chambers (2011: 137) describes *Vigil* as Aslam's fictional 'refutation of the Taliban's destruction' of Afghanistan. He informed her that he wanted to tell 'the Taliban, "although I may not be able to stop you in real life, in my mind and my book you won't succeed in destroying th[e] Buddha" ' whose ruined visage is a powerful presiding presence in the novel, nor – presumably – the Central Asian syncretism it signifies (137). *Vigil* is an eloquent, erudite and not unproblematic attempt to use this culture to "answer back" to those who perpetrate such apparently nihilistic acts in Islam's name.

The story unfolds at a lakeside house near the small town of Usha, occupied by Russians in the anti-Soviet war, ruled by the Taliban after the communist collapse and civil conflict, and presided over in the narrative present – circa 2004 – by an unholy alliance of US intelligence and Afghan warlords. It is home to Marcus, an elderly English doctor and Muslim convert whose connection to Afghanistan long predates the Taliban's advent. The ceilings are studded with impaled books; its walls are covered with mud-smeared paintings; and a perfume factory concealing a partially buried Buddha head is housed in its grounds.[19] Marcus' memories of his Afghan wife Qatrina, also a doctor, and of his daughter Zameen, both of whom were abducted and executed during the Soviet and Taliban regimes, also haunt this lonely space. Despite his losses, Marcus remains, keeping vigil for his grandson, Bihzad, whom he believes survived Zameen. Characters of radically different worldviews converge here seeking sanctuary, aid and answers: Lara, a Russian Christian art historian trying to trace her brother, a Soviet soldier; David, a CIA agent and Zameen's lover, desperate to discover who caused her death 20 years before; Casa, a young Afghan trained in jihadi camps and injured on a covert operation; and Dunia, a schoolteacher contemporary. They make 'links out of separations', or a 'kinship of wounds', while power struggles rage between rival Taliban- and American-backed warlords (Aslam 2008: 87; 430). But the spell breaks when Dunia is kidnapped, Casa returns to the conviction that Allah wants him to have no ties, David dies trying to prevent his suicide, and Lara leaves the world-weary Marcus to find ways to memorialise the graveless dead.

As in Rushdie's *Shalimar*, *Vigil*'s protagonists' affiliations and affinities are largely divided between aggressive, strategic and to some extent devout political and ideological affiliations and "softer" tendencies to be drawn by spiritual and aesthetic affinities, the pursuit of which has both local import and international implications. In *Vigil* more than *Maps*, Aslam figures aspects of Islam itself (rather than distorted elements of Pakistani Muslim tradition) as having belligerent, anti-scientific, anti-cultural historical associations and connections. He does this in bold, memorable statements that "frame" ensuing digressions. The sound of the *salat-ul-fajr* in Jalalabad, for example, prompts the worldly David's "realisation" that 'the first two words of the call to the Muslim prayer are also the Muslim battle cry' (47). The disturbing impact of this is undiminished when the American is lulled asleep by the muezzin's soporific entreaty: 'Come to worship...Come to happiness' (47). The implication for the wary Westerner in post-2002 Afghanistan is that Islam's resonant invitation to religious comfort – and, by extension, submissive faith – cannot be trusted because it may also summon the faithful masses to sleepwalk back to war.

Such statements seem to paint Islam as warmongering and inherently barbaric, but Aslam asserts that they are expressive of his polyphonic novel's non-Muslim American and Russian characters' opinions, rather than his worldview (2011a: 141). (However, it is harder to discern who is speaking in this even more introspective, elliptic, consciousness-flooded fiction than it is in *Maps*, where Ujala's anti-Islamic taunts are contained mostly in belligerent dialogue directly attributable to him.) Nevertheless, to create fiction in the third millennium which gives sonorous if not unchecked voice to European and Afghan Muslim protagonists' 'love' for the Sufistic 'pictures,...practices and habits' and Buddhist inheritances of their Central Asian homelands, is to pit oneself firmly against those ultra-orthodox Muslims who would outlaw and destroy them (2008: 319–21).

As a liberal humanitarian, culturally Muslim artist, Aslam is specifically opposed to the radically conservative, socially restrictive, anti-cultural strains of "fundamentalist" Islam traceable to ultra-orthodox Sunni theologians like the Mongol-era Ibn Taimiyaa. The ethnographer Jurgen Wasim Frembgen (2012: 39), would – like Aslam – uphold the 'feeling of a common bond and closeness' or '*communitas*' which Sufi aesthetic traditions may inspire. He blames the 'anti-Sufi' Ibn Taimiyaa for 'sharply distinguish[ing] normative Islam' from its daily expression in mystical forms – ecstatic music, erotic poetry – so as 'to marginalize popular, living Islam as heathen' (40).[20] *Vigil* is densely packed with fictional scenes – the riddling of the smiling Buddha relic with bullets; the stoning of the burqa-shrouded Qatrina – which echo real-life incidences of Taliban-inflicted terror targeting icons and practitioners of traditional, expressive, "un-Islamic" arts, from the staged detonation the of Bamiyan Buddhas in March 2001, to the showcase murder of Swat Valley singer Shabana in 2009.[21] In spirit with Frembgen, Aslam (2008: 262) would figure as heroes and martyrs individuals who 'rebel' by non-violent, educative and cultural means 'against the Taliban's insistence that the wings be torn off [Afghan] children'. But in *Vigil* he toes a fine line between the projection and representation of anti-Islamic positions as he struggles to complicate readings that would reduce the conflict in Afghanistan to a simple clash of Eastern and Western cultures.

The militant, political, ultra-conservative Islamic affiliates Aslam brings to life in *Vigil* are partly offset – as in Hamid's *The Reluctant Fundamentalist* and Shamsie's *Burnt Shadows* – by American anti-communist, pro-capitalist, neo-conservative ideological extremists. They function as theoretical counter-balances to 'media representations' of Islamic fundamentalists, emphasising Aslam's 'deep … suspicious[ness] of the idea of "empire" ' irrespective of ideology, and seeming to pre-empt criticisms that he places Islamic expansionism beyond the pale but does 'PR for US imperialisms' (2011a: 140; 145). As near mirror-opposites, Aslam's (2008: 414) militant Americans are indeed *almost* as zealous, robotic and – despite their claims to the moral high ground – as to blame for the brutalisation and destruction of Afghanistan and its people as their Islamist counterparts.

But *Vigil's* articulate American former agents and stealth operatives, affiliated professionally to the CIA, are not (quite) equivalent. They include the middle-aged David Town, "turned" against 'the Reds' – and so towards becoming an employee of the anti-communist Agency – by his brother's death in Vietnam, but made 'fundamentally inconsolable' (and irreconcilable) as a result of Zameen's CIA-orchestrated killing some years later (153, 201). They also include James Palantine, the fresh-faced and increasingly fanatical son of David's former friend and recruiter. The 9/11 attacks may have convinced James that the holders of extreme Islamic beliefs 'ha[d] to be stopped', but his family's commitment to continuing the "business" of the CIA – to defending, the 'sane' US against the 'crazy rest of the world' – long predates that "watershed" moment (328–9).

Both these characters are painted – or are permitted to paint themselves in Aslam's multi-focal fiction – in slightly more sophisticated, intelligent and defensible lights than *Vigil*'s Islamist jihadi types. David asserts he became a 'believer', as a 'result of study and contemplation. Not . . . a personal wound'; although he may be guilty of misinterpreting it, he is widely read in Islamic history and culture and fluent in Pashto (153). James justifies his 'vigilant' treatment of 'sleeper' terror suspects like Casa on the grounds that in the wider scheme of things it could prevent the Taliban replicating 'what they did to the Buddhas of Bamiyan' on US soil – detonating the carved visages on Mount Rushmore (380–1). Sins of omission and commission destabilise the positions these characters adopt. At the time of the Soviet War, David raises no objection to the CIA's cynical staging to Western journalists' eyes of a Russian bombing raid on a refugee camp for Afghan exiles in Peshawar, an atrocity the Americans had the intelligence to prevent. Instead, he justifies this human rights violation on the ideological grounds that: 'the civilised world would see this and condemn Soviet brutality, [and] Moscow [would be] made to rethink its policies' (and avoids an acknowledgment of the fact that the young Afghan communist who rivalled him for Zameen's love would, in the process, be eliminated) (173). In the twenty-first-century context of America's war against the Afghan Taliban, Aslam's descriptions of James's actions, too, prove distinctly uncomfortable reading. This is the case, for example, when he is seen casually supervising the young Islamist militant Casa's blinding with a blowtorch, an act he undertakes on the following "reasonable" pretext:

> I did what needed to be done . . . These people have been trained in how to survive interrogation techniques. For some of them true jihad starts at capture. So we have to be extreme, go beyond their trained endurance. I am just searching for our country's enemies . . . It's nothing personal against this man. (411)

Both David and Casa are prepared to go (or to allow others to go) to unacceptable lengths to defend a cause or principle that their extreme measures actually undermine. The 'refined' diction and 'decepti[ve] . . . objectivity' they deploy when dealing with the constituents of a supposedly 'savage and innately violent' corner of the Muslim world betray an 'epistemological overconfidence' akin to that Salaita (2008: 167–8) identifies among America's 'hypocritical' and 'sanctimonious' white liberals and neoconservatives. Aslam's flawed patriots classify as "cultured" in Salaita's value-loaded conception of that word, and their presence in the novel contributes both in obvious and more insidious ways to its radical Islamic subjects' barbarisation or "un-cultur[ing]".

The two young jihadi militants featured in *Vigil* are the assertive and rigidly Islamist Casa and his junior, Bihzad, a less confident and more religiously porous character. Aslam describes their militant activities, like those of their American "others", in sufficient detail to ensure that no doubt is sown about the roles they take in perpetrating atrocities. Together they are responsible for visiting terrifying physical and psychological attacks on the civilians of Usha: Bihzad bombs the town's American-funded school; Casa distributes an intimidating and admonitory *shabnama* ('Night Letter') to the remainder of its residents (Aslam 2008: 72–4, 166–7). However, while these characters' guilt is not in question, their willingness to participate, and the extent to which they do so freely, remains uncertain. Casa and Bihzad's barely existent civilian prehistories, pathways to radicalisation and modes of indoctrination are revealed in snatches of repressed memory, Qur'anic citation, madrassa-cum-training-camp anecdotes and Taliban commanders' opinions. These pervade their consciousnesses and are reported in cool, "factual" tones:

> Cyanide can be extracted from apricots, Casa knows. He had distilled it at a jihad training camp, injected it into the bodies of creatures. The memory comes to him as he walks past a flowering tree at the edge of a street in Jalalabad city centre, the flowers still not finished emptying themselves of scent this late in the afternoon. (121)

> Because no true Muslim should shrink from killing in cold blood, his jihad training had included slitting the throats of sheep and horses while reciting the verse from the holy Koran which gives permission to massacre prisoners of war. (123)

Essentially, like Rushdie's (2008: 225) child soldiers, abducted by the Ottoman Empire 'to be changed into instruments of the Sultan's will', Aslam's (2008: 222) young Afghan jihadis resemble the stereotypes of brutalised orphan "recruits" *Vigil* itself cynically proposes. They appear as third-millennium products of what Robin Yassin-Kassab (2008: n.p.) terms the 'perverse marriage of the worst of the Deobandi and Wahhabi theological traditions', which licensed the Taliban's 'boy commanders' to 'declare...year zero' on syncretic Afghan culture. And they are easily drawn into 'the mechanism of [an] Islamic world' which functions – according to Aslam (2008: 82) – 'with [military] precision'.

Bihzad, the younger, is presented as a 'war victim', an innocent and unwitting martyr (222). 'Happy' to 'suffer for Islam' and Allah, and genuinely contrite that he experiences 'worldly...wants' (he longs to 'go to England...make something of his life. Even find love'), he only realises in a pre-death epiphany that 'his heart is clamped in someone's fist': his life is not his own (63–4, 66, 69). Conversely, Casa, who guides Bihzad blindfold to his suicidal bombing mission, seems a "natural" affiliate: hardened, knowing, self-sufficient, a 'veteran' in youth (137, 221). He feels affinity for a God who inspires terror and sanctions slaughter: frequently we hear him intone "martial" Qur'anic passages in the first person (122–3). He delights in 'creat[ing] alarm among non-believers', prides himself on his military prowess, and in pre-pubescence sought battle and 'martyrdom' (122, 137). A dedicated affiliate, Casa has also 'studied' his trade, attending Friday prayers, reading weapons manuals, learning passport forgery and acquiring English from Western news coverage of terror attacks (214).

But Casa's grasp of English is poor – parroting rote-learned phrases and 'deciphering' at best – while his knowledge of US and Afghan history is inaccurate and poorly sourced; even Bihzad discerns that the 'fêted warrior' the older boy reveres reads incorrectly from the Qur'an (64, 222). In the polyphonic *Vigil*, the foundations of Talibani Islamic world "knowledge" are easily rocked, particularly by cosmopolitan Westerners like Marcus and David (229, 278). The confidence Aslam's "warrior" affiliates retain in the authenticity of their Islamist personae falters along with this epistemology. As a result, stereotypes of 'war criminal' and 'war victim' are destabilised, allowing "other" civilian Islamic identities to be warily explored (222).

The primary alternative *Vigil* proposes to austere Talibani Islamic pathways, antipathetic to the 'heresy' of 'original thought', are the intellectual and empathetic connections to Afghanistan's Persianate and Buddhist aesthetic traditions cultivated by sensitive European converts like Marcus and secular, Western-educated Afghan women like Qatrina (11).[22] They appear as social and artistic 'innovators', educators and holistic healers in a modern, Central Asian era when 'innovator' has become a 'dirty' word (265). 'Indifferent to the idea of supreme beings', these characters recognise the need to understand belief and be literate in its language and culture if they are to converse with believers and – ultimately – 'change' limited conceptions of Islamic identity which harshly restrict the lives of ordinary Afghans. This is a position Aslam's writing repeatedly endorses (39).

The novel's Afghan Muslim man and woman of science once took an active decision 'to teach themselves about history and religions, about paintings and music', aware that their medical training left them ill-equipped to understand the workings of the (imaginative) world in which they practised (356). This fact is introduced late, as if to underscore its importance as Casa's crisis of Islamic identity intensifies. But the couple are established from *Vigil*'s opening page as collectors and 'readers' of 'the best fiction and poetry' and caretakers of indigenous Afghan art (356). Significantly, the artefacts they treasure include, in the subterranean seclusion of the perfume factory and subsequent annexe of the Kabul Museum, the decapitated head of a Gandhara Buddha sculpture in smiling, meditative pose. This talismanic icon is said to have bled gold tears when the Taliban tried to destroy it, leaving them afraid and confused. Marcus and Qatrina's strategic, cultural affiliations predate the Taliban's idol-smashing and book-burning campaigns, and secretly endure in spite of such intimidation. Again, they point to a very real need – in censorious historical contexts – for space to be carved for a 'genuine' art which 'bring[s] human warmth and longing and complexity to what is two-dimensional in other, lesser hands' (Aslam 2010b).[23]

Edward Said (1993: xiii) observes in *Culture and Imperialism* that for the Victorian cultural critic and author of *Culture and Anarchy* Matthew Arnold, 'culture is a concept that includes a refining and elevating element', which 'palliates, if it does not altogether neutralise, the ravages of a ... brutalising ... existence'. "Culture" appears to be valued for similar reasons by Aslam's intellectuals in the very different contexts of late twentieth- and early twenty-first-century Afghanistan. Its palliative dimension is particularly visible in *Vigil* after the advent of the Taliban, who subject Marcus and Qatrina to violent repression (separation, amputation, execution) because their commitment to curating, creating and disseminating Islamicate 'culture' which 'add[s] colour to Adam's story' threatens to undermine the monotone "Islam" on which the fundamentalists' regime depends (256).

Surveying Marcus' lakeside house in the first decade of the new millennium, when the Taliban's grip on Usha has weakened, the grieving art historian Lara is solaced by the 'kinship of wounds' she finds among the bullet-marked Persianate murals and works of world literature riven with nails, which continue to survive in its rooms (430). Lara notes the tender care Marcus has taken to collect and clean shards of plaster depicting lovers strafed by Talibani gunfire. She uses them therapeutically to construct a 'kind of afterlife ... for [the] obliterated'; to create 'a young man and woman made from the ruins of dozens in this interior' (30). Significantly, these artefacts' curator, Marcus, is transformed in Lara's mind's eye into 'the Sufi'; his treasure house a metonym for 'the ruin of golden Islam, a destroyed *markaz* perhaps and a Zone of Peace' (415–16, 430).[24] The Russian woman's orientalised perspectives of her Muslim convert host and his adoptive Afghan home are personal and subjective. Yet Aslam's narrative repeatedly encourages us to view Marcus in a not dissimilar light: as an Orientalised wise man and harbinger of a "cultured" domestic domain, where fragile rapprochements may be forged between his war-damaged guests.

In fact Aslam's novel suggests that the outlawed culture which Marcus and Qatrina attempt tenderly to conserve may do more than mitigate suffering. It can perhaps stay the hand of those who would inflict it, challenge the grounds on which they do so and provide individuals with a means not only of memorialising but of moving beyond it, using the best of what is salvageable from the past to establish new foundations for society. Marcus remains convinced, for example, that neither the Egyptian hijacker-pilot Muhammad Atta, nor his Al-Qaeda terrorist colleagues, can have been 'educated men in the real sense' of being literate in the humanities and open to 'nuances' of belief (357). The implication is that if they were they could never have perpetrated such attacks. Qatrina's creative solution to the "problem" of their apparent antipathy to "culture" is to combine elements Islamic literalists outlaw as profane within sacred, scriptural frames. In doing so, she presents viewers with iconographic conundrums that challenge pitiless conceptions of Allah and celebrate in his name all living creatures on heaven and earth (as in the *ayat ul kursi*):

The Taliban did not know how to deal with the pictures – each bore one of Allah's names in Arabic calligraphy, the Compassionate One [etc.] – but the words were surrounded by... animals... and humans. They wanted to tear out these details but couldn't because the... curves of the name took up the entire rectangle. (242)

Qatrina's more cautious convert husband, in his acquired Islamic wisdom, prefers to emulate the chivalrous Saladin, countering 'iron' beliefs with 'delicately sharp' scriptural "correctives" (231). When confronted, for example, with Casa's antipathy to the Buddha head, Marcus tries to "explain" that the Qur'an appears not to condemn all forms of sculpted image: 'the Koran itself says the race of *djinns* belonging to Solomon ... decorated his cave with statues' (229).

However, as Said (1993: xiii) warns, cultural attitudes can be divisive when they become 'a source of identity, and a rather combative one at that', and are used to 'differentiate... "us" from "them" '. In *Vigil*, the cultural views Qatrina and Marcus articulate by means of provocative artistic statements and slightly patronising literary-historical talk threaten to alienate and antagonise those whose imaginations, not tempers, they seek to reach. Qatrina is publicly stoned for insisting on an unorthodox wedding she hopes will change attitudes to women; Marcus' seeming exposure of Casa's ignorance about Islam in guided tours of the Gandhara Buddha "idol" and Sufistic wall-paintings later induces in his pupil feelings of revulsion and thoughts of 'annihilation' (Aslam 2008: 255). Both husband and wife place their faith in a high Islamic culture which palliates the grief of already-sensitised European characters while dangerously unsettling their ignorant, volatile, Islamist Others. This seems ironic, given that Aslam appears to have written *Vigil* with the (hypothetical) notion of conversing with the Taliban in mind.

Michael Ondaatje's *Anil's Ghost* (2000) linked the symbolic reconstruction of a damaged Buddha statue to the rediscovering of humanity after genocide. Like that novel, *Vigil*, with its foregrounding of the fallen Bamiyan Buddhas, continues to point to Aslam's conviction in the resistant and potentially transformative capacity of art at a time when Islam is popularly seen as the enemy of all such recourse to the aesthetic. Yet in framing potent icons of intra- and inter-faith tolerance and affinity in Afghan lands as always under threat, his novel functions as a "mausoleum" for them vis-à-vis the onlooking West. It reconfirms depressing assertions about the present predominance of barbaric and iconoclastic 'Islamic' mindsets, even as – like miniaturist Khadim Ali's paintings of the Buddhas – it reveals the past and muted presence of thinkers and makers who might challenge them.[25]

4.2   Khadim Ali

What makes the picture Aslam paints of *Vigil's* Talibani Muslim characters more complex is the fact that impulses of affinity inspired by the natural world and an apparently "un-Islamic" cultural aesthetic continually threaten to override the most absolute of Islamist affiliations. They not only throw the minds of resolute recruits into confusion, but – temporarily, at least – bring about minor shifts in perspective, particularly when they arise organically, in contexts free from Western intervention. (Interestingly Casa assumes all foreigners are aid or charity workers, 'cogs in a machinery of kindness' and 'non-believers'; he would exploit their 'compassionate impulses' but hold their ideas in contempt [Aslam 2008: 213].) Despite Casa's hardened state, for example, he is not immune to nature or to culture's charms. Aslam allows us to glimpse the possibility of him being swayed to 'tentativeness', even tenderness and 'trying not to smile' as a result of finding a bird's nest nestled in a stone sculpture's ear (195). This, we are informed, is 'a discovery so enthralling that [Casa] had wished to share it with another human, the momentary fascination of it making him act out of [what he subsequently convinces himself is] his true [puritanical] character' (213–14).[26] He is similarly affected by the experience of unmediated contact with the "magic" Buddha head by which Lara finds him sleeping in the perfume factory (164). The initial thought of proximity to this 'idol' – like the thought of proximity to the Russian woman, a potential temptress to his Taliban-trained eyes – is a cause of 'distress' (218). But the smiling Buddha becomes in the course of the narrative a listener to whom Casa tries to confide the written 'truth' of his stirring humanity – until, that is, his pen's failure to write persuades the petulant and superstitious youth that 'Allah doesn't want him to' (377–8).

Kamila Shamsie (2009d: 76) has lamented the fact that 'there is too small a space for those-who-oppose-attacks-on-Islam and also oppose-violence-in-the-name-of-Islam' to be heard, both in Pakistan and the West. It is interesting therefore that in Aslam's novel it is Casa's encounter with his contemporary Dunia, a local schoolteacher, over a shared prayer-mat at Marcus' house that perhaps has the most profound impact on his psyche. For, this young woman seems to fit Shamsie's description of the kind of practising Muslim to whom both "the West" and its Islamist "other" should give ground. Casa and Dunia's five daily 'trysts' over the *janamaz* offer a potential opportunity for the two differently devout Afghans to assert and counter radically opposed Islamic views, for example, about whether 'the source of prayer [should be] delight', as it is for the gentle, Sufistic Dunia, or 'fear of Allah's retribution', as it is for her Wahabi opposite (Aslam 2008: 319, 321). But they also provide a window of time in which two isolated souls can explore the humanity that may connect them, as Dunia attempts to do when she rubs kohl into Casa's cheek after seeing his praying body in danger of being engulfed by flame, leaving the boy confused (316, 318).

Although he ultimately and aggressively rejects her offering of a smudge of imperfection 'to keep off the bad eye' as the 'practice... of infidels and star-worshippers', Casa is touched momentarily by the girl he must periodically meet because 'they bow towards the same God' (319, 321). Meanwhile her own connection to Allah is strengthened in the struggle to field his 'thorn-like' comments, 'hold his eye' and maintain her firmly humane and life-affirming point of view (319, 321).[27] In Aslam's introspective novel, then, the shared site of prayer provides a rare metaphysical space. Here, hostilities suspended, Afghan Muslims, male and female, with radically different understandings of their faith, may – seeing in one another's prostrations a mirror image of themselves – pause to consider what connects them, rather than what divides, and how they may unite to forge for the future 'a more wholesome and humane representation of [them]selves' (Zahid in Irfani 2008: 18).

However, despite Aslam's "democratic" intentions, his fiction proposes a contemporary cultural hierarchy, placing the enlightened European characters with their compassionate minds and 'rights-bearing bodies' (Gilroy 2004: 89) at the top as the custodians of the apparent best remnants of Afghan and Pakistani heritage.[28] In the end in *Vigil*, he invites our gaze to linger not on the subtleties of faith that divide and could unite the would-be Afghan lovers, but 'The heroes of East and West slaughtering each other in the dust of Afghanistan' like 'sides in Homer's war', while the Buddha's chained visage is airlifted to a museum space secured by the British Army (Aslam 2008: 426, 429–33). The channels Aslam opens up for communication between two different types of people, those sympathetic to a heterodox personal, spiritual and aesthetic Islam, and those who cling unquestioningly and superstitiously to a brutal and absolute ideology or faith, eventually collapse when they become too close, or explode in a shared embrace. As in *Maps*, the more open, humane and flexibly affiliative characters who survive are left lingering on the periphery. From this vantage point they bear agonised witness for readers to the mutual pains suffered and inflicted by warring factions irrespective of faith or ideology, as Aslam (2010b) believes they should.[29] But they also intervene to bury the symbolic remains of a time of greater religious tolerance deep in the Afghan sands or the dusty corner of a foreign archive: fragments shored against a culture's ruin which they are too terrified to risk restoring to its indigenous inheritors. In Aslam's "mausoleum" fiction we return, ironically, to a state of cultural impasse.

To adapt the terms of Agha Shahid Ali (1997: 21) in his poem 'Tonight', affective 'idols' and articulate, empathetic Muslim girls, conveniently vanished and hidden from view, will never 'convert' the alienated and demonised Talibani 'infidel' to a more humane Islamic vision of the world, whatever his affinitive impulses. It is not the novelist's job to attempt this.[30] Indeed, for Aslam or any other writer to do so could be to risk reducing a nuanced intervention to a highly dubious fictional rerun of the civilising mission, with "good" cultured and "bad" barbarous Muslim stereotypes cast in the major roles (see Salaita 2008: 137–9). But Aslam (2010b, 2011a: 140–1) stresses in framing interviews and epigraphs the importance of turning imaginatively and discursively towards Taliban and warlord, making all characters 'human', and using art as an 'instrument against injustice' or a means to 'prevent...radicalization'. Given this emphasis, one might have expected him to have afforded militant Islamists greater scope for development *as humans* in the sensitive, perceptive *Vigil*.[31]

Archived hopes

Discussing postcolonial writers after 11 September in her essay, 'Migrating from Terror', Margaret Scanlan (2010: 267) suggests that:

> While they are much too subtle and ironic to assume the mantle of our unacknowledged legislators, they transform that fault-line [between the binaries of – for example – Islam and the secular West] into a living, breathing space in which the human consequences of rigid and lethal polarities become visible.

Her essay takes a broader sweep than this book – Scanlan discusses the work of Libyan exile Hisham Matar and Indian writer Kiran Desai in addition to Mohsin Hamid. Yet I would argue that her statement, particularly the second part (about transforming the 'fault-line[s]' into a 'living breathing space') more fittingly applies to the intricate landscapes and interiors painted by Aslam than the rather stifled theatres of confrontation constructed by Hamid.

In Aslam's fiction the "world" reader is invited to kneel at the 'bottom of the cross', to use an image from 'Where to Begin': to bear terrible, tragic, global witness to the human toll taken as a result of a seemingly eternal clash, if not of warring faiths then of Western and Eastern imperialist regimes, in which each side is significantly wounded, each significantly to blame (Aslam 2010b).

Yet, while he encourages a recognition of the mutuality of "global" wounds, Aslam re-places the emphasis on the need for ultra-orthodox Muslims to change. He depicts the perception of violent 'offence' to Islam and attacks against 'anti-hardliners' as 'primarily an intra-Muslim affair and only secondarily concerned with the non-Muslim world' (Shamsie 2009d: 3–4, 6).[32]

From our safe and privileged "global" distance, then, we are invited to extend imaginary compassion – albeit to discrepant degrees – to Pakistani and Afghan perpetrators of Islam-inspired violence, and to their victims and families. We are asked to consider how greater access to the secular, expressive and faith-inflected arts – particularly indigenous (South and Central Asian) ones – can put beleaguered Muslims back in touch with diverse images of humanity, thus providing solace, extending awareness of heterodox inheritances, and expanding understandings of 'kin' and 'fellowship' (Aslam 2008: 10). And we are encouraged to imagine that, by remaining open to the possibility that connections can be forged through an affinitive recognition of a mirror-like oneness, the most "enlightened" and self-sacrificing of Aslam's characters may lay the foundations for an "moderate", ethical modus vivendi: for a means of "holding converse" with and countering the radically opposing worldviews of warlords and Islamists (Aslam 2008: epigraph, 2010b).

As I have argued, however, this "converse" is in fact constantly frustrated in Aslam's mausoleum fiction: Marcus and Dunia's attempts to refine or "re-culture" Casa using Sufi practices and Buddhist artefacts are wasted on the ultimately unmovable Islamist subject; the heterodox traditions they treasure are subsequently erased or withdrawn. In the novels of Kamila Shamsie, to which I now turn, it is the conduct of the "cultured" Western and Western-educated characters – by contrast – which comes under greatest scrutiny. The next chapter of this book proceeds to consider how her fictions challenge the very basis on which corrective or combative conversations with Islamic "others" are sustained, and question the ethics of judging ordinary Muslim "strangers" based on assumptions about their religious affiliations and attitudes.

5

Stranger Intimacies – The Novels of Kamila Shamsie

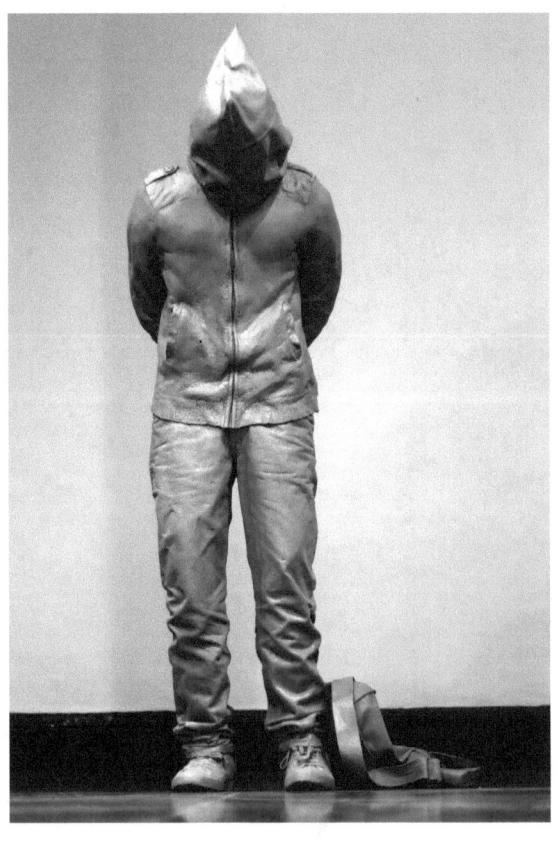

5.1 Saud Baloch

Prologue: 'Do Not Feel Safe. The Poet Remembers'

If something terrible is happening in the world, I want to know about it...I will see what the problem is. I will see who the villain is. And I will bring him to trial by writing the book...'Do not feel safe. The poet remembers.'

(Aslam 2012)[1]

What is one Afghan?...Maybe he's guilty, maybe not. Why risk it?

(K. Shamsie 2009b: 362)

Nadeem Aslam's striking comments, made immediately prior to the publication of his fourth novel, underscore the author's belief that, acting on the courage of his moral convictions and clarity of insight, he must use his fiction to unmask the "warlord" or terrorist and cast him cowering into his cell. This antagonist is envisaged not as a potential partner who may be held in 'converse' – as the epigraph to *Vigil* (2008: n.p.) may imply – but as a subject fit for global inter-rogation, exposure and, finally, "poetic" indictment at the novel's triumphal close.

If Aslam sets out to show his readers what he knows of the world, why it is as it is, and who is to blame, his female contemporary Kamila Shamsie, as the above quotation ('What is one Afghan?') emphasises, repeatedly questions how we know what we see when we look at it, and whether it is morally defensible to bring our cir-cumscribed comprehension and values to bear to condemn those others with whom we share the planet (2009b: 362).[2] Her 2009 novel, *Burnt Shadows*, opens with a man shackled, interned and anticipat-ing receipt of 'an orange jumpsuit' (Shamsie 2009b: 1). But there is no sense of vindication here, nor is the reader given any means by which to "know" how to interpret the scene that Shamsie's 'Prologue' frames. We are confronted only with the consequences of condem-nation: subjugation, confusion and dehumanisation; and with the answerless question: '*How did it come to this?*' (1).

It is my contention that Shamsie crafts in her (geo)political nov-els, from *Kartography* (2002b) to *Burnt Shadows* (2009b), a decentred, Muslim, female fiction of global unknowing, suspended judgements and intimacy with strangers. She attempts – in a phrase borrowed from *Broken Verses*' uncertain heroine Aasmaani – to use it to 'move ... the debate' around the performance and policing of global, Islamic identities at a time of "war on terror" 'to ... that accountable space' of open, uncensored, public discussion (Shamsie 2005a: 288). And in doing so she creates contemporary global narratives which refuse to resolve into any simple, mobilizable epistemology of the world.

This chapter proceeds to argue that Shamsie's novels make readers party to intense experiences of intra- and intercultural alienation and connection, seen through analytical and self-critical elite transnational Pakistani and, later, Asian and American eyes. Her narrative outcomes are increasingly contingent on her female protagonists' realisation that positions of isolation and introspection are both unsustainable and unethical in an interconnected globe: they must interest themselves as a matter of urgency in the worlds that exist beyond their windows.

The author, Kamila Shamsie

Raised in Karachi, educated in America and now resident in London, Kamila Shamsie is a transnational and increasingly activist Pakistani writer and commentator who for many years has lived between these radically different cosmopolitan spheres. She comes from an affluent Muslim emigrant family with a strong commitment to literature and a tradition of producing articulate – and resistant – women writers whose biographies stretch back over several generations to pre-Partition Lucknow.[3]

The acceptance of Shamsie's novels by Bloomsbury marks the realisation of a childhood 'great dream – publication by a house at the centre of English literature' (Shamsie 2009a: n.p.). Her literary fictions are increasingly ambitious. But they remain grounded – as her mother has been at pains to point out – by an inherited, predominantly matrilineal appreciation of how 'the written word mattered so deeply' in subcontinental colonial contexts, and continues to matter in postcolonial Pakistan's uneasy, gendered, national and neo-colonial environments (K. Shamsie in M. Shamsie 2012: 176). Shamsie has undeniably been impressed by the ability of the post-Independence 'Indo-Anglian' fiction championed by Salman Rushdie (1997: x) to 'bedazzle ... the literary world' with its 'uniquely ... hybrid South Asian sound' (M. Shamsie 2009: 141). Yet her writing is shaped by a desire to better its depictions of Pakistan (K. Shamsie 2010: n.p.), and to augment her colonial and postcolonial antecedents' attempts to 'capture the essence of Urdu literature and its culture' in English-language novels (M. Shamsie 2009: 141). Shamsie studied creative writing with the Kashmiri poet Agha Shahid Ali in Clifton, New York and in Massachusetts. Her awareness both of the potency of 'words', and of how 'silence' may provide room for 'pause' and reason to 'search between' them for alternatives, was sharpened under his tutelage (2002a: 23, 25–6).[4] Her novels indicate a similar commitment to cultivating a political aesthetic.

Shamsie's fiction establishes, without what Brennan (1997: 39) terms 'a flattening out of influences', affinitive connections with European, North American, South Asian and other "world" writers and artists. These include Joseph Conrad, Italo Calvino, Rainer Maria Rilke, Faiz Ahmad Faiz, Sadequain and Michael Ondaatje, in addition to Agha Shahid Ali.[5] Their works, which Shamsie more often critically interweaves as intertexts than reverentially invokes as paratexts, represent alternative philosophical and aesthetic approaches which have expanded the author's conception of the world and of how it may be perceived and represented in literature.

Shamsie's biography has followed a similar tripodal trajectory to that of her compatriot Mohsin Hamid. She came of age in a period of Pakistani history overshadowed first by Prime Minister Zulfikar Ali Bhutto's nuclear programme and, subsequently, by General Zia's Islamisation scheme and his regime's complicity in the arming of Afghan mujahideen in the war against the Soviets. Her decentred perspective on Pakistani and world politics has perhaps been most profoundly shaped by this experience, after which, she states, it seems impossible to see 9/11 as an event which occurred in a vacuum, 'the Ground Zero of history' (Shamsie 2011a: 158). Instead, as her commentary and fiction show, Shamsie views this and other geopolitical phenomena – which may be attributed to a "clash of civilizations" or used to justify "terror wars" – through the prisms of different national, regional, individual and group histories (Shamsie 2012: n.p.). She seeks to draw attention not only to long-standing abuses on several sides, but to insidious inequalities in 'cultural power' that persist between countries like Pakistan and America when it comes to their global communication (2011b: 218).

When questioned about her political and religious perspectives, the author has described herself as a 'secular feminist', with the caveat that 'the Islam [she] grew up among didn't make distinctions between the sacred and the secular' and that the 'intermingling of traditions makes it hard to separate religion and culture' (2011b: 219, 223). Shamsie has also stressed that she 'dislike[s] people making generalisations about the "Islamic world"', and that attitudes to feminism and its contemporary manifestations in twenty-first-century Pakistan are anything but homogenous (214, 219).[6] Her relationship to national and international writing and realpolitik, as to Islam and to feminism – whether Western or "Third World" – should therefore be understood as refractory and reflexive.

Knowing: The exotic and its expectations

The "world" literature Shamsie is committed to creating in *Kartography* (2002b), *Broken Verses* (2005a) and *Burnt Shadows* (2009b), the three novels she has produced in the aftermath of the "war on terror", might better be termed "global".[7] It is written with a highly contemporary consciousness of its potential for misinterpretation, excerption and fetishisation in a material world where supposedly authentic, informative and indigenously produced (Islamic) culture has become a powerful commodity, whether for those who would champion or those who would vilify it and the epistemologies it may be claimed to reproduce. And it is shaped by a concomitant awareness of its capacity to engage a "world" of readers with alternative, transnationally informed and locally inflected perspectives of "subaltern" Muslim affiliations and affinities that can engender ordinary cosmopolitan re-cognition, compassion and respect, as well as often-problematic geopolitical anxiety.

Shamsie's pre-2001 novels, *In the City by the Sea* (1998), a magical fable of political oppression, and *Salt and Saffron* (2000), a post-Partition tale of inter-class romance, earned their author the ambiguous accolade of 'our new multi-culti Nancy Mitford; a global girl who does love in both hot and cold climates' (Trapido, in Shamsie 2000: back cover). The entertainment value of a tongue-in-cheek 'multi-culti' exotica and erotica (that is, of affairs of the heart either thwarted by, or permitted to pass beyond, internal and international borders, often explicitly referenced) was an important theme in these early fictions (Shamsie 2000: 1–2). Thick descriptions of mouth-watering South Asian cuisine, a source of comfort and cause of desire for its consumers, rounded off with comical hybridisations of canonical English literary texts ('such stuffed chillies as dreams are made on'), were also staple fare (Shamsie 1998: 62). In these sharp-witted stories of upper-class cosmopolitan Pakistani life, Shamsie has presented attitudes to everything, from the desirability of 'racy *desi*' men who come from 'the not-us' part of town, to the ethics of indulging in the pursuit of 'élitist Third Worlder' narratives, and the creation of saleable 'political art' (2000: 28, 31, 182; 1998: 18). But the intimate, "insider" perspectives she has offered have been nothing if not acute, critical and ironising.

Like other Anglophone writers who appear to have risen with the current wave of interest in Pakistani writing, Shamsie has been and remains quite alert to the potential commerciality of her work. She is also aware that – by dint of her subcontinental Muslim genealogy and transnational biography – she may be expected to deliver variations on a theme of Huggan's (2001) 'postcolonial exotic', enhanced in 'Af-Pak' settings – as Hamid et al. (2010: n.p.) wryly surmise – not by 'paisley designs' but 'bombs/minarets/menacing men in shalwar kameezes' and 'burkhas'. Post-2001, Shamsie continues to blend anticipated cosmopolitan "Pakistani" and newly interesting "Islamic" tropes and themes into romantic and Asia-centring historical English-language fictions. These offer complex, local, cosmopolitical responses to questions of "global" concern.

The two novels Shamsie produced in the early years of the third millennium, *Kartography* (2002b) and *Broken Verses* (2005a), are both largely Karachi-based and narrated from the first-person perspectives of two upper-class, educated and urbane, but also peculiarly insular, young Pakistani women. *Kartography* follows the struggles of the schoolgirl and (later) college student Raheen in a contemporary Karachi rent by "communitarian" violence. We watch as Raheen begins reluctantly to trace the features of a pre-1971 map of 'Pakistan split..., but undivided', seen on a spinning, 'out of date' globe, in the faces of her closest friends and family, with anguishing results (Shamsie 2002b: 1). *Broken Verses* (2005a) is narrated by the brittle, bereaved Aasmaani. It describes a grown-up daughter's desperate attempts to "investigate" the known circumstances of her feminist mother's disappearance and the death of her dissident step-father

'The Poet' in the late 1980s, about which she would remain in elaborate denial. Both novels unfold through romantic plot lines: the pursuit of Aasmaani's quest rides on her relationship with her questionably motivated new boyfriend Ed; Raheen's intimacy with her childhood soulmate and would-be lover, Karim, relies on her recognition of his otherness and the limits of what he perceives as her elite cartographies.

Although ponderous in theme, these novels appear more overtly "multi-culti" in content, lighter and cruder in their characters' flippant-seeming exhibition and integration of South Asian 'exotica or erotica' (Yadav in Reddy 2002: n.p.), than the Ondaatje-esque *Burnt Shadows* (2009b). The latter continent-crossing saga of a middle-class, mixed-race Asian family's enforced peregrinations is overshadowed by the images of a Japanese woman charred by American atomic bombs and a Pakistani man shackled as a suspect in the ongoing "war on terror". It may be considered to offer more geopolitically "exotic" perspectives than its youthful antecedents.

Graham Huggan's (2001: vii, xi) *The Postcolonial Exotic* (to which I referred in my opening chapter) sets out to examine 'the varying degrees of complicity between local oppositional discourses and the global late-capitalist system in which [they] circulate and are contained', drawing attention to the commodification of postcolonial texts and the exploitation of a lucrative trade in 'Oriental(ist)' exotica by multicultural or "Third World" authors like Rushdie. In Huggan's reading of postcolonial literary production, and Indian English literature in particular, its privileged cosmopolitan writers spectacularise the local for the enrichment of the consuming global; they ironise the exoticising imperial and post-imperial gaze, but risk sacrificing cultural specificity and political force along the way (80–1).

Importantly, Huggan's work highlights the 'dilemma' faced by those who attempt to 'account for cultural difference without at the same time mystifying it' or 'promote the cultural margins without ministering to the needs of the mainstream' (31). And it identifies the ways in which writers operating within a discourse of the exotic may manipulate its tropes in order to some extent to critique them. He demonstrates how they use 'unsettling techniques' – the 'counter-ethnographic' depiction of metropolitan South Asia; the foregrounding of sanitising, romanticising, depoliticising and 'spectacularising' processes by which these are reified into aesthetic objects; the transformation or negation of the tourist's gaze; and the interrogation of 'celebrity glamour' and national representativeness – to 'resist' and 'rewrite ... social text[s] of continuing imperial dominance' (x, ix, xi, xv). Huggan describes 'Indo-Anglian' novels thus 'designed as much to challenge as to profit from consumer needs', as 'strategically exotic', yet not unproblematically so (x–xi). As he cautions, the 'ironic self-consciousness' their authors deploy in dealing with "exotic" materials 'might also be seen as precisely the commodity form – the symbolic capital – on which the[y] have made their reputations as reader-friendly, and also wryly sophisticated ... novelists' (xi).

All Shamsie's post-2001 novels feature content which seems deliberately designed to pique and problematise the shifting interests of the international 'alterity industry' Huggan (vii) identifies, which thrives – in the words of one of her archest characters – on 'Exporting Exotica to the West' (Shamsie 2002b: 240). All bear analysis as "strategically exotic" texts in his sense. In *Kartography*, secular Western feminist myths about veiled women's lack of agency turn back most obviously on the East Coast-educated Raheen, who balks as she watches her beautiful, womanly best friend Sonia cover her hair and tug at her sleeves prior to meeting Zia, their childhood companion, at Sonia's family home. Raheen attempts to intervene in what she presumes is Sonia's submission to conservative male oppression:

> 'Is it your father?' I asked. 'Is he making you do the hijab bit?'
>
> 'Raheen!' Zia's voice quavered. 'She does have a mind of her own.'
>
> 'Thanks, Zia. Raheen, stop asking bakwaasi questions. We have a lot to talk about that's more interesting than my wardrobe.'
>
> (Shamsie 2002b: 151–2)

Sonia dismisses Raheen's concerns, taking command of the conversation and making plain that such narrow thinking interrupts the more complacent course of their deep-running friendship. She also scoffs at the 'foreign-returned' Zia's attempt politely to "respect" her seeming "difference" and articulate the social and moral values that may underpin her choice of modest dress, despite his lack of personal affinity with them: ' "customs of proper behaviour" ... which rubbish-wallah sold you that line, Zia? I know you don't see the point in any of it' (153, 155). Both the transnational characters' attempts to interpret Sonia's sartorial shift as the result of patriarchal pressures or cultural conformity rebound on them; Sonia's negations make them seem less mature and more ignorant of the realities of what matters to Muslim women who remain in their home country (148). In Shamsie's countering fiction, the potentially repressive causes of South Asian "Muslim" female behaviours which trouble a "liberal" West are enquired into but left hanging. Meanwhile the object of Western-influenced "concern" gains subjectivity as she refuses to acknowledge a problem – Sonia meets Raheen's initial 'What's going on?' with the answer 'We are Muslim women', and no further elaboration.[8] She retains the right to 'disagree about religion' (148) and, in her frank refusal either to concede or argue – and thereby participate in a 'politico-exotic' 'conversion of politics . . . into a source of aesthetic play' (Huggan 2001: 12, 81) – Sonia wins a degree of bland and un-exotic, if apparently apolitical, autonomy.[9]

Elsewhere in the novel, Shamsie uses the same privileged metropolitan characters' ironic splicing of Western pop culture with the late-1980s Karachi setting to highlight how the city's elite, bilingual residents may "spectacularise" or repackage it as alluring and enticing for a curious, foreign market. On a night-time cruise in a borrowed Mercedes, with Status Quo's 'In the Army Now' blaring loud, Zia and Raheen sing at the top of their voices, drowning out the pop stars and rendering inaudible any residential street sounds with the darkly comic hybrid lyrics: 'Bijli [electricity] fails in the dead of night/Won't help to call "I need a light"/You're in Karachi now' (85). This scene and music are cut abruptly when a gunman attempts to apprehend the couple by embedding a volley of bullets deep into the body of the car, nearly penetrating Raheen's skin. When the shooting ceases, the words 'They cannot protect you from this . . . And what else?' surface and repeat in her ineptly processing mind (87, 89).

The teenagers' frivolous transformation of their native city into a depoliticised adventure playground for the thrill-seeking rich is portrayed less as an act of naivety than one of wilful blindness. Shamsie marks it as implausible, unsustainable and irresponsible in a metropolis where 'affluence and lack [sit] cheek by jowl', and residents regularly confront 'factional', 'ethnic', 'sectarian' and seemingly 'random violence', which may in fact be orchestrated 'by someone who want[s] Karachi terrorised' (2000: 196; 2002b: 259).

Kartography's youthful protagonists' search for entertainment and sensation in their 'always dual' (331) metropolis is undermined and replaced in Shamsie's fiction, but not with the kind of knowing, sardonic, 'politico-exotic' initiation into postcolonial Pakistan's failings which Brennan (in Huggan 2001: 12) might expect. Instead, it instates a considered and contextualised critique of its cosmopolitan elite. In particular, it targets their conscious negation of the complex affiliations and affinities of those less privileged "strangers" who populate the city in which they would feel at home, and suggests they must deepen their understanding of these, and acknowledge how their lives interconnect.

The touristic gaze, much problematised from internal and expatriate perspectives in *Kartography*, is engaged and first comically, then chillingly inverted in *Burnt Shadows'* post- and neo-imperial contexts. This is the case, for example, when the Delhi-departed Muhajir Sajjad takes Harry, his American (and unbeknownst to him, CIA-operative) friend, on a tour of Karachi's opulent 'bazaar of seafood' (Shamsie 2009b: 159). More than the diversity of its fish, or the Pakistani ethnic and faith nations that crowd into the market's melting pot to hawk their catch, Harry's host seeks to showcase his city's most "authentic" natives to his foreign guest:

> Sajjad ... caught hold of a fisherboy and directed Harry's attention to him ... 'But these are the original inhabitants of Karachi. The Makranis. They're descended from African slaves. See?' He pointed to the boy's hair and features in a way that made the American deeply uncomfortable but clearly didn't bother the boy in the least. (160)

Sajjad's point is to draw attention to Karachi's untiring history of absorbing the world's fluctuating tides of enforced migrants – enslaved Africans, displaced Afghans, ousted Indian Muslims fleeing the horrors of Partition – including himself. If Harry is to "see" this he must set aside his amused and patronising racial, tribal and religious presumptions. These include the view that Sajjad has reverted to type, transforming – like 'every Pakistani' – into a chancing 'tour guide at the sight of a foreigner', or capitulated to an easy patriotism, conveniently forgetful of his Dilli disdain for what he once perceived as a culturally inferior location (160). Shamsie's novel seems to hint that

Harry should also consider his own culpability in relation to Sajjad's displacement and self-consciously futile, exilic nostalgia, which are woven carefully into the novel's polyphonic fabric by the omniscient narrator. When asked how he feels about the circumstances that led to his reluctant Karachiite incarnation, Sajjad tells the American: 'now I say this is my life, and I must live it', and attributes this attitude to an apparently neutral yet loaded 'Pakistani resignation' (161). This, he asserts, amounts to 'a completely different thing' from the submissive 'Muslim fatalism' Harry would map onto him (162). Sajjad's carefully chosen words certainly invite further investigation in the light of the provincial and geopolitical context of this section of the novel. That is, the situation of near ethnic civil war in Sindh, exacerbated by an influx of weapons bound for and refugees fleeing from the US-backed anti-Soviet war and facilitated by "Kalashnikov" culture, which the civilian protagonist neither courted nor condoned (Lieven 2011: 303, 315).

The role that the Western media play in creating celebrities out of photogenic activists and resistant artists of "exotic" origin is most knowingly described and challenged in the novel *Broken Verses*, which itself is set in 2002, at the start of Pakistan's cable TV boom (Shamsie 2005a: 4). In the earlier stages of the novel, Aasmaani wryly explains how her British-educated mother Samina rose to sudden fame as ' "Pakistan's Gypsy Feminist" ' in the inequitable political climate of the 1970s (87). A foreign film crew caught the activist's fiery, "ethnic" 'beauty' and 'new-minted' zeal for justice on camera and a laudatory magazine article was circulated globally:

> The Canadian film team must have scarcely been able to believe their luck that day – everything about her cried out 'I'm ready for my close up!' She was wearing a plain white kurta, a thick karra on her wrist . . . and had her hair tied back with a scarf. And she could speak with passion and intelligence and flashing grey-green eyes. (87)

Later, when Aasmaani listens to the audio from a 1986 debate in which Samina went head-to-head with a hard-line Maulana, Shamsie reminds us how the female activist's assumed anglophone affiliations may be held against her by Pakistani Muslims who wish to present them as a threat to an exclusionary, patriarchal, global order.

Attempting to uphold, for example, the "Qur'anic" requirement for female head-coverings, the Maulana seeks patronisingly to designate Samina as ignorant outsider, ill-versed in '*our* Holy Book', thus bolstering his own Islamic authenticity and authority (284). He says: ' "the devil can cite the scriptures to his own purposes". I could mention verses from *our* own tradition . . . but I suspect the Shakespeare of the West might carry more weight with *you*' (284–5, my italics).

More interesting than Shamsie's "knowing" depiction of the dubious benefits of Western press intervention is her portrayal of the way that *Broken Verses*' celebrity figures – 'feminist icon', trail-blazing actress, political Poet-aesthete – whose fame was cemented by local press and artistic intelligentsia, are scrutinised by a young, media-savvy generation out of love with politics (32, 87–8). Typified by the cynical, elite, disaffected Aasmaani, these inheritors are forced in Shamsie's narrative to 'rethink' and 'try to understand' how the attractive, resistant, internationally recognised icons they worshipped in childhood relate to the composite, contradictory Pakistani selves on whom the spotlight seldom falls, yet with whom they share a home (332). Her younger characters are also made to reconsider what the implications of such understandings may be for narratives of "representative" national character.[10]

What sets Shamsie's "global" fictions apart is the fact that their frames of reference are not limited to those which seem to be prescribed by Huggan's "postcolonial exotic" parameters. They encompass but extend beyond a sense of address to the West's imperial interest in spectacles of South Asian exoticism, shifting the focus to contemporary anxieties about Islamic difference or otherness both at home and abroad. Arguably, they are more interested in matters of internal domestic concern and their relation to neo-imperialist or 'unipolar' (Gilroy 2004: 65) geopolitics than the legacies of colonialism. They struggle self-consciously to circumvent a simple replication of elitist perspectives and to contend with multiple marginal, migrant and dominant viewpoints. The attitudes and positions they present are not easily assimilated; they rarely make for comfortable reading.

Reactions to "exotic" content staged in *Kartography* and *Broken Verses*' pages become a means of enquiring into how Pakistan's more privileged classes "read" and interpret the social fabric of their subcontinental Muslim homeland from positions of distance and proximity which simultaneously limit and enhance their perspectives. *Burnt Shadows* goes on to explore the detrimental effect expectations of an Islamic "exotic" cultural otherness can have on the relationships of intra- and intercultural strangers between whom 'differential relations of power' exist, both in twentieth-century Asian and in contemporary North American contexts (Huggan 2001: ix–x). Considered together, these global fictions offer a substantial critique of the roles privileged transnationals can play as 'gatekeepers [of] authentic access' to scenes of South Asian Muslim otherness.[11]

Questioning: Complex affiliations

In considering the rise of the Indian English novel, Gopal has asked: 'What does it mean that *the world reads and believes that it comprehends* "India" through Rushdie [(English)]...rather than...Qurrutalain Hyder (Urdu)?' (2009: 2, my italics). Shamsie herself is a writer who is indebted to world literature in English for its insights; indeed she claims to have 'discovered' the world – or at least, its metropolises – through reading 'Anglophone novels set Elsewhere' (2010: n.p.). But she is also extremely aware that if the reading (Western) "world" interprets and believes that it comprehends "Islamic" Pakistan and Pakistanis as they are authorised for global consumption by South Asian anglophone writers with agendas more in tune with market demands, then its understanding will only ever be partial.[12] Her knowing treatment of "exotic" content reveals that she cannot see 'tiptoeing away' from the 'landmines' she acknowledges 'exist around the particular stories from Pakistan that most interest the world', or from the finding ways to write about them, as a 'legitimate course of action' (Shamsie 2007a: n.p.). She cannot abnegate responsibility in a third-millennium republic of letters whose leaders' at times 'odious' coverage of Islam requires serious rebalancing (2007b: n.p.).

Instead, she deals with the twin problems of positionality and representation by producing increasingly geopolitical world fictions which "respond" from situated, self-critical perspectives. They answer back to the totalising visions of an irrational, absolute and 'unreformed Islam' (Mishra 2012: n.p.) offered in 9/11's wake by a mostly white, Western, male establishment with whom the Indo-Anglian Rushdie may be bracketed. And they are also written in questioning relation to the more ambiguous literary interventions of her immediate Pakistani associates Aslam and Hamid, whose slippery and elegiac novels depict Islam more subtly – as complex and multiply affiliated – but also perhaps operate insidiously to reconfirm stereotypes of young Muslim men as tragically un-cultured or dangerously unreadable.[13]

The novels Shamsie has produced in an era of "war on terror" are inscribed with globally anticipated tropes of a stereotypically "fundamental" Islam and Islamic identity, and endeavour to map related affinitive and affiliative trajectories in South and Central Asian lands. Hence certain resemblances can be traced between them and the post-9/11 novels of the other three writers discussed in earlier chapters. In *Broken Verses*' contemporary narrative strand Shamsie (2005a: 59–60) figures as 'the beards' the groups of religious conservatives who gain political ground in the North-West Frontier Province, and threaten to curb women's rights, citing compliance with 'the guidelines of Islam' as their justification. Her synecdochic shorthand might contribute to the mystification of religious fundamentalists who dedicate themselves to wielding the Holy Qur'an as a tool for discipline and punishment, transforming them into faceless, menacing but ultimately mockable Islamist bogeymen.

The early morning call to prayer intrudes upon her critical and resistant metropolitan protagonists. The compelling vision of a beached mermaid with which *Broken Verses* begins – and which proves central to the reader's understanding of Aasmaani's hauntedness – breaks with her recollection of how, on moving into a new Karachi apartment, she had chosen the child's nursery over the master bedroom. She had settled there in hope of finding shelter from the barrage of aural assaults that would come from an uncomfortably proximate mosque. 'My sister had warned me, [it] broadcast fiery sermons just before the dawn azaan', Aasmaani informs us, ' "If you sleep there, you'll wake up angry every morning", Rabia had said' (2). Statement made, she steps abruptly, naked, from her bed and the chapter shifts from a lyric to a brittle, sarcastic, prosaic tone. It is as if – with the brute, quotidian intrusion of Pakistan's harsh "religious" realities – our largely secular heroine's hope of retaining space to fathom what thwarts the progress of her intellectual and emotional life is shattered.

In *Broken Verses*, too, Aasmaani's surly and disillusioned lover, "Ed" (aka Mir Adnan Akbar Khan), bemoans his post-9/11 unemployment and exile from his adoptive New York. Ed turns bitter when recalling what happened in the aftermath of the Twin Towers' collapse: 'I was laid off because I'm Muslim', he angrily asserts, after expressing his nostalgic love for the life he led in America, and for the feeling he relished of being 'a New Yorker' until 'that September day' when the World Trade Center collapsed (45–6). A 'caveman' volatility seems temporarily to consume this haughty and highly educated Pakistani 30-something, turning him suddenly 'from light to dark, from joker to knave'; Aasmaani reinterprets it seconds later as a kind of controlled aggression: Ed is a man who 'only play[s] with masks' (46–7).

It may be possible to cite the inclusion of such seeming trademarks of the Pakistani 'horror brand' (Hamid et al. 2010: n.p.), excerpted from their novelistic contexts, as evidence of how Shamsie's world fiction perpetuates Western (feminist) myths even as it attempts to complicate them. Yet any marginally more comprehensive analysis of *Kartography*'s, *Broken Verses*' and *Burnt Shadows*' complex contents would make this critique hard to sustain. For the plots of Shamsie's third-millennium novels revolve around the repeated puzzling of supposedly enlightened Anglo-European and Asian "readers" of subcontinental Muslim society and culture. Not only do Shamsie's fictions anticipate and 'interrupt' – to borrow Derrida's (in Cherif 2008: 66) term – limited and habitual epistemologies which are conspicuously mapped onto the bodies of South Asian Islamic characters. *Burnt Shadows*' intertextual allusion to and reworking of E.M. Forster's 1924 novel *A Passage to India* through Sajjad's tentative seduction in colonial Delhi of his British employers' Japanese visitor is a notable instance (Shamsie 2009b: 92–112). They also endeavour to replace descriptions of Islamic affiliations and affinities which position Muslims as alien and other with depictions of ordinary Islamic connections which are grounded in local domestic and political realities.[14] The "dis/sociative" quality of Shamsie's fiction perhaps distinguishes it from that of the other authors examined in this book, whose fiction either presents readers with prejudged "bad Muslim" ciphers; sets out from a position of "knowledge" to bring Islamic villains to trial in its pages; or playfully renders judgement of the central Pakistani pro/antagonist impossible by obscuring his features with smoke and mirrors.[15]

In their fictions, Muslim Pakistan's largely undifferentiated ethnic and "sectarian" communities are depicted as patriarchal, hostile

and violent (or as passive recipients of that violence), with orthodox Muslims of Sunni tradition usually cast – as in Aslam's *Maps*
or Rushdie's *The Enchantress* – in the role of would-be perpetrators of anti-Sufi and anti-Shia persecution. Yet where Aslam may
fail, as Rehana Ahmed (2015: 171) rightly notes, to create 'space
for the idea of Muslim culture as a force of community coher-
ence, strength and resistance in the face of racism and other types
of inequality', I would argue that Shamsie begins to make room
in her novels for 'a cultural communitarianism that is not oppressive'. In *Kartography* she presents us, courtesy of the novel's heroine,
Raheen, with an altogether different vision of how, in contemporary Karachi, the religious practices of Shia Muslims are permitted
to continue. In doing so she revises understandings of the capacity
of diverse and apparently divided Islamic communities for a kind of
productive cohabitation which simultaneously negates yet is contingent on the existence of established boundaries (in this case of gender
and religious denomination).

Kartography draws to a close in 1995, when security forces mounted
an indiscriminate crackdown on the protestatory, self-defensive and
militant Muttahida Quami Movement (Immigration and Refugee
Board of Canada, 1996: n.p.). In the same period Raheen's personal
life spirals out of control, her closest relationships thwarted by the
discovery of her Muhajir father's historic expression of racist contempt for her boyfriend's mother's 'Bengali blood line' as tensions
escalated in West Pakistan with the advent of the Bangladesh War of
Independence (Shamsie 2002b: 232). Yet it is at this time of regional
turmoil that the cosseted, Karachiphile narrator interrupts her private
nightmares of being caught in the city's crossfire in order to write her
estranged lover a letter that tells of its 'lunar street[s]' (330, 337).

Raheen informs Karim that during the sacred month of Muhurram
(in which Shiites mourn the slaying at the battle of Karbala of Imam
Hussein ibn Ali, the Prophet Muhammad's grandson), an alley opens
through the interconnecting hallways of a line of houses which
reaches to the rear entrance of the Imam Baragh mosque. Readers
familiar with Karachi's geography will know that Imam Baragh is
located in the ethnically mixed area of Orangi Town. Raheen explains
that the alley permits purdah-observing Shia women – aided by
neighbouring families – to walk from their homes to their place of
worship free of strangers' intrusive gazes (330–1). Its lifespan is brief,

for the street obeys lunar time: it lasts only the course of a month and as long as the moon shines. But, nevertheless, it exists – evidence, for her, of the city's difficult and not easily resolvable dualities (331–2).

At this point in the novel the expatriate Karim, who left Karachi for London and Boston in his early teens following his parents' separation, has become obsessively headline-conscious; he daily scours the online English-language editions of *Dawn* and *Newsline* for death statistics and updates on factional issues (132–3, 147). Monitoring his native city from a globally mediated distance, Raheen's exilic boyfriend sees it as a fearful 'abstraction', one from which – in Raheen's opinion – he remains estranged because he 'lack[s] the heart to make it a reality' (297). Raheen's elegiac epistle to Karim may be seen as an attempt on the part of the story-loving narrator to do just this: to use less told and less sensational narratives of ordinary Karachi lives sustained amongst its diverse streets to make an alienated former intimate 'hear' the cross-rhythms of its 'heartbeat', and hence draw him home (181). Shamsie's fiction suggests, through its heroine, that elite Pakistani ex-pats and locals alike must contemplate their internationally infamous "Third World" city with neither terror nor romanticism, but with an 'unblinking, unsentimental compassion', if they are to find ways to live within it (332). And, they must remain attentive to the 'truth' of its Muslim population's daily pursuit of concomitantly serendipitous and conflicting sectarian religious and ethnic lives which can neither be easily censored nor condoned, if they are honestly and ethically to attempt to re-present the character of this Pakistani metropolis to an expectant globe (332).[16]

Where scriptural Islam and the language of Arabic have generally been presented as instruments of patriarchal oppression, and their affiliates as antipathetic to art, *Broken Verses'* discussion of Aasmaani's potential creation of a poetic, English-language translation of the Qur'an pre-empts and interrupts both these readings. Attending an interview for a media job soon after her somewhat rude awakening, the bored protagonist finds herself attracted by a line of Arabic painted on the unfortunately titled 'Save the Date' or 'STD' television studio's wall (2005a: 3). It is the refrain which threads itself 31 times through the verses of the *Surah al-Rahman* or Chapter of "The All-Merciful", which begins with Allah's gift of speech to man and ends with the gardens of Paradise. It reads, in Aasmaani's rendering:

'Which of your Lord's blessings would you deny?', and – as she eruditely informs us – has been cherished by calligraphers 'for its variedness and balance' (5). For the 'instantly old' and suddenly outmoded 31-year-old heroine it offers a temporary anchor to something older and – by implication – wiser and more substantial either than her latest flippant and studiously apolitical 'media incarnation', or the studio's aspirant bright young things, whose intimidating commitment to 'progressive thought' appears to shine through their eyes (4, 10).

It seems significant that it is the eloquence *not* of the bejewelled calligraphy which so delights Aslam (2006: 67; 2011b: 77) and his characters, but of the phrasing and lexis of the single line of Arabic text, which might repulse or confuse them, that triggers in Shamsie's Aasmaani a wistful and affectionate memory of the conversation that took place between her mother and The Poet, her avuncular 'Omi' (Shamsie 2005a: 5, 166). Samina suggests that her precocious, idealistic and still-idolising daughter should make a career of translation, learning Arabic so as to rework the Qur'an politically 'into both English and Urdu, in versions free from patriarchal interpretations' (5). The poet requests that his young protégé consider the Surah al-Rahman aesthetically 'especially for me', and vie to 'top' his 'beautiful' transpositions of its most lucid and ponderous verses with new renderings of her own (5). The Qur'an is positioned as a result not as an inherently tyrannical and patriarchal text of 'unarguable absolutes', as it is for Rushdie (in Mishra 2012: n.p.), a book of pre-scripted censures which some greater Islamic (male) authority may impose. Rather, it appears as a complex and challenging literary work, comprised of dark and light materials – apocalyptic visions of the split sky 'redden[ning] like a rose or stainèd leather', the granting of 'articulate speech', promises of 'virginal houris' (Shamsie 2005a: 5) – and open to reinterpretation. In Shamsie the sacred text is transformed into a 'realm of polyphony, doubt and argument', which Mishra (2012: n.p.) notes Rushdie has sought to reserve as the stamping ground of the secular novel.

In *Broken Verses* the Qur'an remains an awe-inspiring book, but also one which Shamsie implies the Prophet's progressive, female, Muslim inheritors must nevertheless struggle to make their own – if, that is, they are convinced that dialogical strategies of resistance and recuperation are preferable in contemporary Pakistan to the self-preservatory ones of silence, inaction, or (dis-)contented 'repose' (Shamsie 2005a: 137–9). Yet it is important to note that although she is personally attuned to language's 'aesthetic – its music', and passionately committed to her chosen profession, Shamsie is too conscious of the limited reach of literary fiction in a 'largely illiterate country' to fetishise (novel) writing as a 'politically crucial art', or a means to present perfect models of Pakistani feminist resistance (2002a: 24, 2011b: 225). Hence perhaps it takes the entirety of *Broken Verses* for her sceptical and reluctant third-millennium protagonist to conclude that it *may* in fact be viable to use newly independent private TV channels to continue her upper-class mother's still meaningful project of 'mov[ing] battles towards abstract space' and 'forc[ing] tyranny to defend itself in language' in order to expose it to debate, and so weaken its hold (2005a: 336). And it is the living, spoken word, as expressed through contemporary and populist media – documentaries, drama, poetry, song – in which *Broken Verses'* strong-minded female characters invest greatest hope. That is, hope not of individually dictating action or winning 'ultimate victory' (as they might in Aslam), but of collectively 'remind[ing the nation] of all the components of its character', creating a matrix within which Pakistan's Muslim, female citizens may attempt to forge resistant pathways of their own (2005a: 335).

Shamsie's treatment in *Burnt Shadows* of the often over-determined and politicised act of *namaaz* and its emotional effect on young affiliates to anti-Soviet jihad is also instructive when considering the dis/sociated position her fiction adopts in comparison, say, to Aslam's *Vigil*, and how it replaces more polarised perspectives of Muslim prayer rituals with similarly situated but alternatively dual and political ones. In *Burnt Shadows* the two excitable teenage protagonists Raza and Abdullah pray in an austere mountain setting which seems to make them more susceptible to a powerful overflow of feelings of religious awe and wonder. Shamsie informs us that, as 'the setting sun dulled all the sharp edges of the world … Raza saw the beauty in the moment and it was with a true sense of reverence … that he laid his pattusi [blanket] on the ground and stepped onto it' to pray, catching Abdullah's eye and nodding in a shared recognition of common 'emotions' as he did so (Shamsie 2009b: 229).

Yet the context is important to establish before proceeding with such a reading. The scene takes place in the early 1980s at a makeshift 'prayer space' overshadowed by a gun tree beside a 'cluster of tents' on a borderland plateau not far from the frontier city of Peshawar (226, 229). The middle-class, polyglot Karachi schoolboy Raza, masquerading as an orphaned ethnic Hazara, has accompanied his newfound refugee friend Abdullah here, having convinced the hesitating Afghan Pashtun to join the mujahideen. Raza, who has planned to deliver Abdullah to the camp and mysteriously 'vanish' back to the safety of his aunt's house in Peshawar, is by this stage a highly reluctant participant in his own 'grand adventure', panicking, afraid and conscious of his foolishness (213, 226). Abdullah, by contrast, appears to have regained confidence in his mature, long-standing commitment to drive the occupying Soviets out of the 'hell' that has become his homeland and, for future generations, 'restore it to Paradise', as he rejoins his Pashtun brothers on Afghanistan's threshold (216).

Raza is woken by an older, 'green-eyed' man at the camp and told (but not forced) to join the other men beside the tree; performing the *namaaz* appears an important step to proving his masculinity and kinship with the 'first Muslims, in the deserts of Arabia' (228–9). Both boys are born Muslims, and we are told that Raza has memorised the Arabic words of prayer whose 'literal translation' he still does not know, while Abdullah is likely to view the region's 'ancient rock carvings' as 'the work of infidels' (212, 330). But neither Raza nor Abdullah's horizons have been set by the teachings of an ultra-conservative madrassa. Each has attended a school at which he appears to have excelled – at least, that is, until his education was disrupted by international and internal conflicts; Abdullah retains a reverence for books and desire to learn English, Raza an interest in teaching and a gift for languages (197–200).

Neither character's naturally pious participation in this seemingly spontaneous and unfettered Islamic act of worship can be interpreted as disinterested when his place in the novel's geopolitical "big picture" is understood. Yet *Burnt Shadows*' portrayal of the spiritual and fraternal stirrings of these 'still so unformed', praying youths, caught in the 'confusion of still-forming nation[s]' and described from Raza's wide-eyed point of view, is genuine (182). We have no reason to question that Raza believed he 'felt the words of prayer enter his mouth from a place of pure faith', found a sense of shy affinity with his Afghan friend as they mutually contemplated their entry to a state of martyrdom, or discovered 'meaning in every muttered syllable of Arabic' he embraced for his own purposes (230). Nevertheless, when considered in the context in which he experiences them – as a spectator at the scene of his Afghan "brother's" potential self-sacrifice, and as a petitioner for deliverance on purely selfish grounds ('*Lord, Allah, let me escape this place*') – Raza's feelings of closeness both to Abdullah and to God appear morally compromised (230). As in her Karachi-based novels, Shamsie provides 'no simple answers' (2002b: 331) nor easy paths to inter/national judgement of the Muslim characters she creates and critiques as she shifts the terms of world literary engagement away from stereotypical visions of 'thugs' and 'angels' (Hamid 2007b: 204), and towards the sensitive depiction of ordinary, globe-tethered citizens.

Un-knowing: Global, decentring perspectives

Kartography's description of the lunar streets is prefaced with a quotation from the Italian novelist Italo Calvino. The citation appears, given the telltale parenthetic intervention, and Raheen's earlier reference to writing a paper based on Calvino's *Invisible Cities*, to have been selected by the protagonist to accompany her love letter to Karim. But it may also act, by proxy, as an epigraph for Shamsie's novel, and indeed her global fiction as a whole. It reads:

> *There are two ways to escape suffering* [the inferno where we live every day]. *The first is easy for many: accept the inferno and become such a part of it that you no longer see it. The second is risky and demands constant vigilance and apprehension: seek and learn to recognize who and what, in the midst of the inferno, are not inferno, then make them endure, give them space.*
>
> (Calvino in Shamsie 2002b: 330, author's
> square brackets)

On a scale first local then global, Shamsie's decentred, (South) Asian female protagonists both 'seek and learn to recognize who and what...are not inferno', and make room for them. These women: Raheen, Aasmaani, and especially Hiroko, function as cautious, self-conscious agents for the demystification, differentiation and humanisation of Islam and ordinary Muslim Others who have been made 'acceptable' targets for demonisation, even decimation, in geopolitical climates inflamed by the "war on terror" (2009b: 362).

Migrating beyond the 'limited circles' of 'intima[cy] with...intimates' which *Kartography* sought to trouble, and into the states of global "un-knowingness" and 'intima[cy] with strangers' described by the more diasporic *Burnt Shadows*, these Asian heroines lay bare the historical politics and prejudices that give rise to subjugation (2002b: 331–2). They point to the precariousness of basing a "knowledge" of others on paranoid, self-centred "readings" of their supposed performance to type, and to the perils of placing apparently insignificant people in the 'little corner' of our world's 'big picture' (2009b: 362). And, having waymarked these hazards, they proceed to extend an unconditional commitment to the diverse individuals they encounter. This may resemble the 'translocal solidarity' described by Gilroy (2004: 88–9) in *After Empire*. However, in developing that concept the sociologist seems to place the emphasis on the charitable 'alleviation of suffering' conferred by Western cosmopolitans with 'rights-bearing bodies' on peoples in post-imperial regions (such as Palestinians in the Gaza strip) who are less mobile and less privileged (89). Shamsie's non-Western, transnational female protagonists, with their subaltern bodies and distrust of hierarchies, eschew this; they instead invest in the 'open communication', which Gilroy also envisages, functioning not as patrons or martyrs in relation to global others, but as equal, common citizens (89).

It is Hiroko Tanaka, *Burnt Shadows'* perspicacious East Asian protagonist, who provides the most sustained focalising point for a humane and critical consideration of who or what is "not inferno" in Shamsie's "war on terror" fictions. Hiroko is a migrant character with a strong sense of the cosmopolitan 'morality' described by Kwame Anthony Appiah (2006: xiii); she is acutely conscious that 'each person [she] know[s] about and can affect is someone to whom [she] has responsibilities'.[17] Hiroko's near innate 'disdain...of official attitudes towards foreigners' puts her at odds, in Shamsie's words, with the ' "us versus them" ' mentality of her native Japan's 'xenophobic [wartime] society' – and, indeed, with all societies which condone the inimical treatment of strangers (Shamsie 2011a: 158). Despite her transnational affinities and the easy camaraderie she establishes with other peoples in countries which are far from her homeland, she remains firmly uninterested in 'belonging to anything as contradictory and damaging as a nation', whether Pakistan, America or a global *ummat al-Islamiyah* (2009b: 204).[18] In short, Shamsie's most arresting heroine cultivates a position that is not only decentred but also scrupulously unaffiliated as she attempts to engage with planetary others whose nominal regional, cultural or religious allegiances make them vulnerable to xenophobic attacks.

When we first encounter Hiroko as a conscripted munitions worker in wartime Nagasaki, her capacity to combine rectitude and anarchy with a hint of Raheen's 'unsentimental compassion' is already apparent (2002b: 332). In a period when Western cosmopolitans and indigenous artists have been branded 'traitors', factories deemed 'more functional than schools and boys...more functional as weapons than as humans', she has been dismissed from her job as a German teacher for remaining loyal to her 'iconoclastic' father (2009b: 7, 13). A dissident artist, Matsui Tanaka dared to challenge his neighbours' ostentatious memorialisation of a "heroic" schoolboy's kamikaze attack. Hiroko has also fallen in love with the 'fugitive' Berliner, Konrad Weiss, who has abandoned 'a once-beloved country he long ago gave up on trying to fight for or against' and sought solace in tales of late nineteenth- and early twentieth-century Nagasaki's cosmopolitan world, about which he plans to write (12, 18).

This young woman's status as a perhaps elective but hardly privileged migrant is also conferred early in *Burnt Shadows'* narrative. Following the death of her father and fiancé on 9 August 1945, when America exploded its second atomic bomb "Fat Man" over Nagasaki, the city's medical facilities are 'overrun' (Shamsie 2009b: 61). Suffering from radiation poisoning – she is severely burned on her back – Hiroko has little choice but to accept a friend's offer to admit her to a Tokyo hospital for treatment. When life there as a translator for the Americans becomes unbearable, she feels compelled to seek 'departure' (48). She treads a path alone to pre-Partition Delhi, where Konrad's married half-sister Elizabeth (formerly "Ilse" Weiss) and her English husband James Burton live. Hiroko travels not in a bid to claim some widow's due, but in hope of help securing work and a future as something more than the 'explosion-affected person' the Western world would reduce her to being: more than a Japanese 'hibakusha' (49).

In India, and for the rest of her long life, Shamsie's resilient and resolute subaltern heroine vehemently refuses to allow herself to be defined by the physical and mental scars of the nuclear holocaust – by the 'story of the bomb' (222–3). Her subsequent peregrinations take her to the newly carved Muslim Pakistan as the convert wife of James' legal assistant, to late-1990s New York after India performed its Operation Shakti tests. Yet throughout them she will not forget the irreparable damage done as a result of President Truman's decision that it was 'acceptable' to 'expend' thousands of supposedly threatening Japanese lives in order to 'save' American ones (62, 362). Hiroko's enduring disquiet about the ease with which such international acts of inhumanity are justified in Western circles makes her reticent to assume complete knowledge of the proclivities of those South and Central Asian Muslims with whom she comes to share a home. However, it must be stressed that the non-judgemental compassion towards Muslims which Shamsie's global fiction uses Hiroko to enact is ultimately disinterested: driven first by moral principle, although underpinned by traumatic personal loss and sensitivity to Islamic nuance gained through marriage and international migration.[19]

Hiroko functions most powerfully as an agent for the demystification, differentiation and humanisation of ordinary, peaceful South Asian Muslims in *Burnt Shadows'* final section, which is takes its title – 'The Speed Necessary to Replace Loss' – from *The English Patient* (1992), Ondaatje's equally epic post-war novel of converging international lives (Shamsie 2009b: 245, 365).[20] This concluding, contemporary part of Shamsie's novel takes place in a post-9/11 New York whose patriotic populace's attitude to immigrants has 'shifted' and 'shrunken' in the aftermath of the World Trade Center attacks (289). In the metropolis' suddenly self-defensive and suspicious climate, Afghans and 'Arab'-looking men of military age are reduced to potential Islamist combatants (326–7). Even the most benign invocations of Allah now meet with a frosty reception in a city-space where allusions to the Prophet Mohammad's sympathetic sentiments once were socially acceptable (289). Yet it is at this time that Hiroko, who since 1998 has tacitly accepted the Manhattan penthouse refuge and openly embraced the companionship offered by her old friend Ilse Weiss, recalls with joy the conversations she had with the city's migrant South Asian taxi-driving population prior to the Twin Towers' collapse, and tries to sustain these precious relationships into an uncertain future (263).

On arriving in New York, desperate to know whether Pakistan has responded 'in kind' to India's recent nuclear tests, Hiroko takes a risk, blurting out in Urdu to a possibly Indian or Pakistani yellow cab driver, 'Has Pakistan tested yet?' (287). Immediately thereafter the affable 'Omar from Gujranwala', a new-minted American citizen, draws the elder woman under his wing, responding first "in kind" by answering her anxious question in Urdu, then 'switch[ing] to English to say, "Welcome to my country, aunty" ' (288). Omar's genial remark, which makes a mockery of the idea of discrete identities or exclusive claims to belonging, 'mark[s] the start of her love affair with New York' (288). It is an affection which the 'uncivic' aspects of the city's response to 9/11 may jeopardise but not ultimately extinguish, so long as people of a similarly hospitable spirit – Hiroko included – remain within it (289).

In the conversation that follows the East Asian woman and South Asian man's initial, 'flirtatious' showcasing of their acquired Pakistani and American affiliations, Omar plunges into serious talk, telling Hiroko about the 'Major cab strike' against the introduction of new regulations with which he is involved (288). This politically active Punjabi migrant's animated tone feels familiar to Hiroko; it reminds her of 'her former students in 1988 when boys who had once sat at the back of the class were out on the [Karachi] streets, waving the flags of their political party and singing songs of victory' (288).[21]

Yet it is important to note that in this brief encounter Omar appears as a man whose sentiments may seem knowable to Shamsie's decentred Asian protagonist, and yet who wishes – in order that they might be better understood – for his national and political affiliations to be "un-known". When Hiroko begins to enquire into the number of taxi drivers who are Indian and the number who are Pakistani, apparently treating the two as separate entities, he makes a request:

No, no, please...Don't ask how it's possible that we can strike together when our countries are in the middle of planning for the Day of Judgement. It's what all the journalists ask. Aunty, we are taxi drivers, and we're protesting unjust new rules. Why should we let those governments who long ago let us down stop us from successfully doing that? (288)

Practical solidarity in the face of the restrictions imposed by authorities is what Omar wishes to place on display here.

Seating herself always in a respectfully distant but receptive position, 'behind the passenger-side seat[s]' of the New York taxi cabs she orders, Hiroko continues to listen to their drivers' stories and not to question but to 'talk . . . to them about their lives' (309). Shamsie's narrative emphasises that it is thus, through discourse and not through confrontation, that Hiroko's comprehension grows of the many personal as well as political matters that preoccupy 'this varied group of migrant workers' (309).[22] The reader's awareness of the diversity of a particular (Pakistani) quotient of New York migrants and of the kaleidoscopic nature of their human concerns is thereby expanded. So too is this community's continuing need to insist that group outsiders accept on trust what they claim to be the truth about their attitudes and motives. Even as it widens the parameters of what – filtered through the Hiroko's consciousness – the global reader may "know" about Subcontinental others, Shamsie fiction uses the cosmopolitan protagonist's experiences to inculcate an understanding that we may learn more about such subalterns by being prepared not to question, but to listen, and to let personal presumptions and societal preconceptions go.

When it comes to Hiroko's encounter in New York Public Library's 'cavernous [presumably Rose Main] reading room' with Abdullah, the Afghan man who at the age of 14 encouraged her son Raza to join him in training for the anti-Soviet mujahideen, this "un-knowing" approach is everywhere in evidence (309). Now, in 2002, following a knock on the door from the FBI, the terrified Afghan, who has been working for nine years in New York illegally as a cab driver, is on the run, and Hiroko has agreed – at Raza's proxy behest – to smuggle him into Canada, from where he can be transported to Afghanistan.

In the reading room, she tentatively approaches a 'broad-shouldered, dark-haired . . . straight-backed' figure whose 'fingers rest . . . very lightly on the page of a book', 'not knowing' whether he bears the identifying mark of the Afghan man she is meant to meet or, if he does, 'what kind of man she w[ill] find' (309, 313). When his eyes meet hers and he slides away to another table, perhaps for privacy, perhaps because he at first cannot see Raza's face in her Japanese features, an old man with arched eyebrows "explains": 'Afghan. They don't like women' ("their" attitudes to books remain unmentioned!).

This prompts Hiroko to extend her hand to rest on Abdullah's arm, a determined gesture that demonstrates her 'refusal to accept that analysis', her preparedness to keep an open mind (310).

As Hiroko listens, asking only short, unassuming, echoing questions that barely interrupt his narrative flow, Abdullah quietly explains that, having stayed with the Afghan guerrillas until the final remaining Soviet troops were withdrawn in 1989, but never seen the hoped-for peace, he has come to the US out of economic expediency. In 1993 he accepted his brothers' decision that he was most likely to survive the journey across; the prospect of their youngest brother earning 'a real living' in America was deemed a better option for his family, despite the risks, than his remaining in Karachi as a truck-driving refugee (313). Now, faced with the prospect of his enforced return, Abdullah attempts to make the best of it, telling Hiroko that after a nine-year absence in which his child was born: 'I'll see my son, my wife. The light of Afghanistan. It's not so bad?' (314).

Shamsie paints a nuanced picture, through Hiroko's unflinching, compassionate, maternal gaze, not of 'the boy who drew [her son] into a life of violence but only [of] a man' – dutiful, sensitive, 'uncertain' about his future – who 'understood lost homelands and the impossibility of return', yet fought for and will journey back to them (313). This is a man who – understandably, given his circumstances – may glance with guarded 'suspicion' at the Japanese woman who seats herself beside him in the exposed public space of the American library, but whose eyes express a longing to have that sentiment 'overturned' (310). One who will also, after the briefest acquaintance, 'reverently' share his bibliographic finds – photographs of Afghan couples in scenes of vibrant, peacetime life, long destroyed by cluster bombs – or unthinkingly lift a veering drunk from his new-made companion's path, placing him gently out of the way of harm (311, 313). Like the intimate strangers Raheen encounters in *Kartography*'s city of 'no simple answers', and the estranged parental figures whom *Broken Verses*' Aasmaani seeks better to know, *Burnt Shadows*' former mujahid ultimately appears as a peaceful man with a difficult past and future who seems to struggle with all 'human soul[s]' for the 'luxury' of finding 'humanity in repose' (Shamsie 2002b: 331; 2005a: 139).

Neither Abdullah nor Omar's faith affiliations surface in their conversations with Hiroko, a woman whose first allusion to Islam has been to confirm with her future husband, Sajjad, that 'the spider is beloved of Muslims' (Shamsie 2009b: 59). What religious sympathies they have remain implicit; they are something the secular Japanese-Pakistani convert finds no reason to challenge.[23] Shamsie has assented to Harleen Singh's idea that *Burnt Shadows* is 'positioned precisely against...a narrowing of topic' (Singh in Shamsie 2011a: 158) in "war on terror" novels to the events of 9/11 and to the question of 'why Muslims become terrorists' (Shamsie 2011b: 223). Instead she uses Hiroko to unsettle the assumed right of Western non-Muslims to second-guess the quality of the beliefs held by 'peaceful Muslims' whom they view as 'potential terrorists' (223). And, by bringing this self-righteous attitude into historical and political perspective, Shamsie points to its negative impact on contemporary, globally interconnected individuals and communities. In this way, she partly demystifies the process whereby peaceful people are turned to violence, but eschews a direct engagement with Islam and Muslims themselves (or their values and beliefs) as a "problem".

The most forceful instance of this unsettling of Western perspectives comes at *Burnt Shadows'* climax, when the novel has shifted gear from cross-continental romance to international thriller. Ilse's patriotic American granddaughter Kim has insisted – despite her 'unshakeable faith in a world that allowed all protests...to take place within a legal framework' – on driving Abdullah over the Canadian border on Hiroko's behalf, knowing that the old lady's Pakistani passport and non-Western features are unlikely to smooth her dealings with the immigration officials (2009b: 329). Kim is a woman whose sentimental, ex-CIA father Harry once believed could 'alone be counted on to engage the world without doing any harm' (174). Yet, since 9/11, she has begun visibly to 'stiffen' at the sight of 'a dark-haired man doing something with his shoes' in a Manhattan Park and, since Harry's death in Afghanistan where he was working as a private military contractor, to question whether 'one Afghan man' can be trusted not to 'send [her] world crumbling' or – in an echo of her father's words – to 'do no harm' (276, 326).

Committed to keeping her promise, but deeply 'uneasy' about aiding the deliverance of an illegal Muslim migrant reported to have fallen foul of federal authorities, Kim is increasingly discomfited by her and Abdullah's stilted attempts at conversation on the drive from New York to Montreal, which seem only to confirm her assumptions about his attitudes to 9/11 and Islamic affiliations. When Abdullah tries, 'choosing his words carefully', to describe the only other journey he has made beyond the metropolis prior to this departing trip – to a Massachusetts mosque with other Central Asian, North African and Eurasian Muslims at the time of Ramadan – he initially arouses Kim's amusement by describing the group's confused response to American road signs (341–2). But Abdullah soon stumbles onto thornier ground with a comment that Kim construes as an allusion to his Muslim companions' pre-9/11 comprehension of American vulnerability: of the country's unpreparedness for the unsignalled World Trade Centre attacks. With this the 'pang' of 'liberal guilt' Kim had thought she felt for a man who could not 'take for granted [the] ability to enter and exit nations at will' quickly abates (340).

Kim's tension only increases with the Afghan's truncated description of his friends' encounter with a shed truckload of stuffed toys on their night-time drive home. She is convinced that Abdullah curtails the story of his return trip in order to circumvent a confession that the group of idol-hating Muslims 'cut right through...the pink bunny rabbits' scattered over highway, appalled by a 'grotesque' and absurd image of Islamic barbarity and intolerance which is of her own conjuring (343). The reader is made party to the fact that, at Abdullah's request, the men had driven close enough to the fallen cargo to take in 'armloads of rabbits and bears' as they passed, delighting in 'fur softer than anything the men had touched in years', and at the idea of being able to present them as gifts to their children (343). But he is wary of mentioning this, lest his sharp American patron consider him a thief; and she, lost in fantasy, shows no inclination to invite her own disillusionment.

Most detrimental to their attempts at dialogue and, ultimately, Abdullah's chance of freedom, is Kim's refusal to 'feel uncomfortable' when the Afghan thoughtfully observes that America should seek – perhaps through proximity – a better understanding of the 'disease' (war) which it liberally spreads in foreign lands, and determination instead to interrogate and discredit as 'mad' the 'system of belief' that may inform his decentred perspectives (344, 346). Even Abdullah's endorsement of Kim's assertion that Hiroko is 'an amazing woman', which she makes in a supposed 'last' bid to 'establish common ground', proves unsatisfactory (345). He assents by alluding to the fact that Hiroko has secured her son and husband a place in heaven because she converted to Islam. 'Even martyrs who die in jihad can't do so much for their family', he concludes, 'It's written in the Quran' (346). But she, deaf to the Afghan's suggestion that it seems 'wrong' for the same 'honour' not be extended to the convert, is interested only in channelling her misplaced feminist outrage at his supposed reduction of Hiroko to 'a launch pad for her husband and son's journey to...paradise' into an acerbic attempt to enlighten him as to the erroneousness of his understandings of Islam:

'Have you read the Quran?'

'Of course I have.'

'Have you read it in any language you understand?'

...'I understand Islam,' he said tensing.

'I'll take that to mean no. I've read it – in English. Believe me, the Quran says nothing of the sort. And frankly, what kind of a heaven is heaven if you can find shortcuts into it?'

...'Please do not speak this way.'

'Tell me one thing...' Unexpectedly, such a rage within her...'If an Afghan dies in the act of killing infidels in his own country, does he go straight to heaven?'

'If the people he kills come as invaders or occupiers, yes. He is shaheed. Martyr.'

...'He is a murderer. And your heaven is an abomination.'

'We should not speak any more.' (346–7)

It is almost as if, in this decentred global fiction, the roles of *Vigil*'s Casa and Marcus are reversed: here thoughts of 'annihilation' crowd Kim's mind, while Abdullah patiently tries to point to a more nuanced understanding of Islamic belief and culture (Aslam 2008: 255). Yet the reality remains in *Burnt Shadows* that it is the incensed, Islamophobic US citizen who wields greatest power. Whatever the rights or wrongs of her Muslim interlocutor's perspectives, no space can exist for an inoffensive and expansive dialogue about the Islam he understands differently when the "knowing" American claims the moral high ground and remains on the defensive. The confused Kim's inability to listen or give credence to the "other", less easily digestible, "side" of Abdullah's story of Islamic affinity and affiliation – to his reverence for those who accept his God, his trust that 'Allah protect' all those who have helped him, and his desire to resist oppression – not only puts an end to dialogue (Shamsie 2009b: 353). It also leads, when Kim reports Abdullah to the authorities, to the arrest of another Central Asian Muslim who 'did nothing wrong': Hiroko's son Raza, who is presumably thereafter detained at Guantanamo; to the marginalisation of this man's concerns; and to the impoverishment of his betrayer's humanity (363). It is Hiroko's bold attempt to spell this out to Kim in the penultimate pages of the novel, rather than mock or mourn the tragedy of an Islamic East and secular West's ultimate irreconcilability, that makes plain the difference of the perspectives Shamsie offers in her "war on terror" fiction.

Re-entering the narrative after Raza's arrest, Hiroko takes issue with Kim's claims that her 'training' in dealing with suspected threats should exonerate her 'suspicion of Muslims', and hence her betrayal of Abdullah's trust; that her recent bereavement might make a paranoid, self-saving attitude to the world outside her window comprehensible (293, 360–1). In censoring her friend's attitude to strangers ('I think you're too scared and angry to be allowed to make a judgement', 'You condemn a man based on five minutes of conversation', 'You don't even know you're lost'), Hiroko makes historic links to similar such moments, from the familial to the geopolitical, in which humanity is abandoned (361). She reminds Kim of her grandmother Ilse's ill treatment in Delhi in 1947 of Sajjad: in an echo of *A Passage to India*, 'for all of two minutes [the colonial wife] thought [her husband's Indian assistant] was a rapist' when she saw him touching the scars on her Japanese guest's back (361). Finally, Hiroko makes more shocking links between Kim's 'crime' of privileging her own life and freedoms over those of the Muslim Abdullah, and international atrocities – the internment of the Jews under the Nazis, the nuking of Hiroshima and Nagasaki, and the post-9/11 targeting of Afghans – which were permitted to pass because more powerful nations saw them as necessary to the preservation of European or 'American lives' (62, 361–2). To Shamsie's migrant Asian protagonist's mind, there is no choice to be made when it comes to judging the potential threat posed by another's ties of nation or faith. For her the risk of losing touch with humanity and becoming part of 'the inferno' is too great: she must seek to know that part which is 'not', and let it live (2002b: 330).

Rendering forgiveness redundant

Perhaps most significantly, Shamsie's "war on terror" fictions dare to imagine through their decentred female Muslim characters that different people may – as humans – find ways to connect and cohabit without needing either to deny or to justify the religious and cultural affiliations and affinities which international entities may seek to render suspect. The position she adopts is not unproblematic. It requires that her predominantly Western world readers distance themselves sufficiently from complex and compromised Islamic characters to be able to situate their actions in inter/national contexts of conflict, or recognise their capacity – in the midst of "the inferno" – to extend an 'unexpected embrace' when a relative stranger is in need (2009b: 322). These flawed figures include Raheen's Muhajir father Zafar, a man perhaps too proud of his link as an emigrant to the 'Muslims of Mecca' to 'be absorbed' into the potential melting pot of Karachi, despite his disquiet at rising ethnic violence (Shamsie 2002b: 224). They also include Abdullah's brother Ismail, a farmer who welcomes the stability brought by the Taliban regime but refuses to entertain external 'concern' about its impact on his daughters (2009b: 320).

'No simple answers' are forthcoming in Shamsie's novels when it comes to appraising the bearings that very different manifestations of South and Central Asian Islam have on the actions of her Muslim characters. This is not because the "true" nature of their affiliative alignments and affinitive emotions are obscured, as in Hamid, but rather because they are necessarily portrayed as diverse and multiple – always unpredictably, usually surprisingly, and often reassuringly so. From *Kartography* to *Burnt Shadows*, Shamsie's decentred heroines work their way towards an understanding that: 'We have to every day live with the truth and every day find a way towards unblinking, unsentimental compassion that renders forgiveness irrelevant' (2002b: 332). Reading the world through their eyes, Shamsie's global fictions start to set an agenda for an alternative, critical, Asian- and Islam-inflected geopolitical consciousness which encompasses but does not rush to judge the perspectives of those characters who continue to be consigned to 'the little corner of the big picture', as it is configured by the West (Shamsie 2009b: 362).

6

Writing Contemporary Islam –
An Ambiguous Project

6.1 Jamil Baloch

This book has explored how four South Asian Muslim writers have responded to demands for "coherent" accounts of Islamic faith ties in the first decade of the third millennium, and situated the dominant discourses of the West-led "war on terror" as central to their internationally marketed English-language fiction. It has argued that their globally oriented novels operate in different ways not simply to reveal, but also strategically to occlude, complicate and re-culture the wide-ranging (Islamic) affiliations and affinities which animate their Muslim characters. Some of the individual works examined may ultimately reconfirm the Western stereotypes they attempt to rewrite. Others circumvent them entirely, hinting at but refusing fully to reveal the religious proclivities of their protagonists. Still others strive to deconstruct stereotypes and de-centre Western perspectives and priorities, daring to envisage a world where, as humans, Muslims may cohabit with others convivially, needing neither to apologise for nor to disclose the religious attachments which global hegemonies may seek to render suspect. Considered collectively, they demonstrate an attempt to revise modern "knowledge" of the Islamic world, countering rigid interpretations with narratives centred in a range of South and Central Asian locations, and periods of cosmopolitan (Islamic) civilization, which bring the more flexible and open dimensions of Muslim culture and societies to life.

This book acknowledges the partiality of the portraits which the selected authors offer as they attempt to reframe (in English) their Muslim subjects' potential to connect with diverse intra- and intercultural others. It notes a tendency to privilege relationships formed on the basis of a shared affinity for aesthetic culture, "Sufistic" philosophy or "universal" humanitarian principles, rather than a mutual interrogation of political differences or potentially divisive doctrinal issues. *Writing Islam* also recognises that some novels, such as those by the diasporic writers Aslam and Rushdie, continue to indulge "exotic" appetites, or reinforce Eurocentric ways of seeing. It also points to how certain highly resistant texts like Hamid's *The Reluctant Fundamentalist* remain susceptible to appropriation by dominant political and cultural forces. Yet, as I have argued, such fictions may be interpreted as "authentic" exposés of radical Islamist mindsets less as a result of their authors' "authoritative" provision of inside perspectives and more because of their readers' compulsion to mine them for pathological insights. For this book also highlights the selected writers' use of certain formal strategies, which demonstrate their capacity to negotiate the tensions of being seen to act as Muslim spokespeople, as it analyses how far their geopolitically engaged and embedded texts intervene in hegemonic discourses around ("suspect") Islamic identities. It indicates how Hamid stages, for example, a young Muslim man's "confession" which implicates its foreign audiences; and how Shamsie constructs a historical narrative which de-centres predominant Western readings of "world" history and uses Islamic characters to challenge the ethics of judging planetary "others". It suggests that these writers are particularly effective in circumventing dominant narratives: they confound the world reader's search for "insight"; bring into view alternative perspectives of Asian Muslim experiences of affiliation and affinity; and undermine assumptions about how (devout) Islamic identifications limit Muslims' capacity to converse with the rest of world.

Ultimately, I maintain that the works of world literature which Rushdie, Hamid, Aslam and Shamsie have produced in the wake of 9/11 *do* attempt to reorient Western readers' perspectives. They invite audiences to redirect their attention onto diverse spheres of global connection (beyond "moderate" Sufistic and "fanatical" Islamist ones), and to reconsider how far their Muslim characters' sense of self is informed by proximity to these spaces. In so doing, each one also refocuses its international readership's attention on the matters of geopolitical concern which its author deems most urgent. These include the threat posed not only to the Western world but also to heterodox South and Central Muslim multiculture by absolutist Islamist affiliates, and the negative impact that the policing of Islamic identities has had on multiply affiliated Muslim subjects/suspects. They also encompass the need to find a way of holding converse with and about Islamic peoples, founded on an 'unsentimental compassion which renders forgiveness redundant', and a vital suspension of judgement (Shamsie 2002b: 332). On reflection, "orienting" is perhaps a suitably ambiguous term. It hints at the potential reactivation of perspectives complicit with the (neo-)imperialistic agendas of a global literary marketplace, but also points to a re-centring of (South) Asian visions, which realign global Muslim identities with multiple spheres. As such it may be aptly posed as a means to describe the complex ways in which the novels of Rushdie, Hamid, Aslam and Shamsie are implicated in the (fictional) unravelling of the Islamic affiliations and affinities, which have engendered such consternation and curiosity in the post-9/11 decade.

Writing Islam argues that the discourses of the "war on terror" have had a profound influence on the intractable Islamic perspectives produced by transnational South Asian Muslim authors who remain conscious of the complex geopolitical contexts in which they write. This book both identifies the narratives which frame the authors and texts which form its focus, and investigates the strategies they have deployed to differentiate, deconstruct and de-centre dominant discourses. Considered together, the fictions in English produced by South Asian authors of Muslim background provide a nuanced perspective on contemporary Islam, unsettling crude stereotypes and pessimistic East–West binaries, and writing rather of a world defined by ambiguities and even – occasionally – of hope.

Notes

1 Writing Islam from a Contemporary South Asian Muslim Perspective

1. The perpetrator was actually Timothy McVeigh, an American Gulf War veteran and agnostic, whose protest was anti-government.
2. Here Said builds on his 1978 critique of the Occidental exoticising of Eastern subjects. In *Orientalism*, Said emphasises the 'socially constitutive role of Orientalist (or Eurocentric) discourse' in creating a 'fantasmatic' Orient which it identifies as 'real' (Lazarus 2004: 10). He also asserts that there 'are cultures and nations whose location is in the East, and their lives, histories and customs have a brute reality obviously greater than anything that could be said about them in the West' (Said 1978: 5). These ideas, and those posited in *Covering Islam*, remain relevant because of the continued production in Western/ised discourses of a fictional non-Western, Muslim "Other", with whose "reality" the novels examined in this book all appear to engage.
3. This quotation is taken from 'The Second Plane', an article first published in *The Guardian* on 18 September 2001 and subsequently collected in *The Second Plane* (2008).
4. Amis', Hitchens' and Rushdie's opinions on aspects of American foreign and British domestic policy in the years following the 9/11 attacks are not homogeneous, but their attitudes to (radical) Islam, neoliberal, neo-conservative and atheistic in tendency, are largely in sympathy. Rushdie's (2002) book of essays was dedicated to Hitchens, who championed his cause after the 1989 fatwa.
5. The most controversial of Amis's (quoted in Dougary 2006: n.p.) comments has been the assertion he made that 'the Muslim community will have to suffer until it gets its house in order'. Measures suggested to ensure this included travel restrictions, the strip-searching of people who looked Pakistani or Middle Eastern and deportation. What Amis described as 'discriminatory stuff' intended to 'hurt...the whole community', Terry Eagleton (2007a: xi) later exposed as a regime of 'calculated harassment of a whole population' aimed at 'humiliating and insulting certain kinds of men and women at random'.
6. Hereafter *Maps for Lost Lovers* will be referred to as *"Maps"*.
7. Standing at a greater geographical remove from Pakistani fiction in English, Indian writer Amit Chaudhuri (2009: n.p.) has hesitated to link its burgeoning to rapid changes in the geopolitical landscape. Yet he has heralded novelists like Rushdie, Hamid, Aslam and Shamsie (whose novels *do* connect with such alternations in direct and in oblique ways) as

'a 21st-century phenomenon, appearing at a time when the new supposed fundamentals...suddenly seem frayed'. For him, these authors are 'interestingly poised: implicated in both the unfolding and the unravelling of our age'. Such observations, coupled with contemporary critical discourses surrounding Muslim representation in wider spheres, open up ground for a multidimensional consideration of how contemporary South Asian Muslim writers contribute to this "unravelling".

8. These might include, for example, 'Muslim cosmopolitanisms' constituted on the Afghanistan–Pakistan frontier. According to Hopkins and Marsden (2011: 137–8), these differ significantly from the models apparently prescribed by a 'militant' "global Islam" often assumed to have replaced them. Hopkins and Marsden's argument is that 'transregional forms of Muslim identity' in liminal, frontier spaces 'encompass people who enact their identities in relation to a wide range of ethnic and linguistic markers, [and] varying forms of doctrinal tradition'. Furthermore, 'such identity formations...involve the forging of connections *between...Muslims* who have experienced the differential effects of...imperialism' (137, my italics). These 'connections' may, in their account, 'illuminate the nature of Muslim thought and self-understanding' (138–9).

9. Damrosch (2003: 14) asserts that 'works by non-Western authors...are always particularly liable to be assimilated to the immediate interests and agendas of those who edit, translate and interpret them'.

10. Morey explains that Spivak prefers 'planetarity' because she believes 'it allows Otherness to flourish while eschewing mastery and enshrines respect for difference', whereas "world" and "globe" 'have become contaminated by their association with globalisation and a particular hegemony' (21).

11. Hereafter *The Wasted Vigil* will be referred to as "*Vigil*".

12. Aslam's (2008) *Vigil*, for example, is praised in the novel's front papers as: 'arguably the best novel available on the current situation in the Middle East. The jihadists, the warlords, the crusading Americans – all are given voice...There's no whitewash...just authentic writing.'

13. As I do so I remain aware that while the authors' 'subjective experience' may be 'taken to validate [fictional] representations of [Islam] ...there is also an "objective" dimension to [their] texts which...[requires] critical examination' (Mondal 2012: 38). In other words, I understand the subjective experiences dramatised in the novels to be shaped not simply by their writers' "inside" knowledge of Muslim South Asia, but – crucially – by these global authors' personal attitudes and political agendas.

14. This accent both mimics that deployed by a particular class of Pakistani and 'resonates with many Western preconceptions about Islam, or about people from the Muslim world', Hamid (2008b: 46) has said – prejudices he wishes to use his fiction to expose.

15. Hereafter *The Enchantress of Florence* will be referred to as '*The Enchantress*'.

16. I allude here to Rushdie's phrase, 'the Empire writes back to the centre' which Bill Ashcroft, Gareth Griffiths and Helen Tiffin (2002) used as the

title for their study of the capacity of postcolonial literature, Indian writing in English in particular, to resist, reconstitute and replace dominant imperial narratives.

17. Mamdani (2004: 15–18) discusses the popular distinction drawn between 'good' ('modern', 'peaceful') Muslims and 'bad' ones ('premodern', 'inclined to terror'), which he deems the result of judging individuals of faith according to political affiliations, not cultural or religious identities. This division he reveals as false: 'there are no readily available "good" Muslims split off from "bad" Muslims, which would allow for the embrace of the former and the casting off of the latter' (15).

18. It seems important here to note that internationally acclaimed anglophone novels like Hamid's *The Reluctant Fundamentalist*, with its arch, even arrogant-sounding transnational Pakistani protagonist, and Aslam's morbid and nostalgic *Vigil*, celebrated at national events such as the Karachi Literary Festival, have provoked a range of (negative) responses from local readers for various reasons. These include irritation with the predominance of privileged cosmopolitan characters; boredom at the provision of Islamic history lessons; and (at times misguided) accusations that the critical and political perspectives they offer are anti-Pakistani and anti-Muslim. Yet, despite continuing debates in Pakistan (resembling those described by Brouillette (2007b: 34–5) about the relative "authenticity" and representativeness of English-language fiction ostensibly produced by a small elite for a "world" market (as opposed to literature produced in (other) vernacular languages for "indigenous" audiences), anglophone writing is not necessarily the preserve solely of the upper classes – or may not remain so. For, as Zahra Sabri (2013b: n.p.) notes, the establishment of a 'firm market' for Pakistani English fiction abroad may have allowed 'for more diverse types of local writers to be published, noticed, and also promoted' at home. Such authors could hail from an 'emerging' 'class...for whom speaking English is not necessarily a function of a profound Westernisation of culture and lifestyle' (ibid: n.p.). This class may include Omar Shahid Hamid, author of the Christian cop-and-convict thriller, *The Prisoner* (2013), or Shazaf Fatima Haider, who wrote *How It Happened* (2012), a witty Shia-Syed family romance. Sabri (2013: n.p.) cites the latter as a novel which, although written in English, and hence accessible to foreign audiences, does not make 'local readers...feel disoriented'. Such fiction may provide different challenges and insights to "First World" readers than those produced by the globally oriented novelists; for its readers must accept perhaps that there are local 'context[s] where things' – such as faith affiliations – 'do not always need an explanation' (ibid: n.p.).

2 Enchanted Realms, Sceptical Perspectives – Salman Rushdie after 9/11

1. Other critics offer a more cautious account of the privileging of a secular, syncretic, Sufi Islam in 'liberal Indian discourse', such as that deployed

by writers like Rushdie (Kabir 2009: 20, 145). Ananya Jahanara Kabir suggests that this promotion *may* result in the (positive) 'reinsert[ion of] spirituality into the praxis of the everyday', displacing 'narratives of religion-driven partialities and schisms' (21). However, it could also culminate in the (too) simplistic 'defus[ing]' of Islam's 'significations of a threatening otherness' at a time when what is most 'troubling' about that faith to 'national imaginar[ies]' needs to be explored, rather than a 'malleable Islam' more crudely proffered as a foil to rigid Muslim positions (20–1). I would suggest that both these dynamics are at play in the novels I examine by Rushdie, and in those of Aslam considered in the fourth chapter.

2. The identities and positions Rushdie articulates vis-a-vis subcontinental Islam are informed by the secularism Jawaharlal Nehru adopted after Independence, which was linked to a revised historiography of India 'as a "composite culture" ' and 'syncretic, tolerant civilization' (Srivastava 2008: 23). According to Achin Vanaik (1990: 148), Indian secularism 'does not favour the development of a progressively non-religious state', unlike European models. While Rushdie might personally favour the relegation of religion to the private sphere, he nevertheless endeavours in his novels (*The Enchantress* especially) to entertain 'secularism, myth and belief' as 'worldviews' which may jostle for equal validity – as do others of my writers, Aslam in particular (Srivastava 2008: 23, 25).

3. *Kashmiriyat* was always a fictional notion. As Victoria Schofield (2000: xii–xiii) points out in her Preface to *Kashmir in Conflict*:

> [As] Sir Owen Dixon...noted in 1950, the difficulty of resolving the future of the state [of Jammu and Kashmir] was compounded by the fact that it was 'not really a unit geographically, demographically, or economically' but 'an agglomeration of territories brought under...One Maharaja'....What [he] noticed from the outset was that with peoples of such diverse origins nominally united under one political authority, whatever the outcome of a unitary plebiscite, there was bound to be disappointment from amongst the minority...As...Sumantra Bose, has recognised, the challenge was always to find a middle ground between 'communal compartmentalism and the chimera of non-existent oneness'.

4. This seems in tune with the novelist's broadly binary reading of Islam in Kashmir expressed in June 1999 (Rushdie 2002: 305–7). In this column, written at the time of the Kargil crisis, he described 'mullahs and radical Islamists, who characterise the struggle to "liberate" (that is, to seize) Kashmir as a holy war' as an external, Pakistani force, whereas:

> Ironically, Kashmiri Islam has always been of the mild Sufistic variety, in which local *pirs*, or holy men, are revered as saints. This openhearted, tolerant Islam is anathema to the firebrands of Pakistan. (306)

Historians like Victoria Schofield (2000: xiii–xv) might agree – in more complex terms – 'That what began as a more secular movement in the valley [of Kashmir] for greater political liberty became one with "Islamist" overtones arose directly from the changes occurring within Pakistani society and influences from Afghanistan'; and that, lamentably, 'In the crossfire of multiple objectives remain the lives, and sadly often violent deaths of men, women and children caught up in a deadly war of words and weapons, which seems unending.' Yet she, and other scholars of the region's conflict (for example Mridu Rai (2011: 277), who points to how Kashmiri Muslims have 'defied assimilation within an Islamist rhetoric that fails to recognise their regional specificities'; or Peer (2010a), who points to the attraction to his contemporaries of the Salafi fundamentalist-reformist movement, discussed below), would illuminate the greater diversity of Kashmiri political and moral positions in relation to "Islamism", which the fiction writer, in his satirical reconstruction of post-Second World War history, strategically omits or obfuscates.

5. The Sufistic affiliations also seem conveniently to be frozen in time – part of a bygone era. There is no space in Rushdie's darkly comic tale of terror for a realistic portrayal of those politically committed Kashmiris whose retention of a link to religious tradition may lend gravitas to their leadership of resistance movements. The journalist Basharat Peer (2010b: 81) describes, for example, in the article 'Kashmir's Forever War', how the head of the separatist Hurriyat Conference coalition, Omar Farooq, 'deftly mixed his roles as modern politician and the head cleric in Kashmir's Sufi tradition, leading his followers in a sing-song voice humming Kashmiri and Persian devotional songs and then moving effortlessly to the question of Kashmiri politics' as he commemorated the death of his cleric father, who was assassinated in 1990. Peer goes on to mention both Farooq's shouting of crowd-pleasing slogans ('Kashmir is for Kashmiris!...We will decide our destiny'), which win him the support of 'excited young' Srinagaris; and the politician's sustained attempts to engage with Indian and Pakistani governments regarding a peaceful settlement and the demilitarisation of the region, 'often at a high personal price' (81).

6. Interestingly, such Islamist types as *Shalimar*'s iron mullah closely resemble the 'rather forbidding old men glassy-eyed with righteous indignation' whom Anshuman Mondal (2008) remembers as being responsible for the burning in Bradford in 1989 of copies of *The Satanic Verses*. For the youthful Mondal, they represented 'the archetypal Other – exotically attired, speaking broken English in thick "foreign" accents and fanatically propagating the rhetoric of the mullahs in Tehran' (1). Mondal argues that these fantastic figures, often mistakenly associated with an older generation of Muslim immigrants whose Islamic attachments clash with the duties of multicultural citizenship, have lingered too long in the popular consciousness as stereotypes of a more fundamental Islam. Meanwhile, the increased 'religiosity' or 'turn to Islam' of the angry young men who joined the crowds that day has, until very recently, been under-researched and little represented or understood (2).

7. In Part One of 'Step Across this Line', one of his 'Lectures on Human Values' Rushdie emphasises the importance of ideas contained in the Sufi Muslim poet Fariduddin Attar's story *The Conference of the Birds* (Rushdie 2002: 407–9). Here the creatures expand the possibilities of what they can be by transgressing the limits prescribed by others, eventually becoming their own gods. Rushdie sees this as a vital step towards 'advanced civilisation', founded on 'several individualisms...merged into a collectivity' (409).

8. In her review of the novel, Kamila Shamsie (2005b: n.p.) states that Ali, 'prompted...by...a comment [made] during the Gulf war that Muslims have no culture', deliberately set out to counter this claim in this fourth instalment of his *Islam Quintet* by depicting instead 'times when learning and culture were synonymous with Islam – and appreciated as such by the most enlightened Christians'.

9. Economist and philosopher Amartya Sen (2005: xiii) suggests in a work which Rushdie cites as a source in *The Enchantress'* concluding bibliography, that 'the contemporary relevance [of this Indian Muslim emperor's cultivation] of the dialogic tradition and of the acceptance of heterodoxy is hard to exaggerate'.

10. The role of Indo-Persian culture in shaping South Asian Muslim identities, specifically – and fascinatingly – the influence of Persian epic on the contemporary Pakistani and Afghan 'cultural unconscious' (including that of a 'jihadi milieu'), is something that the academic Suroosh Irfani (2010: 37) explores in detail in his recent article, '*Shahnamah* – The Other Story'.

11. Akbar's commitment to Islam is substantiated by historical accounts. Amartya Sen (2005: 289), for example, notes that:

> When [Akbar] died in 1605, the Islamic theologian Abdul Haq concluded with some satisfaction that, despite his "innovations", Akbar had remained a good Muslim. This was indeed so, but Akbar would also have added that his religious beliefs came from his own reason and choice, not from "blind faith", or from "the marshy land of tradition".

3   'A Devilishly Difficult Ball' – Mohsin Hamid's *The Reluctant Fundamentalist*

1. While *The Reluctant Fundamentalist* has been well received by Western reviewers and prize-awarding bodies, and Hamid has been a high-profile guest at South Asian literary events such as Jaipur and the Karachi Literature Festival, praise for his novel has not been universal, nor has it remained uncontested. Pakistani audiences, from academics to students and lay readers, have described feelings of repulsion for its central antagonist, who has been seen rather as a misrepresentation and an unnecessary perpetuation of a negative stereotype.

2. This is a pressure registered in a recent fiction by the character of Mo Khan, the American and nominally Muslim protagonist in Amy

Waldman's novel *The Submission* (2011), whose plan for a garden wins the competition to design a memorial at Ground Zero. Frustrated when it seems his success will be denied, he resolves to flirt with the fears of the American populace, refusing to promote the "normal" (non-threatening) Muslim self-image that would mollify and reassure them:

> He would not…reassure anyone that he was 'moderate' or 'safe' or Sufi, whatever adjective would allow Americans to sleep without worrying he had placed a bomb under their pillow. It was exactly because they had nothing to worry about from him that he wanted to let them worry. (78)

Mo's rebellious thought perfectly encapsulates the dilemma of the Muslim-as-"problem" after 9/11, forced to articulate his "good Muslim" credentials or, remaining silent, be assumed to belong to the dark side.

3. His approach is utterly unlike that of the protesting 'Islamic Rage Boy' figure, Shakeel Ahmad Bhat, whose unkempt, ranting visage has been fetishised as an icon of 'pathological anti-Western fanaticism' while the potentially rational or political portent of his words has passed without comment (Morey and Yaqin 2011: 27). Nor does Hamid's attitude resemble that adopted by the reasonable-sounding Muslim ' "refusenik" ' (94) whom Morey and Yaqin also describe. This figure, critical of the supposed 'complicity of a mindless, monolithic Muslim community that has been cowed by rampant Saudi-inspired extremism', has come to stand for the (often reformed) "good" Muslim type in the contemporary Western press (94–5).

4. Examples of scholarly interest include Paul Jay's (2010) discussion of *Moth Smoke* as a transnational and post-postcolonial text and Cara Cilano's (2011) consideration of what the novel may reveal about mental strategies for dealing with the traumatic events of 1971. The treatment of the novel in these is fairly brief; neither writer deals with *Moth Smoke* exclusively.

5. Hamid has also appeared on other "flagship" British news and current affairs programmes, such as BBC 2's *Newsnight* (Quirkstir 2008), where he was called upon to offer a response to the Mumbai terrorist attacks of 2008.

6. In this book, Lieven (2011: 4) introduces his protagonist, Pakistan, as ' "Janus-faced" ': 'divided, disorganised, economically backward, corrupt, violent, unjust, often savagely oppressive and home to extremely dangerous forms of extremism'; yet he also characterises it as a country which ' "moves", and is in many ways surprisingly tough and resilient as a state and a society'.

7. Morey and Yaqin's (2011) chapter in *Framing Muslims* on 'Muslims, Multiculturalism and the Media: Normalization and Difference' (44–78) offers a more extensive discussion of how the mainstream media has set the agenda when it comes to the discussion of 'Muslim issues'.

8. See, for example the strapline from *The Times* on *The Islamist*'s front cover, which describes the memoir as 'a complete eye-opener' (Husain 2007).

9. Changez observes that a 'confession' can 'implicate...its audience', depending on their response: 'Reject it and you slight the confessor; accept it and you admit your own guilt' (Hamid 2007b: 80).

10. Interestingly, the 'political events' that certain Book Club readers thought the novel foreshadowed were not solely the stereotypical turns to the "dark side" of militant Islam and acts of "jihadist" terror one might expect the Western reader to anticipate (Mullan 2011). They also included the violent reciprocations of individuals who might resemble Changez's shadowy, paranoid interlocutor. Mullan notes, for example, that one reader observed:

> 'There is a lot of prescience in this book,'...referring to the 'incident in Lahore' (the arrest of an American CIA agent who shot two men who had threatened him in the street). 'It could have come straight out of the pages of the novel.'

11. Within the body of the novel, Changez draws attention to his capacity to use language creatively to gain the trust and respect of his American colleagues in phrases such as: 'I was aware of an advantage conferred upon me by my foreignness, and I tried to utilize it as much as I could' (Hamid 2007b: 46).

12. In his article, 'Bad Faith', Mondal (2012: 37) draws attention to this quotation from *The Daily Telegraph*, which is reprinted in the endpapers of *The Islamist* (Husain 2007). Mondal observes that Husain's memoir has been circulated as recommended reading in the corridors of Whitehall, and has informed government thinking and policy with regard to tackling Islamic extremism, 'due in large part to the conviction that general lessons for our times could be drawn from this personal account of one young man's experience of certain radical "Islamist" movements' (37).

13. *The Reluctant Fundamentalist* was first published by Hamish Hamilton and then by Penguin in 2007.

14. Davids' presumption appears to be that contemporary America and Pakistan as portrayed in *The Reluctant Fundamentalist* provide no place for a young Muslim to work through identitarian issues, although what evidence the novel provides for this remains unspecified.

4 Re-culturing Islam – Nadeem Aslam's Mausoleum Fiction

1. As mentioned in this book's introductory chapter, Salaita (2008: 1–2) argues that Muslims have been relegated to the realm of the 'uncultured' in Western imaginations, construed not only as 'unrefined', barbarous, and premodern, but also 'complicit...with terrorism'. This Arab-American scholar himself would reject the label 'cultured' because he associates it with 'white liberals' and neoconservatives whose 'platitudes about tolerance, diversity and coexistence...engender sanctimony', and

because their 'refined conversations [have] overt[aken] the world, delegating people into intellectual categories, demarcating civilizational essences, [and] prioritizing rights of expression' (167–8).

2. Interestingly, and perhaps controversially, Bhatti concludes her article with the following statement:

> Maybe it is time to expose this Pakistani culture in an effort to subvert and rescue the deteriorating image of Pakistan, and export [its] knowledge widely so that images of antiquities such as the renowned fasting Buddha... become the future associations with the nation and its people. (2010: 32)

This prospect may seem unlikely, given the Muslim country's prevailing cultural climate; indeed, Bhatti acknowledges that she may appear to 'chase for a utopian fantasy' in searching for a way to revive 'the increasingly forgotten vision for the nation that embraces an unbiased inclusive history and diversity' at an early stage in her piece (30). But she also stresses that what she is striving toward is less ambitious and hence perhaps more realistic than that: 'the recognition of possible alternatives that are not hampered by official national ideology or blinkered by conservative imagination' (30). Aslam seems to be in sympathy with Bhatti's sentiment and (as I will go on to discuss) to explore through his fiction – *Vigil* in particular – what he considers to be the achievability of this goal.

3. Bruce Lawrence (2012: 21) uses Marshall Hodgson's term 'Islamicate' (and the related 'Persianate') to describe 'aesthetic or literary elements' that are the result of an 'elision' of religion and (secular) culture and of the sharing of Islamic and non-Islamic traditions in a Muslim Cosmopolitan context.

4. Interestingly, the model to which Aslam returns when discussing morality and his aesthetic ethos is Christian:

> With Christ came the idea of the 'brotherhood of man': I am good towards you because you are my sister/brother... Buddhism and Hinduism ... preach compassion, but... without this same sense of strangers' relationships involving filial obligation (2011a: 145);

> A work of art can be a powerful instrument against injustice... Think of a crucifixion scene... by Giotto. A man is being tortured ... He is dying and this dying is being witnessed not by strangers but *by... his friends*! They are at the bottom of the cross, their own agony as visible as his... *And all of this is being watched by us.* (2010b)

Christ is a powerful icon; however, Islamic tradition seems notably absent here. Examples of Islam-inspired (or Qur'an-enshrined) tolerance and compassion are not entirely lacking in Aslam's fictions, however. In the short story 'Punnu's Jihad', for instance, a Yemeni man eases the Pakistani protagonist's religious guilt with an adapted saying from the Hadith. 'There is a kind of tree whose leaves do not fall... in that it is like an ideal Muslim', he tells the anxious Punnu, 'But Allah understands if we don't succeed in being perfect in this imperfect world' (2011b: 77).

5. In my opinion, Aslam presents the suffering human as something more than that. His bound, bleeding and brutalised figures – Leila, Punnu and Qatrina – appear almost as instant icons of martyrdom. Their pain, beautified and intricately described, stirs the reader, creating a feeling of awful excitement, which I would describe as a sense of the "sublime"; the disturbing affect of this has been noted by critics (for example, Adam Mars-Jones 2008: n.p.).

6. Aslam's concept of "mirror-written" fiction relies on an assumption of the universality of human sentiments and passions and a faith in the visionary eye of the author-poet. This notion resembles those outlined by Romantic writers such as Percy Shelley (1977: 485), for whom a poem was 'universal', 'the creation of actions according to the unchangeable forms of human nature, as existing in the mind of the creator, which is itself the image of all other minds'.

7. Tony Vaux notes in *The Selfish Altruist* that in a 'new global era', which may 'show Western power seizing hold of humanitarian principles and distorting them', those who attempt to stand for "the human" must continually strive for 'impartiality', interrogating the 'interests [that lie] behind any expression of "concern" or humanity', 'carefully defin[ing] their] relationship with those who claim ... [their] values', and ensuring 'concern for "the person in need" ... include[s] all who are in need, not just those we happen to favour' (2001: 17, 42).

8. Aslam's tendency to foreground certain characters' human "universality" may – as Kadir (2004: 7) warns – be 'a function of the universalising impulse in the cultural optic of those [privileged bodies] doing the worlding' in 'world literature'. It could betray Aslam's desire to 'circumscribe the world [and its people] into manageable global boundaries' in order to bolster a particular civilisational view (Kadir 2006: 73).

9. Amis appears unable to entertain Rumi's notion, to which Ziauddin Sardar has since sought to draw attention, of 'Islam as love and all Muslims as "a community of spirit": "join it, and feel the delight of walking in the noisy streets, and being the noise", [Rumi] wrote' (2012: 4).

10. Their compassionate, self-sacrificial commitment to rehabilitating a small part of the Muslim world seems in keeping with that of the ordinary, heroic citizen-protagonists in the poems of the revolutionary left-wing Punjabi poet Faiz Ahmad Faiz (1911–1984), to whom Aslam dedicates *Maps* and whose work has been strikingly redeployed by artists and politicians who would resist religious oppression in contemporary Pakistan. The following lines from his poem about the execution of Ethel and Julius Rosenberg as enemies of state, *Ham Jo Taarik Rahon Mein Maray Gaiy* ("We Who Were Murdered in the Darkest Lanes"), for example, were quoted in Pakistan's House of Parliament by Aasia Nasir, a Christian member of the National Assembly, in protest at the murder of cabinet member Shahbaz Bhatti, who spoke in favour of a Christian women sentenced to death under blasphemy laws:

> Why complain? Holding up our sorrows as banners,
> new lovers will emerge

from the lanes where we were killed
and embark, in caravans, on those highways of desire…
it's because of them that we went out to make the world our own
we who were murdered in the darkest lanes.
(Faiz, translated by Waqar Ahmad in Nasir 2012: 249)

11. In 'A Plea for Enlightened Moderation', published in *The Washington Post*, General Pervez Musharraf (2004: n.p.) proposed a two-pronged strategy to tackle Islamic militancy and the West's mistrust of the Muslim world. This was based on an Islamic commitment to 'shun militancy and extremism' and focus on advancement through 'individual achievement' and 'socioeconomic emancipation', and on a Western undertaking to 'seek to resolve all political disputes with justice' and 'aid in the socioeconomic betterment of the deprived Muslim world'. In describing the strategy's 'Muslim part', Musharraf emphasised, as Aslam does, the importance of individual 'introspection' as a means to social maturation. He also stressed the need to recall and resurrect Islam's 'glorious past… as the flag bearer of a just, lawful, tolerant and value-oriented society' which stakes 'faith in human exaltation through knowledge and enlightenment'. The then president of Pakistan, however, seemed to invest greater hope in the achievability of a 'renaissance' among his 'brother Muslims' than his artistic counterpart has since displayed in his fiction.

12. In her review of the novel, Kamila Shamsie (2004: n.p.) described Kaukab as a character who, 'in the hands of a lesser novelist, [could] have become a monster', but instead:

> She is transformed into a woman entirely human, entirely heartbreaking…she is the voice of condemnation raised against all transgressions from orthodoxy and also the voice telling us: 'Islam said that in order not to be unworthy of being, only one thing was required: love.'

Thus Shamsie anticipated Aslam's criteria for a compassionate but uncompromisingly realist fiction, as set out in 'Where to Begin' and his interview with Chambers (Aslam 2010b; 2011a: 140).

13. Despite Aslam's seeming commitment to 'referenc[ing] … every headline-grabber' (Brace 2004: n.p.) when exploring the 'issue' of "honour" crimes in diasporic South Asian Muslim households, his novel implies no link between such domestic tragedies and political, religious extremism. The lovers' murders are not 'colored with the lens of a nationalist antiterror rhetoric' (Morey and Yaqin 2011: 75), as is usually the case, but instead are re-presented as a focus for Dasht-e-Tanhaii's multi-faith residents' 'humanitarian concerns'.

14. Aslam's (2010b) enthusiasm for a faith that foregrounds the cultivation of a love for what is human which may emulate the love expressed by the divine is evident in 'Where to Begin':

> I love thinking about religion and how it attempts to put something other than money and sex at the centre of human discourse – it puts

love there. As Borges said: 'I give thanks...for love, which lets us see others as God sees them.'

15. Similarly, Aslam's novella *Leila in the Wilderness* exposes the corruption of 'holy personages' at a desert shrine when, at the heroine's mother-in-law's behest, they administer mind- and soul-cleansing treatments to 'help' the sonless Leila conceive a male child; nail her to a bed; and provide crude implements to sever the magical wings of hope and longing that sprout spontaneously from her back (2010a: 41–5).

16. Since writing 'A Sufi Saint', Sabri (2013a: n.p.) has sought to emphasise in private correspondence with me that (in her opinion) the championing of Sufism as a "heterodox" opponent to an "orthodox" Islam is itself based on a misapplication of the term "orthodox" to Islam;

> The truth, in [Sabri's] view, and in the view of some leading non-Western and Western scholars of Islam, is that it is difficult to distinguish within Islam any such thing as 'orthodox' Islam (especially given the lack of an organised Church or priests, at least among the majority Sunni sect) to which 'heterodox', 'Sufi' Islam can be presented in attractive juxtaposition.

She has also stressed that 'in fact if "Sufism" (which [is] a relatively new, Western term; the term we [Pakistani Muslims] have traditionally tended to use being "*tasawwuf*") is interpreted as the mystical dimension of Islam, then it actually becomes mainstream Islam, rather than a deviant variant'.

17. Katherine Pratt Ewing (1997: 11, 14) points to a tendency among 'modernist' intellectuals to reconstruct (simplified) versions of 'the histories Pakistani Sufis claim for themselves', which are in fact comprised 'of a complex set of resistances and identifications', as they attempt both to 'reconstitute' their South Asian Muslim 'roots' and to raise objections 'to the fixity of [Islamic] tradition'. Such appropriations are particularly apparent in *Maps* as Aslam attempts to articulate more "moderate" Muslim positions through the figure of Shamas.

18. The epigraph from the front pages of *The Wasted Vigil* is as follows:

> And the poet in his solitude
> turned towards the warlord in a corner of his mind
> and gradually came to look upon him
> and held a converse with him.
> DAULAT SHAH OF HERAT, *Tazkirat-ush-Shuara*, 1487
>
> (Aslam 2008: epigraph)

19. Marcus' treasure-filled home appears to the reader as a miniature *Ajaib Ghar* (house of wonders). In Shaila Bhatti's (2010: 30) terms, such a building 'may...appear as a problematic sign of nineteenth-century [or colonialist, Orientalist] display narrative', but also suggest a 'panoply of exhibits [which] is ideal in thinking about revisionism of [Afghan] history and culture'.

20. An enthusiastic exponent of Sufi mysticism, Frembgen's emotional accounts of journeys in Pakistan ("the land of the Sufis") read 'more like a kind of travel fairytale' than conventional ethnography, as Simone Falk notes (dust jacket, Frembgen 2012: n.p.). They should be treated as partial, somewhat Orientalised reflections.

21. In January 2009, as Frembgen (2012: 41) notes, Shabana's body, 'riddled with bullets, [and covered] with banknotes and CDs... [was] exhibited on the main square of the town of Mingora as a deterrent to "immoral shows" '. For Frembgen, it provided a poignant illustration of how 'the militant Sunni Taliban poison and destroy their own Pashtun culture... which, along with a cult of masculinity, also cultivates a romantic spirit and appreciation of beauty' (41).

22. The attraction of Sufi religious traditions such as saint worship, dependent on a more visceral draw, features in *Vigil* and – as in *Maps* – is made specific to an Afghan Muslim female underclass. But its depiction here is more cursory, and seems touched with a greater geopolitical sadness. Aslam (2008: 173) reminds us, via the aid-working Zameen, that the long-buried Muslim saint to whose grave the women of refugee-flooded Peshawar travel to address their complaints is 'often the only person in this life they could question without impunity and accuse of neglect'. Such comments reflect the unbelieving and socially conscious author's personal disquiet when contemplating Muslims' dependence for support on godly intercession and desire for reunion with the divine, particularly if they are living in impoverished communities and war-torn lands open to exploitation. Aslam (2010b) has described himself as 'deeply moved' and 'at times shaken to the last cell in [his] body' by the sight of 'the destitute and helpless' flocking to kiss the 'walls and floors' of Pakistani mosques. But such observations also indicate his enduring consciousness that places like the saint's mausoleum, seen by the Islamist Casa as 'contrary to the pure form of Islam [which] had to be destroyed', also function as present-day sanctuaries for an Islam that permits dissent and doubt (2008: 334). The cathartic effect of communing rituals remains in *Vigil*, but it is largely by means of aesthetic encounters that Sufism's subversive spirit is kept alive in the novel.

23. This is in keeping with contemporaneous cultural discourses within Pakistan about the importance of reclaiming of an Indo-Persian Islamic culture underpinning Pakistan's South Asian Muslim identity as a counter to the Islam of the Taliban (e.g. Irfani 2010).

24. The paintings, intended, for courtship, celebrate the five senses in vibrant scenes of animate and inanimate life centred on Islamic customs such as the Ramadan fast. Drawing the guest to the topmost room dedicated to 'love, the ultimate human wonder', they may also inspire her to reach for divine love (Aslam 2008: 12–13).

25. Haema Sivanesan's 'Bamiyan Notes' (2011) also seems relevant to a consideration of how artists may intervene in the destruction of symbolic artefacts in order to produce artworks which retain traces of that

violence, but integrate them into new, hopeful images with a healing effect. Sivanesan discusses Pakistani miniaturist Khadim Ali's 2008 installation project, which focused on the Bamiyan valley in which the Taliban-detonated Buddhas were situated. Also being home to members of Afghanistan's Shia Hazara minority, this place seemed to her to 'locate ... the fault-lines, ideological divides and inequalities, that underline the current conflict' (54). She emphasises that Bamiyan's ruined Buddhas simultaneously 'conserve a violent and traumatic history' of the Taliban's attempted erasure of the syncretic identities of Hazaras who claim kinship with the statues' creators, and bear witness to this people's 'role in Afghanistan's history' (55). The Hazaras' 'ambition to reconstruct' the Buddhas 'suggests a process of recuperation ... of remaking or rehabilitating history and identity – to restore a symbolic order ... dignity and a sense of belonging' (55).

Full reconstruction may be impossible, even undesirable, however (Clark 2011: n.p.). Ali's paintings, like Aslam's novel, attempt it in partial, miniature form, giving a similar sense of the imperilled Buddhas' enduring vulnerability. In *Untitled 2007* (4.2), Ali replenishes an emptied niche, depicted in golden tones, with the spirit of a serene-faced, spherical Buddha. This icon seems at once indestructible and dangerously oblivious to the tiny, colourless Taliban fighter who penetrates its shell. Images of resilience are juxtaposed with those of continuing threat, resulting – as in *Vigil* – in ambiguous scenes in which (pre-)Islamic cultural connections are preserved but this heritage's future appears uncertain, and hope of its unprotected survival naive. Yet where Ali's miniature appears primarily to restate a cultural problem and simultaneously – by shrinking the Talibani soldier and making the meditating Buddha loom large – to invest faith in the prevalence of his peaceful mentality, Aslam's anglophone fiction places the emphasis on the importance of outside bodies' physical salvaging of the artefacts that, almost talismanically, seem to encapsulate such powers.

26. For this incident, Aslam (2006: 68) surely takes inspiration from a childhood memory of his ultra-orthodox uncle's encounter with a toy bird in which the man seemed to recognise 'the possibility of beauty within something he loathed'. Its fictional resurfacing points to the mature author's need to bear witness to the spark of humanity he believes must exist in the mind of the most entrenched Islamist, to remind readers – as the well-meaning disaffiliate David reminds the Islamophobic James – that even the most apparently diabolic is 'the child of a human, which means he has a choice and he can change' (2008: 413).

27. In this Dunia resembles the 'pure-hearted Sūfis' Iqbal describes as 'seekers after God and possessors of the truth', 'who see ... God in the light of [their] own *khudi*' (Mir 2007: 168).

28. Paul Gilroy (2004: 89) states that 'where the lives of natives, prisoners and enemies are abject and vulnerable, they must be shielded by others, endowed with those more prestigious, rights-bearing bodies that can inhibit the brutal exercise of colonial governance'. I borrow from him

when I describe characters like Qatrina, Marcus and David because they seem to resemble those cosmopolitan 'others' Gilroy identifies as empowered to extend 'translocal solidarity' – in this case – as a counter to the Taliban's brand of Islamist imperialism; they place themselves in the line of fire, literally and metaphorically, when they try to shelter and save ordinary Afghans like Dunia and Casa from rape, murder and "jihadi" suicide.

29. Aslam (2010b) wrote in 'Where to Begin':

> I ask myself if this is what a novel or a story can be – that the reader is locked in a space with the victim and the perpetrator and those who love the victim. Imagine if we were there at Abu Ghraib, in those terrible rooms and hallways, and imagine if the parents of the men being abused were there too, watching. But then it's not 'watching'. It's 'witnessing'.

30. The original line from Ali's (1997: 21) poem is: '*Lord,* cried out the idols, *Don't let us be broken;/Only we can convert the infidel tonight'*.

31. Aslam (2011b) perhaps attempts this in the apocalyptic 'Punnu's Jihad', a poetic, realist but less polyphonic short fiction, which exposes the workings of a Pakistani orphan's consciousness during the process of his re-categorisation (but not religious radicalisation) in October 2001. Joining the Afghan fight against a punitive West as a medical auxiliary, Punnu is forced into soldiery by a Talibani mullah, sold to the Americans as an Islamist terror suspect, and recast as a candidate for extraordinary rendition. Aslam sketches his experiences almost exclusively from inside-out, creating an internal, Islam-inflected dialogue which demonstrates Punnu's political perspicuity, spiritual and philosophical depth of thought, delight and wonder at nature and culture, righteous anger at global inequalities, and enduring Sufistic desire to persevere in a greater jihad, wrestling with darkness towards perfection in Allah's 'imperfect world' (77). Punnu's vivid dream of the battlefield provides an example:

> They lay all around ... slaughtered, stinking, cleansed at last of the burden of being ... and he stood above their corpses, puffing out wide flowers of breath into ... a dawn light so pure ... He wanted Allah to appear and explain it all ..., not just watch from His high distance through unappalled eyes. Punnu hadn't known he could summon such deep feelings ... he was enraged at the peace ... on other parts of the planet, and in grief he cursed the lives that were continuing uninterrupted elsewhere (67).

But, unlike Casa and Bihzad, the self-possessed Punnu proceeds to harm no one or thing in the name of any cause. He causes injury to a warlord's lackey and dreams of denuding a prayer book of leaves for self-protection only. He feels guilt for imagining ill-doing and offers aid to those who will betray him, incapable of deserting fellow Muslims or negating their 'dreams of justice', until he is shackled 'with zip-locks' and bundled into a US helicopter, his capacity for planetary interaction crudely suspended (78–9). Before Punnu closes his eyes at the story's end in a martyrish gesture of surrender to geopolitical forces beyond his control, the mis-taken, disempowered Muslim suspect 'casts a spell on the world, telling it to last until he awakens' (79). Ten years after 9/11, Aslam invites the reader to imagine what story Punnu would tell if he were released from imposed bonds and assumed affiliations and free to pursue a humane, affinitive jihad-al-akbar of his own.

32. Shamsie defines 'anti-hardliners' as: 'a varied group that includes moderate Muslims, secularist Muslims, non-Muslims etc.: in short, those who, for varying reasons, oppose the ascendency of the hardliners...who call for [punitive] violence in the name of religion' (2009d: 6).

5   Stranger Intimacies – The Novels of Kamila Shamsie

1. Aslam made this statement in a public discussion of his then forthcoming fourth book, *The Blind Man's Garden* (2013). This novel returns to Afghanistan and to Pakistan at the time of 9/11 to consider how that geopolitical 'hinge moment' (Aslam 2012) exacerbated pre-existing tensions. The quotation is from 'You Who Wronged', Czesław Miłosz's poem on the death of the dissident poet Osip Mandelstam, written in 1950. It concludes:

   Do not feel safe. The poet remembers.
   You can kill one, but another is born.
   The words are written down, the deed, the date.
   And you'd have done better with a winter dawn,
   A rope and a branch bowed beneath your weight.

   (Miłosz 2001: 103)

2. References to "Shamsie" hereafter will refer to the writings of Kamila Shamsie, unless otherwise indicated.

3. For a full discussion of these relatives' movements and legacies, see M. Shamsie (2009, 2012).

4. Shamsie (2002a: 26) vividly recalls in 'Agha Shahid Ali, Teacher' being set the task of creating a poem using only the words which were contained in an Amnesty International article. She describes it as 'a lesson in working with the language of journalism to create moments of lyricism', and 'a demand that we search between words like "torture" and "deprived" to find "touch" and "skin" ', which 'had the effect of making every word we used seem like a sought after thing' (26). This questioning sensibility seems fundamental to her novelistic reworking of often over-determined and dehumanised or desensitised images, particularly in *Burnt Shadows*, with an illustration from which this chapter began.

5. Brennan (1997: 39) criticises "Third World" cosmopolitan writers who have 'found recognition first in English' on account of their juxtaposition of 'alien cultural elements' because he assumes their intention is 'not to

show (like E. M. Foster in *A Passage to India*) a cultural dissonance, mutual incomprehensibility, but rather unity and complementarity' which, for Brennan, is too simplistic. This, he argues is 'not a matter of individual style' but 'borrowed from the meetings and mixings of distinct national and ethnic styles on American streets' (39). However, Brennan identifies as different literature such as that written first in Arabic and Urdu which he suggests draws on a culture whose 'sense of history ... source materials ... literary allusions, and assumptions' are 'not a part of the common knowledge of Western readers', and whose 'aesthetic strategies are therefore too independent to be pedagogical' (43). Shamsie's Islam- and Urdu-inflected English-language fiction would seem both to fall into the latter category, and to demonstrate the complementarity and disparity of other world literature.

6. Ruvani Ranasinha (2012: 209–10) has argued persuasively that Shamsie's fiction 'enacts the fault-lines within contemporary discourses of feminism and the need for an alternative framework to conceive Pakistani women beyond the totalising conceptual categories of both "Islam" and "feminism" '. She describes it as being 'animated by the theoretical insights of "Third World" feminist and postcolonial feminist scholarship'; and she observes that it 'attempts to gesture towards a range of progressive gender possibilities framed within a discourse of human rights that transcends discourses of cultural imperialism' (211–12).

7. I avoid describing this as "post-9/11" fiction. Shamsie (2011b: 222) has firmly stated that '9/11 wasn't the turning point' for a shift in the way she views the world. Rather:

> It was the war on terror ... America's invasion of Afghanistan in October 2001. That's when the war on terror came to Pakistan. In 2002, Pakistan's religious parties became serious players in the government for the first time, and at that moment I thought the world had changed.

8. These might be read as what Gayatri Spivak (1988: 308) describes as 'displacing gesture[s]' or 'unemphatic, ad hoc, subaltern rewriting[s] of ... social text[s]' in 'Can the Subaltern Speak?', her consideration of Western epistemological bias, how the discourses of imperial and patriarchal hegemonies function both to construct and to silence marginal subjects, and the (im)possibility of subaltern self-representation.

9. Brennan's criticisms of the formulaic "Third World" cosmopolitan fiction he later termed 'politico-exotic' (Huggan 2001: 11–12) include the view that 'to be political has become a selling point' for its authors, who 'join an impassioned political sarcasm ... with ironic detachment, employing humor with a cosmic, celebratory pessimism' (Brennan 1997: 41). It may be possible to lodge this claim against writers like Mohammad Hanif in *A Case of Exploding Mangoes* (2008a), but not Shamsie: she may deploy irony, irreverence and sarcasm, but her fiction is anything but morbidly "celebratory" in its portrayal of concerns about contemporary local and

global political trends and formations, from which her characters can never remain "detached".

10. Significantly, Aasmaani begins to believe that 'character is just an invention', a fiction which 'allows us to go through the world with ... ease' but obscures 'what we can't begin to consider...: that there is no consistent "I", only a somewhat consistent outward form that houses a vast set of possibilities', held together by a (self-) imposed 'narrative of character' (142–3).

11. Considering 'the problem of access to the cultural other by the touring classes', which Shamsie seems to raise and challenge thorough the casts of her fiction, Sarah Brouillette asks the following questions:

> Who [presumes to be able to] access ... the [South Asian, Muslim] cultural other, which forms of access are legitimate, and who may judge? ... How do postcolonial 'writers/thinkers' [and crucially all empowered "global" citizens] establish themselves as gatekeepers to any presumed authentic access, or, alternatively disavow the very requirement that they take on such roles? (2007a: 25)

12. Shamsie notes in particular the inauthenticity of Rushdie's depictions, to which her fictions may provide correctives: 'The only time I recall reading about Karachi in novels was in Salman Rushdie's early works ... But [his] vibrant, dynamic Bombay felt far more Karachi-like to me than his versions of Karachi' (2010: n.p.).

13. Shamsie has indicated, for example, her annoyance at Aslam's assumption that a new Nagasaki-based novel must be her ' "9/11 book" ', and that her knowledge and experience of Pakistani Muslims' 'religious feelings' as a Karachi-raised expatriate is very different from his British one (2011b: 214–15). While praising Aslam and Hamid's sustained engagement with 'issues' of extremism, she has sought to distance her writing from both their 9/11-centring novels, stressing that she is 'always interested in Pakistan's alternative narratives, rather than the stories of the military and extremists' (225).

14. In conversation with Mustapha Cherif, Derrida asserts that: 'To relate to the other, as other, is ... to respect the interruption ... [E]ven if one recognises this insurmountable dissociation in ... between us, to live together is to be able to recognise the dissociation and interruption' (in Cherif 2008: 66).

15. In describing Shamsie's novels as *"dis/sociative"*, I mean to point to their conscious incorporation of – and hence *sociation* with – myths of "Islamic" Pakistan which may be considered of interest to "world" readers, and which have variously been given fictional life by her South Asian (male) literary associates. Simultaneously, I seek to give weight to her attempts to distance, withdraw, separate – or dissociate – her depictions from the insights offered by these supposed representatives, and to adopt (at times radically) alternative interpretative slants, which render redundant the binary epistemologies of contemporary and historic Islamic customs and practices widely available in the West. This still dialogical

strategy is altogether different from the perhaps similar-sounding one of 'disengagement from your country [America] by mine' advocated by Hamid's (2007b: 203) ambiguous and fictional Changez.

16. Brouillette (2007a: 18) hints that 'closeness, community, intimacy and solidarity' have been weighted with too much 'authority' by postcolonial critics like Huggan, for whom 'access to what's "real" can require the valuing of [such] forms of identification with "what is morally superior to rationality and distance in social relationships" ' (18). Shamsie's account of intersectarian cohabitation in contemporary Karachi seems to eschew this criticism, opening as it does a window onto a scene of intimacy which arises only as a result of 'rationality' and respect for social 'distance', a window which quickly closes.

17. Appiah (2006: xiii) acknowledges in *Cosmopolitanism: Ethics in a World of Strangers* the negative connotations that the term 'cosmopolitanism' has acquired ('celebrations of the "cosmopolitan" can suggest an unpleasant posture of superiority towards the putative provincial'). Yet he has 'settled on' it because it encompasses two 'intertwin[ing]' strands: first, 'the idea that we have obligations to others'; second, that 'we take seriously the value not just of human life but of particular human lives' (xv).

18. Her approach to exchanges with global others may, in this regard, resemble the 'partial cosmopolitanism' which Appiah (2006: xvi–xvii) proceeds to advocate: Hiroko 'sides neither with the nationalist who abandons all foreigners nor with the hard-core cosmopolitan who regards her friends and fellow citizens with icy impartiality'.

19. Derrida states that for a relationship to be established between oneself and a respected, interruptive other, a 'leap' of faith must be made in the 'darkness that is the lack of knowledge', even as we seek to 'accumulate the most knowledge and critical awareness possible', for 'the difference between an opening up and a closure depends ... on the *responsibility taken in the midst of risk*' (in Cherif 2008: 60, 75).

20. The Sri Lankan-born Canadian author's novel closes where Shamsie's has begun: with the dropping by America of its atom bombs over Hiroshima and Nagasaki. *Burnt Shadows* seems haunted both by Ondaatje's (1992: 284–5) Indian British Army sapper Kip's initial 'shock and horror', and by his deep contained anger, as he realises what this means: the betrayal of the 'fragile white island that with customs and manners and books ... somehow converted the rest of the world' (283). Shamsie's novel also seems governed by Kip's sense of restraint, even contempt, on contemplating all those who – convinced of their moral superiority and in control of history – would 'bomb ... the brown races of the world', make them feel 'this tremor of Western wisdom' (284, 286). For although he rages: 'All those speeches of civilisation from kings and queens and presidents ... such voices of abstract order. Smell it. Listen to the radio and smell the celebration in it. In my country, when a father breaks justice in two, you kill the father' (285, author's ellipsis), Kip cannot execute the English patient; his choice is rather to give the 'slip' to his hypocritical world.

21. In Pakistan, 1988 was the year when General Zia was killed in a plane crash and Benazir Bhutto's centre-left, democratic socialist Pakistan People's Party swept to power, making Bhutto Pakistan's first woman Prime Minister.

22. Appiah (2006: xv) emphasises that being 'cosmopolitan' entails not only 'tak[ing] seriously...the value of human life' and 'particular human lives', but also 'taking an interest in the practices and beliefs that lend them significance'. He goes on to state that:

> Cosmopolitanism shouldn't be seen as some exalted attainment: it begins with the simple idea that in the human community, as in national communities, we need to develop habits of co-existence: conversation in its older [obsolete/archaic] meaning, of living together, association. (xviii–xix)

Hiroko's "un-exalted" cosmopolitan approach is a kind of 'habit...of co-existence' that embraces this principle of 'taking an interest' and of 'conversation' (xv, xviii–xix). But in Shamsie better relations (and understandings) are established – as we have seen, and will go on to see – not just through passive cohabitation, but through active investment in "conversation" in the more current sense of that word: through the reciprocal 'interchange of thoughts and words; familiar discourse or talk' (*OED Online* 2013c), which may lead to a deeper appreciation of and respect for others' principles and motivations.

23. Shamsie informs us that Hiroko 'felt about those who believed in religion' as 'about people who believed in the morality of their nations': 'it was baffling, it seemed to deny all reason, and yet she would never be the one to attempt to wrestle the comfort of an illusory order away from someone else' (2009b: 329) or allow it to limit her understanding of their capacity for humanity. At least, that is, while they remain peaceful, and do no harm.

Bibliography

Ahmad, J. (2011) *The Wandering Falcon*. London: Hamish Hamilton.

Ahmed, R. (2015) 'Creative Freedom and Community Constraint in Nadeem Aslam's *Maps for Lost Lovers*', in *Writing British Muslims: Religion, Class and Multiculturalism*. Manchester: Manchester University Press, 154–82.

Ali, A. (1940) *Twilight in Delhi*. New York, NY: New Directions, 1994.

Ali, A. S. (1997) *The Country Without A Post Office: Poems 1991–1995*. New Delhi: Ravi Dayal, 2000.

Ali, T. (2005) *A Sultan in Palermo*. London: Verso.

――――. (2008) *The Duel: Pakistan on the Flight Path of American Power*. London: Simon & Schuster.

Amis, M. (2008) *The Second Plane: September 11: 2001–2007*. London: Jonathan Cape.

Anderson, B. (1991) *Imagined Communities: Reflections on the Origins and Spread of Nationalism*. London: Verso.

Appiah, K. A. (2006) *Cosmopolitanism: Ethics in a World of Strangers*. New York, NY: W. W. Norton & Company.

Ashcroft, B., Griffiths, G. and Tiffin, H. (2002) *The Empire Writes Back: Theory and Practice in Post-Colonial Literatures*, 2nd edn. London: Routledge.

Aslam, N. (1993) *Season of the Rainbirds*. London: Faber and Faber, 2005.

――――. (2004a) *Maps for Lost Lovers*. London: Faber and Faber, 2005.

――――. (2004b) 'Nadeem Aslam: A Question of Honour'. Interview with Nadeem Aslam. Interviewed by Marianne Brace for *The Independent*, 11 June. [Online] Available at: http://www.independent.co.uk/arts-entertainment/books/feat ures/nadeem-aslam-a-question-of-honour-6167858.html (Accessed 31 May 2013).

――――. (2006) 'God and Me', *Granta 93: God's Own Countries*, 66–8.

――――. (2008) *The Wasted Vigil*. London: Faber and Faber, 2009.

――――. (2010a) *Leila in the Wilderness, Granta 112: Pakistan*, 7–53.

――――. (2010b) 'Where to Begin', *Granta*, 29 September. [Online] Available at: http://www.granta.com/New-Writing/Where-to-Begin (Accessed 31 May 2013).

――――. (2011a) 'Nadeem Aslam'. Interview with Nadeem Aslam. Interviewed by Claire Chambers for Chambers, C. *British Muslim Fictions: Interviews with Contemporary Writers*. Basingstoke: Palgrave Macmillan, 132–55.

――――. (2011b) 'Punnu's Jihad', *Granta 116: Ten Years Later*, 59–79.

――――. (2012) *The Blind Man's Garden* [Public discussion with Arifa Akbar at *South Asian Literature Festival*, Bush Theatre, London], 4 November.

――――. (2013) *The Blind Man's Garden*. London: Faber and Faber.

Aslam Khan, U. (2010) 'The National Language: Uzma Aslam Khan'. Interviewed by Ollie Brock for *Granta*, 18 October. [Online] Available at: http://www.granta.com/Online-Only/The-National-Language (Accessed 29 May 2013).

Aspden, R. (2011) '*Moth Smoke* by Mohsin Hamid – Review', *The Observer*, 1 May 2011. [Online] Available at: http://www.guardian.co.uk/books/2011/may/01/moth-smoke-mohsin-hamid-review (Accessed 29 May 2013).

Baig, M. A. (2009) *Sifar Se Aik Tak: Cyberspace Ke Munshi Ki Sargazasht*. Lahore: Sanjh Publications.

Bayoumi, M. (2008) *How Does It Feel to Be a Problem? Being Young and Arab in America*. New York: Penguin Press.

BBC News. (2006) 'Writers' Statement on Cartoons', 1 March. [Online] Available at: http://news.bbc.co.uk/1/hi/world/europe/4764730.stm (Accessed 19 July 2013).

Bennett, R. (2007) 'Shame On Us', *The Guardian*, 19 November. [Online] Available at: http://www.guardian.co.uk/uk/2007/nov/19/race.bookscomment (Accessed 9 July 2013).

Bhatti, S. (2010) 'What Can Museums Do For Pakistan?', *Sohbet: Journal of Contemporary Arts and Culture*, 1, 23–32.

Brace, M. (2004) 'Nadeem Aslam: A Question of Honour', *The Independent*, 11 June. [Online] Available at: http://www.independent.co.uk/arts-entertainment/books/features/nadeem-aslam-a-question-of-honour-6167858.html (Accessed 31 May 2013).

Bradley, A. and Tate, A. (2010) *The New Atheist Novel: Fiction, Philosophy and Polemic after 9/11*. London: Continuum.

Brennan, T. (1997) *At Home in the World: Cosmopolitanism Now*. Cambridge, MA: Harvard.

Brouillette, S. (2007a) *Postcolonial Writers in the Global Literary Marketplace*. Basingstoke: Palgrave Macmillan.

——. (2007b) 'South Asian Literature and Global Publishing', *Wasafiri*, 22 (3), 34–38.

Brown, K. E. (2010) 'Contesting the Securitization of British Muslims: Citizenship and Resistance', *Interventions*, 12 (2), 171–82.

Bunting, M. (2007) 'We Were the Brothers', *The Guardian*, 12 May. [Online] Available at: http://www.guardian.co.uk/books/2007/may/12/religion.news (Accessed 29 May 2013).

Camus, A. (1957) *The Fall*. Translated by Justin O'Brien. London: Hamish Hamilton.

Chambers, C. (2011) *British Muslim Fictions: Interviews with Contemporary Writers*. Basingstoke: Palgrave Macmillan.

Chaudhuri, A. (2009) 'Qatrina and the Books: *The Wasted Vigil* by Nadeem Aslam', *London Review of Books*, 27 August. [Online] Available at: http://www.lrb.co.uk/v31/n16/print/chau01_.html (Accessed 19 July 2013).

Cherif, M. (2008) ' "Separation or Connection" in *Islam and the West: A Conversation with Jacques Derrida*', Translated by Teresa Lavender Fagan. Chicago: University of Chicago Press, 55–76.

Cilano, C. (2011) *National identities in Pakistan: The 1971 War in Contemporary Pakistani Fiction*. London: Routledge.

Clark, L. (2011) 'Reconstructing Afghanistan's Bombed Buddhas of Bamiyan', [Online] Available at: http://www.wired.co.uk/news/archive/2011-03/

01/afghanistan-buddhas-of-bamiyan-reconstruction?page= all (Accessed 31 May 2013).

Clements, M. (2014) 'Enchanted Realms, Sceptical Perspectives: Salman Rushdie's Recent Fiction', in Chambers, C. and Herbert, C. (eds.) *Imagining Muslims in South Asia and the Diaspora: Secularism, Religion, Representations*. London: Routledge, 127–41.

Currie, G. (2011) 'Let's Pretend: Literature and the Psychology Lab', *The Times Literary Supplement*, 2 September, 14–15.

Dalrymple, W. (2009) *Nine Lives: In Search of the Sacred in Modern India*. London: Bloomsbury, 2010.

Damrosch, D. (2003) 'What is World Literature?', *World Literature Today*, April–June, 9–14.

Davids, M. F. (2009) 'The Impact of Islamophobia', *Psychoanalysis and History*, 11 (2), 175–91.

DeLillo, D. (2007) *Falling Man: A Novel*. New York, NY: Picador, 2008.

Dougary, G. (2006) 'The Voice of Experience'. *The Times*, 9 September. [Online] Available at: http://www.ginnydougary.co.uk/2006/09/17/the-voice-of-experience/ (Accessed 19 July 2013).

Eaglestone, R. (2010) ' "The Age of Reason was over...an Age of Fury was Dawning": Contemporary Fiction and Terror', in Boehmer, E. and Morton, S. (eds.) *Terror and the Postcolonial*. Oxford: Wiley-Blackwell, 361–9.

Eagleton, T. (1996) *Literary Theory: An Introduction*. 2nd edn. Oxford: Blackwell, 1997.

——. (2007a) *Ideology, An Introduction: New and Updated Edition*. London: Verso.

——. (2007b) 'Only Pinter Remains: British Literature's Long and Rich Tradition of Politically Engaged Writers has come to an End', *The Guardian*, 7 July. [Online] Available at: http://www.guardian.co.uk/commentisfree/2007/jul/07/comment.politics/print (Accessed 29 May 2013).

Elliott, F. (2011) 'In Pakistan, Words Really Do Matter – Mohsin Hamid, Bestselling Author of *The Reluctant Fundamentalist*, tells Francis Elliott why he braved critics and gunman to return to his homeland', *The Times* (Features section), 23 April, 9.

Faulks, S. (2009) *A Week in December*. London: Hutchinson.

Forster, E. M. (1924) *A Passage to India*. London: E. Arnold & Co.

Frembgen, J. W. (2012) *Nocturnal Music in the Land of the Sufis: The Unheard Pakistan*. Translated by Jane Ripken. Lahore: Oxford University Press Pakistan.

Gandhi, R. (2014) *The Legacy of the Mahatma* [Keynote speech at the *Karachi Literature Festival 2014*, Beach Luxury Hotel, Karachi, Pakistan], 7 February.

Gilroy, P. (2004) *After Empire: Multiculture or Postcolonial Melancholia?* Abingdon: Routledge.

Gopal, P. (2009) *The Indian English Novel: Nation, History, and Narration*. Oxford: Oxford University Press.

Gora, T. A. (2013) *Rung Mahal*. Karachi: Aaj.

Granta (2006) *Granta 93: God's Own Countries*.

—— (2010) *Granta 112: Pakistan*.

Greene, G. (1955) *The Quiet American*. London: Heinemann.

Gurnah, A. (ed.) (2007) *The Cambridge Companion to Salman Rushdie.* Cambridge: Cambridge University Press.

Habermas, J. (2001) 'The Postnational Constellation and the Future of Democracy', in Pensky, M (ed. and trans.) *The Postnational Constellation Political Essays.* Cambridge, MA: Polity, 58–112.

Haider, S. F. (2012) *How It Happened.* New Delhi: Viking.

Hamid, M. (2000a) 'Changing of the Guard'. [Online] Available at: http://www.mohsinhamid.com/changingoftheguard.html (Accessed 9 December 2011).

Hamid, O. S. (2013) *The Prisoner.* India: Pan India.

——. (2000b) 'Lives; International Relations'. [Online] Available at: http://www.mohsinhamid.com/internationalrelations.html (Accessed 29 May 2011).

——. (2000c) *Moth Smoke.* London: Granta, 2001.

——. (2000d) *Moth Smoke.* Reprint, London: Penguin, 2011.

——. (2001a) 'Lives; The Countdown', *The New York Times Magazine,* 30 September. [Online] Available at: http://www.nytimes.com/2001/09/30/magazine/lives-the-countdown.html (Accessed 29 May 2013).

——. (2001b) 'The Usual Ally', *TIME Magazine,* 1 October. [Online] Available at: http://www.mohsinhamid.com/theusualally.html (Accessed 31 May 2013).

——. (2003a) 'Gunning for War', *TIME Asia Magazine,* 20 January. [Online] Available at: http://www.time.com/time/asia/features/asia_iraq/viewpoint.html (Accessed 17 May 2011).

——. (2003b) 'The Pathos of Exile', *TIME Asia Magazine,* 11 August. [Online] Available at: http://www.mohsinhamid.com/thepathosofexile.html (Accessed 31 May 2013).

——. (2003c) 'We're All on the Same Side', *TIME Asia Magazine,* 10 March. [Online] Available at: http://www.time.com/time/magazine/article/0,9171,428183,00.html (Accessed 29 May 2013).

——. (2006) 'I Love This Dirty Town', *New Statesman,* 9 October. [Online] Available at: http://www.newstatesman.com/node/154496 (Accessed 29 May 2013).

——. (2007a) 'My Reluctant Fundamentalist', *Powell's Books.* [Online] Available at: http://www.powells.com/essays/mohsin.html (Accessed 31 May 2013).

——. (2007b) *The Reluctant Fundamentalist.* London: Penguin, 2008.

——. (2007c) ' "Reluctant" Success'. Interview with Mohsin Hamid. Interviewed by Jennifer Reese for *Entertainment Weekly,* 13 June. [Online] Available at: http://www.ew.com/ew/article/0,,20042152,00.html (Accessed 29 May 2013).

——. (2008a) 'An Interview with Mohsin Hamid'. Interviewed by Amina Yaqin for *Moving Worlds,* 8 (1), 111–122.

——. (2008b) 'Mohsin Hamid in Conversation'. Interview with Mohsin Hamid. Interviewed by Amina Yaqin for *Wasafiri,* 23 (2), 44–49.

——. (2008c) 'End of a Beginning', *Time Magazine,* 21 August. [Online] Available at: http://www.time.com/time/magazine/article/0,9171,1834456,00.html (Accessed 29 May 2013).

——. (2008d) 'The (Former) General in his Labyrinth'. [Online] Available at: http://wetellstories.co.uk/stories/week6/ (Accessed 29 May 2013).

——. (2009a) 'It Had to Be a Sign. Time to Move the Family to Pakistan', *The Guardian*, 23 November. [Online] Available at: http://www.guardian. co.uk/commentisfree/2009/nov/23/london-family-pakistan-hope-tolerance (Accessed 29 May 2013).

——. (2009b) 'Slaying Dragons: Mohsin Hamid Discusses *The Reluctant Fundamentalist*', *Psychoanalysis and History*, 11 (2), 225–37.

——. (2010) 'A Beheading', *Granta 112: Pakistan*, 191–5.

——. (2011a) 'Guardian Book Club: *The Reluctant Fundamentalist* by Mohsin Hamid: Week Three: Mohsin Hamid On Writing *The Reluctant Fundamentalist*', *The Guardian*, 14 May. [Online] Available at: http://www. guardian.co.uk/books/2011/may/14/mohsin-hamid-reluctant-fundamen talist-bookclub?intcmp=239 (Accessed 29 May 2013).

——. (2011b) *'Moth Smoke' and Pakistan after Bin Laden*. [Seminar discussion with Amina Yaqin for *Framing Muslims*], 25 May. [Online] Available at: http://framingmuslims.org/event-archive/193-moth-smoke-and-pakistan-after-bin-laden.html (Accessed 29 May 2013).

——. (2011c) 'Silencing Pakistan', *The Express Tribune*, 4 June. [Online] Available at: http://tribune.com.pk/story/181760/silencing-pakistan (Accessed 29 May 2013).

——. (2011d) 'Terminator: Attack of the Drone', *The Guardian*, 7 November. [Online] Available at: http://www.guardian.co.uk/books/2011/nov/07/short-story-mohsin-hamid (Accessed 29 May 2013).

——. (2013a) 'It's all about you: Mohsin Hamid on his new novel – a self-help book and second-person life story', *The Guardian*, 23 March, 15.

Hamid, M., Hanif, M., Mueenuddin, D. and Shamsie, K. (2010) 'How to Write About Pakistan', *Granta*, 23 September. [Online] Available at: http://www. granta.com/Online-Only/How-to-write-about-Pakistan (Accessed 29 May 2013).

Hanif, M. (2008a) *A Case of Exploding Mangoes*. London: Jonathan Cape.

——. (2008b) 'Karachi Calling', *The Guardian*, 24 June. [Online] Available at: http://www.guardian.co.uk/world/2008/jun/24/pakistan.healthand wellbeing (Accessed 29 May 2013).

——. (2011) *Our Lady of Alice Bhatti*. London: Jonathan Cape.

Haque, J. (2011) 'Fear and Cricket: Mohsin Hamid's Pakistan', *The Express Tribune*, 6 February. [Online] Available at: http://tribune.com.pk/story/ 114698/fear-and-cricket-mohsin-hamids-pakistan/ (Accessed 29 May 2013).

Hari, J. (2006) 'Salman Rushdie: His Life, His Work, and His Religion', *The Independent*, 13 October. [Online] Available at: http://www.independent.co. uk/news/people/profiles/salman-rushdie-his-life-his-work-and-his-religion-419902.html (Accessed 31 May 2013).

Hobsbawm, E. (2007) *Globalisation, Democracy and Terrorism*. London: Little, Brown.

Hopkins, B. and Marsden, M. (2011) *Fragments of the Afghan Frontier*. London: Hurst & Company.

Hosain, A. (1961) *Sunlight on a Broken Column*. London: Virago, 1988.

Hoyle, B. (2007) 'Muslim World Inflamed by Rushdie Knighthood', *The Times*, 19 June, 3.

Huggan, G. (2001) *The Postcolonial Exotic: Marketing the Margins*. London: Routledge.

Huntington, S. (1992) *The Clash of Civilizations?* Washington, DC: American Enterprise Institute.

Husain, E. (2007) *The Islamist: Why I Joined Radical Islam in Britain, What I Saw and Why I Left*. London: Penguin.

Hussein, A. (2002) *Turquoise*. London: Saqi Books.

——. (ed.) (2005) *Kahani: Short Stories by Pakistani Women*. London: Saqi Books.

——. (2009) *Another Gulmohar Tree*. London: Telegram Books.

Immigration and Refugee Board of Canada (1996) *The Mohajir Qaumi Movement (MQM) in Karachi January 1995 – April 1996*, 1 November. [Online] Available at: http://www.unhcr.org/refworld/topic,463af2212, 469f2eb02,3ae6a85d4,0,,COUNTRYREP,.html (Accessed 1 January 2013).

Irfani, S. (ed.). (2008) *Transformation*. Lahore: National College of Arts.

——. (2010) 'Shahnama: The Other Story' in Milz, M. (ed.) *Painting the Persian Book of Kings Today: Ancient Text and Modern Images*. Cambridge, MA: Talking Tree, 32–54.

Iqbal, N. (2013) *Surkh Dhabbay*. Islamabad: Dost Publications.

Jalal, A. (2008) *Partisans of Allah: Jihad in South Asia*. Cambridge, MA: Harvard University Press.

Jay, P. (2010) *Global Matters: The Transnational Turn in Literary Studies*. Ithaca, NY: Cornell University Press.

Kabir, A. J. (2009) *Territory of Desire: Representing the Valley of Kashmir*. Minneapolis, MN: University of Minnesota Press.

Kadir, D. (2004) 'To World, to Globalize – Comparative Literature's Crossroads', *Comparative Literature Studies*, 41 (1), 1–9.

——. (2006) 'Comparative Literature in an Age of Terrorism', in Saussy, H. (ed.) *Comparative Literature in an Age of Globalization*. Baltimore, MD: The John Hopkins University Press.

Kapur, A. (2005) 'Little Murders', *The New York Times* 22 May. [Online] Available at: http://query.nytimes.com/gst/fullpage.html?res= 9A0CE7D91030F 931A15756C0A9639C8B63&sec= &spon= &pagewanted= 2 (Accessed 20 July 2013).

Kellner, D. (2002) ' "The Axis of Evil," Operation Infinite War, and Bush's Attacks on Democracy', *Cultural Studies–Critical Methodologies*, 2 (3), pp. 343–7.

Khan Philips, M. (2010) *Beautiful from This Angle*. New Delhi: Penguin Books India.

King, B. (2009) 'Review Essay: Muslim Modernities', *Journal of Postcolonial Writing*, 45 (4), 472–7.

Kureishi, H. (1995) *The Black Album*. London: Faber and Faber.

——. (2004) *My Ear at His Heart: Reading My Father*. London: Faber, 2005.

Lawrence, B. (2012) 'Muslim Cosmopolitanism', *Critical Muslim 2: The Idea of Islam*, 19–39.

Lazarus, N. (2004) 'Introducing Postcolonial Studies', in Lazarus, N. (ed.) *Postcolonial Literary Studies*. Cambridge, MA: Cambridge University Press, 2006, 1–16.

Levi, J. (2000) 'A Pakistani Saga of Fraternal Rivalry', *The Los Angeles Times*, 21 January. [Online] Available at: http://articles.latimes.com/2000/jan/21/news/cl-56017 (Accessed 29 May 2013).

Lieven, A. (2011) *Pakistan: A Hard Country*. London: Penguin, 2012.

Majid, A. (2000) *Unveiling Traditions: Postcolonial Islam in a Polycentric World*. London: Duke University Press.

Malak, A. (2004) *Muslim Narratives and the Discourse of English*. Albany, NY: State University of New York Press, 2005.

Malik, S. (2013) 'A Walk Through the Blind Man's Garden with Nadeem Aslam', *Tribune*, 24 February. [Online] Available at: http://tribune.com.pk/story/511894/llf-2013-a-walk-through-blind-mans-garden-with-nadeem-aslam (Accessed 31 May 2013).

Mamdani, M. (2004) *Good Muslim, Bad Muslim: America, the Cold War, and the Roots of Terror*. New York, NY: Doubleday, 2005.

Mars-Jones, A. (2008) 'Anything to See Those Paper Eyes', *The Guardian*, 12 October. [Online] Available at: http://www.guardian.co.uk/books/2008/oct/12/fiction2 (Accessed 4 June 2013).

McEwan, I. (2005) *Saturday*. London: Jonathan Cape.

——. (2007) 'Martin Amis is Not a Racist', *The Guardian*, 21 November. [Online] Available at: http://www.guardian.co.uk/world/2007/nov/21/religion.race (Accessed 29 May 2013).

Miłosz, C. (2001) 'You Who Wronged', in *New and Collected Poems 1931–2001*. London: Penguin, 103.

Mir, M. (2006) *Iqbal: Makers of Modern Civilization*. London: I. B. Taurus.

——. (2007) *Tulip in the Desert*. Lahore: Iqbal Academy Pakistan.

Mishra, P. (2012) '*Joseph Anton* by Salman Rushdie – Review', *The Guardian*, 18 September. [Online] Available at: http:// www.guardian.co.uk/books/2012/sep/18/joseph-anton-salman-rushdie-review (Accessed 27 December 2012).

Mondal, A. (2007) *Amitav Ghosh*. Manchester, NH: Manchester University Press.

——. (2008) *Young British Muslim Voices*. Oxford: Greenwood World Publishing.

——. (2012) 'Bad Faith: The Construction of Muslim Extremism in Ed Husain's *The Islamist*', in Ahmed, R., Morey, P. and Yaqin, A. (eds.) *Culture, Diaspora, and Modernity in Muslim Writing*. Abingdon, VA: Routledge, 37–51.

Moore-Gilbert, B. (2012) 'From "the Politics of Recognition" to "the Policing of Recognition": Writing Muslims, *Ummah*, Nation and Modernity in Hanif Kureishi and Mohsin Hamid', in Ahmed, R., Morey, P. and Yaqin, A. (eds.) *Culture, Diaspora, and Modernity in Muslim Writing*. Abingdon, VA: Routledge, 183–99.

Moretti, F. (2000) 'Conjectures on World Literature', *New Left Review*, 1 (January–February), 54–68.

Morey, P. (2011) ' "The Rules of the Game Have Changed": Mohsin Hamid's *The Reluctant Fundamentalist* and Post-9/11 Fiction', *Journal of Postcolonial Writing*, 47 (2), 135–46.

———. (2012) 'A Little Corner of the Big Picture: Worlding the 9/11 Novel'. Unpublished book chapter, 1–52.

Morey, P. and Yaqin, A. (2011) *Framing Muslims: Stereotyping and Representation After 9/11*. London: Harvard University Press.

Mueenuddin's, D. (2009) *In Other Rooms, Other Wonders*. London: W. W. Norton & Company.

Muir, K. (2008) 'Rushdie Goes Racy', *The Times* (Books section), 5 April, 6.

Mullan, J. (2011) 'Guardian Book Club: *The Reluctant Fundamentalist* by Mohsin Hamid: Week Four: Readers' Responses', *The Guardian*, 21 May. [Online] Available at: http://www.guardian.co.uk/books/2011/may/21/book-club-reluctant-fundamentalist-hamid?intcmp=239 (Accessed 30 May 2013).

Musharraf, P. (2004) 'A Plea for Enlightened Moderation', *Washington Post*, 31 March. [Online] Available at: http://www.washingtonpost.com/wp-dyn/articles/A5081-2004May31.html (Accessed 31 May 2013).

Nasir, A. (2012) 'J'Accuse: Pakistan', *Critical Muslim 1: The Arabs Are Alive*, 247–253.

Nasta, S. (2002) *Home Truths: Fictions of the South Asian Diaspora in Britain*. Basingstoke: Palgrave.

Nederveen Pieterse, J. (2007) *Ethnicities and Global Multiculture: Pants for an Octopus*. Maryland, MD: Rowman & Littlefield.

OED Online (2013a) 'Affiliate, v.'. in *Oxford English Dictionary*. [Online] Available at: http://www.oed.com/view/Entry/3403 (Accessed: 12 June 2013).

———. (2013b) 'Affinity, n.', in *Oxford English Dictionary*. [Online] Available at: http://www.oed.com/view/Entry/3417?redirectedFrom= affinity (Accessed 12 June 2013).

———. (2013c) 'Conversation, n.' in *Oxford English Dictionary*. [Online] Available at: http://www.oed.com/view/Entry/40748?rskey= QEZa2n&result=1&isAdvanced=false (Accessed 12 June 2013).

Ondaatje, M. (1992) *The English Patient*. London: Picador, 1993.

———. (2000) *Anil's Ghost*. Toronto, ON: McClelland and Stewart.

Peer, B. (2010a) *Curfewed Night*. New York, NY: Scribner.

———. (2010b) 'Kashmir's Forever War', *Granta 112: Pakistan*, 69–87.

Phillips, T. (2005) *After 7/7: Sleepwalking to Segregation*. [Speech to Manchester Council for Community Relations]. 22 September. [Online] Available at: http://www.humanities.manchester.ac.uk/socialchange/research/social-change/summer-workshops/documents/sleepwalking.pdf (Accessed 30 May 2013).

Pratt Ewing, K. (1997) *Arguing Sainthood: Modernity, Psychoanalysis and Islam*. 2nd printing. Durham, NC: Duke University Press, 2006.

Quirkstir (2008) *Newsnight Mohsin Hamid Amitav Ghosh*. [Online] Available at: http://www.youtube.com/watch?gl= GB&hl= en-GB&v= YSReQAZI4mQ (Accessed 18 May 2011).

Rai, M. (2011) 'Making a Part Inalienable: Folding Kashmir into India's Imagination', in Kak, S. (ed.) *Until My Freedom Has Come: The New Intifada*. New Delhi: Penguin, 250–78.

Ranasinha, R. (2012) 'Resistance and Religion in the Work of Kamila Shamsie', in Ahmed, R., Morey, P. and Yaqin, A. (eds.) *Culture, Diaspora, and Modernity in Muslim Writing*. London: Routledge, 200–14.

Reddy, S. (2002) 'Midnight's Orphans', *Outlook India*, 25 February. [Online] Available at: http://www.outlookindia.com/article.aspx?214680 (Accessed 14 December 2012).

Rees, J. (2004) 'Nadeem Aslam', *The Telegraph*, 14 June. [Online] Available at: http://www.telegraph.co.uk/culture/books/3619197/Nadeem-Aslam.html (Accessed 31 May 2013).

Rushdie, S. (1981) *Midnight's Children*. London: Jonathan Cape.

————. (1983) *Shame*. London: Vintage, 1995.

——. (1988) *The Satanic Verses*. London: Vintage, 2006.

————. (1991) *Imaginary Homelands: Essays and Criticism 1981–1991*. London: Granta.

——. (1995) *The Moor's Last Sigh*. London: Vintage, 1996.

——. (1997) 'Introduction', in Rushdie, S. and West, E. (eds.) *The Vintage Book of Indian Writing 1947–1997*. London: Vintage, ix–xxiii.

——. (2001) *Fury*. London: Vintage, 2002.

——. (2002) *Step Across This Line: Collected Non-Fiction 1992–2002*. London: Vintage, 2003.

——. (2005a) 'Interview with Salman Rushdie'. Interviewed by Dan Webster for *The Spokesman Review*, 21 April. [Online] Available at: http://www.spokesmanreview.com/breaking/story.asp%3Fid%3D3821 (Accessed 12 October 2010).

——. (2005b) 'Muslims Unite! A new Reformation will bring your faith into the modern era', *The Times*, 11 August, 19.

——. (2005c) *Shalimar the Clown*. London: Vintage, 2006.

——. (2006) 'Salman Rushdie: His Life, His Work, and His Religion'. Interview with Salman Rushdie. Interviewed by Johann Hari for *The Independent*, 13 October. [Online] Available at: http://www.independent.co.uk/news/people/profiles/salman-rushdie-his-life-his-work-and-his-religion-419902.html (Accessed 31 May 2013).

——. (2008a) *The Enchantress of Florence*. London: Vintage, 2009.

——. (2008b) 'Magical Thinking – Salman Rushdie Interview', Interviewed by Peter Ross for *Scotland on Sunday*, 20 April. [Online] Available at: http://scotlandonsunday.scotsman.com/sos-review/Magical-thinking–Salman-Rushdie.3999048.jp (Accessed 30 May 2013).

——. (2010a) *Luka and the Fire of Life*. London: Jonathan Cape.

——. (2010b) 'Salman's Children'. Interview with Salman Rushdie. Interviewed by Susannah Rustin for *The Guardian*, 2 October. [Online] Available at: http://www.guardian.co.uk/books/2010/oct/02/salman-rushdie-luka (Accessed 30 May 2013).

Rustin, S. (2010) 'Salman's Children'. Interview with Salman Rushdie for *The Guardian*, 2 October. [Online] Available at: http://www.guardian.co.uk/books/2010/oct/02/salman-rushdie-luka (Accessed 30 May 2013).

Sabri, Z. (2012) 'A Sūfi Saint', in Naqvi, M. (comp.) *Festival!* Karachi: Sherazade, 15.

———. (2013a) Email to Madeline Clements, 13 May.

———. (2013b) 'Whose Pakistan, Whose Picture?', *Dawn,* 21 June. [Online] Available at: herald.dawn.com/2013/06/21/whose-pakistan-whose-picture. html (Accessed 28 June).

Safran Foer, J. (2005) *Extremely Loud and Incredibly Close.* London: Penguin. 2006.

Said, E. (1978) *Orientalism.* London: Penguin, 2003.

———. (1983) *The World the Text and the Critic.* London: Vintage, 1991.

———. (1993) *Culture and Imperialism.* London: Vintage (1994).

———. (1997) *Covering Islam: How the Media and the Experts Determine How We See the Rest of the World.* Revised edn. London: Vintage.

Salaita, S. (2008) *The Uncultured Wars: Arabs, Muslims, and the Poverty of Liberal Thought – New Essays.* New York, NY: Zed Books.

Sardar, Z. (2012) 'What's the Big Idea?', *Critical Muslim 2: The Idea of Islam,* 3–18.

Scanlan, M. (2010) 'Migrating from Terror: The Postcolonial Novel After September 11', *Journal of Postcolonial Writing,* 46 (3–4), 266–78.

Schofield, V. (2000) *Kashmir in Conflict: India, Pakistan and the Unending War.* London: I. B. Tauris, 2003.

Sen, A. (2005) *The Argumentative Indian: Writings on Culture, History and Identity* London: Penguin Books, 2005.

Sethi, A. (2009) *The Wish Maker.* New York, NY: Riverhead Books.

Shah, B. (2004) *The 786 Cyber Cafe.* Islamabad: Alhamra.

Shah, S. (2009) 'As the Country Descends into Chaos, Pakistani Writers are Winning Acclaim', *The Guardian,* 17 February. [Online] Available at: http://www.guardian.co.uk/books/2009/feb/17/fiction-pakistan-hanif (Accessed 21 July 2013).

Shamsie, K. (1998) *In the City by the Sea.* London: Bloomsbury, 2004.

———. (2000) *Salt and Saffron.* London: Bloomsbury, 2001.

———. (2002a) 'Agha Shahid Ali, Teacher', in *The Annual of Urdu Studies,* 17, 23–27. [Online] Available at: http://www.urdustudies.com/Issue17/index. html (Accessed 7 December 2012).

———. (2002b) *Kartography.* London: Bloomsbury, 2003.

———. (2004) 'All You Need is Love', *Guardian,* 26 June. [Online] Available at: http://www.guardian.co.uk/books/2004/jun/26/featuresreviews. guardianreview17 (Accessed 31 May 2013).

———. (2005a) *Broken Verses.* London: Bloomsbury, 2006.

———. (2005b) 'Defending the Faith', *The Guardian,* 30 July. [Online] Available at: http://www.guardian.co.uk/books/2005/jul/30/featuresreviews. guardianreview11 (Accessed 30 May 2013).

———. (2007a) 'Another Side of the Story'. *The Guardian,* 14 August. [Online] Available at: http://www.guardian.co.uk/books/2007/aug/14/fiction (Accessed 30 May 2013).

———. (2007b) 'Martin Amis's Views Demand a Response'. *The Guardian,* 19 November. [Online] Available at: http://www.guardian.co.uk/books/

booksblog/2007/nov/19/martinamissviewsdemandare (Accessed 28 December 2012).

——. (2008) 'Jihad for Peace', *The Guardian*, 21 June. [Online] Available at: http://www.guardian.co.uk/books/2008/jun/21/saturdayreviewsfeatres. guardianreview25 (Accessed 30 May 2013).

——. (2009a) 'A Long Loving Literary Line', *The Guardian*, 1 May. [Online] Available at: http://www.guardian.co.uk/lifeandstyle/2009/may/01/kamila-shamsie-books-fiction-women (Accessed 7 December 2012).

——. (2009b) *Burnt Shadows*. London: Bloomsbury.

——. (2009c) ' "International Writing": Past, Present and Future Directions', *Wasafiri*, 24 (3), 99–113.

——. (2009d) *Offence: The Muslim Case*. Calcutta: Seagull.

——. (2010) 'Kamila Shamsie On Leaving and Returning to Karachi', *The Guardian*, 13 March. [Online] Available at: www.guardian.co.uk/books/2010/mar/13/karachi-leaving-london-writing-fiction (Accessed 13 September 2012).

——. (2011a) 'A Legacy of Violence: Interview with Kamila Shamsie about *Burnt Shadows* conducted via email on October 26, 2010'. Interviewed by Harleen Singh, *Ariel* 42 (2), 157–62.

——. (2011b) 'Kamila Shamsie', interviewed by Claire Chambers, in Chambers, C. *British Muslim Fictions: Interviews with Contemporary Writers*. Basingstoke: Palgrave Macmillan, 205–25.

——. (2012) 'What has Malala Yousafzai done to the Taliban? *The Guardian*, 10 October. [Online] Available at: www.guardian.co.uk/commentisfree/2012/oct/10/malala-yousafzai-taliban-misogyny/print (Accessed 22 November 2012).

Shamsie, M. (ed.) (1997) *A Dragonfly in the Sun: An Anthology of Pakistani Writing in English*. Oxford: Oxford University Press.

——. (ed.) (2001) *Leaving Home: Towards a New Millennium; A Collection of English Prose by Pakistani Writers*. Oxford: Oxford University Press.

——. (2006) 'Pakistan', *Journal of Commonwealth Literature*, 41 (4), 161–80.

——. (ed.) (2008) *And the World Changed: Contemporary Stories by Pakistani Women*. New York, NY: The Feminist Press.

——. (2009) 'Sunlight and Salt: The Literary Landscapes of a Divided Family', *Journal of Commonwealth Literature*, 44 (1), 135–143.

——. (ed.) (2011) *Journal of Postcolonial Writing: Beyond Geography: Literature, Politics and Violence in Pakistan* [special issue], 47 (2).

——. (2012) 'Discovering the Matrix', *Critical Muslim 4: Pakistan*, 165–76.

Shelley, P. B. (1977) 'The Defence of Poetry', in Reiman, D. H. and Powers, S. B. (eds.) *Shelley's Poetry and Prose*. London: W. W. Norton & Company, 480–508.

Siddiqi, Y. (2008) *Anxieties of Empire and the Fiction of Intrigue*. New York: Columbia University Press.

Sivanesan, H. (2011) 'Bamiyan Notes', *Sohbet: Journal of Contemporary Arts and Culture*, 2, 52–61.

Smith, Z. (2000) *White Teeth*. London: Penguin, 2001.

Spencer, R. (2010a) 'Literature vs. Fundamentalism: Politics and Morality in J. M. Coetzee's *Diary of a Bad Year*' [Conference paper presented at *Forum on Literature, Terrorism and 9/11*, University of Chichester], 29 May.

———. (2010b) 'Salman Rushdie and the "War on Terror"', *Journal of Postcolonial Writing*, 46 (3–4), 251–65.

Spivak, G. C. (1988) 'Can the Subaltern Speak', in Nelson, C. and Grossberg, L. (eds.) *Marxism and the Interpretation of Culture*. Basingstoke: Macmillan Education, 271–313.

———. (2003) *Death of a Discipline*. New York, NY: Columbia University Press.

Srivastava, N. (2008) *Secularism in the Postcolonial Novel*. Abingdon: Routledge.

Start the Week (2011) BBC Radio 4, 16 May. [Online] Available at: http://www.bbc.co.uk/programmes/b01132kh (Accessed 30 May 2013).

Suroor, H. (2011) 'Pakistan is in Terminal Decline', *The Hindu*, 29 May. [Online] Available at: http://www.hindu.com/2011/05/29/stories/2011052 957041100.htm (Accessed 30 May 2013).

Tillion, G. (1966) *My Cousin, My Husband: Clans and Kinship in Mediterranean Societies*. Translated by Quintin Hoare. Reprint, London: Saqi Books, 2007.

Updike, J. (2006) *Terrorist*. London: Penguin Books, 2007.

Vanaik, A. (1990) *The Painful Transition: Bourgeois Democracy in India*. London: Verso.

Vaux, T. (2001) *The Selfish Altruist: Relief Work in Famine and War*. London: Earthscan, 2004.

Wakefield, M. (2007) 'How the Fanatic Found Peace', *Telegraph*, 17 May. [Online] Available at: http://www.telegraph.co.uk/culture/books/3665174/ How-the-fanatic-found-peace.html (Accessed 14 September 2011).

Waldman, A. (2011) *The Submission*. London: Random House.

We Tell Stories (2008) [Online] Available at: http://wetellstories.co.uk (Accessed 29 May 2013).

Werbner, P. (2002) *Imagined Diasporas Among Manchester Muslims*. Oxford: James Currey.

Wintour, P. (2005) 'Blair Vows to Root Out Extremism', *The Guardian*, 6 August 2005. [Online] Available at: http://www.guardian.co.uk/politics/2005/aug/ 06/terrorism.july7 (Accessed 30 May 2013).

Yaqin, A. (2012) 'Muslims as Multicultural Misfits in Nadeem Aslam's *Maps for Lost Lovers*, in Ahmed, R., Morey, P. and Yaqin, T. (eds.) *Culture, Diaspora and Modernity*. London: Routledge, 101–16.

Yassin-Kassab, R. (2008) 'Within the Rubble', *National*, 10 October. [Online] Available at: http://www.thenational.ae/arts-culture/books/within-the-rubble#full (Accessed 31 May 2013).

Index

191